AF323417

GENDER, CHRISTIANITY AND CHANGE IN VANUATU

Anthropology and Cultural History in Asia and the Indo-Pacific

Series Editors:
Pamela J. Stewart and Andrew Strathern
University of Pittsburgh, USA

This series offers a fresh perspective on Asian and Indo-Pacific Anthropology. Acknowledging the increasing impact of transnational flows of ideas and practices across borders, the series widens the established geographical remit of Asian studies to consider the entire Indo-Pacific region. In addition to focussed ethnographic studies, the series incorporates thematic work on issues of cross-regional impact, including globalization, the spread of terrorism, and alternative medical practices.

The series further aims to be innovative in its disciplinary breadth, linking anthropological theory with studies in cultural history and religious studies, thus reflecting the current creative interactions between anthropology and historical scholarship that are enriching the study of Asia and the Indo-Pacific region. While the series covers classic themes within the anthropology of the region such as ritual, political and economic issues will also be tackled. Studies of adaptation, change and conflict in small-scale situations enmeshed in wider currents of change will have a significant place in this range of foci.

We publish scholarly texts, both single-authored and collaborative as well as collections of thematically organized essays. The series aims to reach a core audience of anthropologists and Asian Studies specialists, but also to be accessible to a broader multidisciplinary readership.

Recent titles in the series

The Anthropology of Morality in Melanesia and Beyond
Edited by John Barker
ISBN 978 0 7546 7185 5

Situating the Uyghurs Between China and Central Asia
Edited by Ildikó Bellér-Hann, M. Cristina Cesàro, Rachel Harris
and Joanne Smith Finley
ISBN 978 0 7546 7041 4

Family, Gender and Kinship in Australia
The Social and Cultural Logic of Practice and Subjectivity
Allon J. Uhlmann
ISBN 978 0 7546 4645 7

Gender, Christianity and Change in Vanuatu

An Analysis of Social Movements in North Ambrym

ANNELIN ERIKSEN
University of Bergen, Norway

ASHGATE

Published by
Ashgate Publishing Limited
Gower House
Croft Road
Aldershot
Hampshire GU11 3HR
England

Ashgate Publishing Company
Suite 420
101 Cherry Street
Burlington, VT 05401-4405
USA

Ashgate website: http://www.ashgate.com

British Library Cataloguing in Publication Data
Eriksen, Annelin
   Gender, Christianity and change in Vanuatu: an analysis of
   social movements in North Ambrym. – (Anthropology and
   cultural history in Asia and the Indo-Pacific)
   1. Social change – Vanuatu – Ambrym 2. Women – Vanuatu –
   Ambrym – Social conditions 3. Christianity – Vanuatu –
   Ambrym 4. Ambrym (Vanuatu) – Social life and customs
   I. Title
   303.4'099595

Library of Congress Cataloging-in-Publication Data
Eriksen, Annelin.
 Gender, Christianity and change in Vanuatu : an analysis of social movements in North
Ambrym / by Annelin Eriksen.
   p. cm. -- (Series: Anthropology and cultural history in Asia and the
Indo-Pacific)
 Includes bibliographical references and index.
 ISBN 978-0-7546-7209-8
 1. Social change--Vanuatu--Ambrym. 2. Ambrym (Vanuatu)--Social life and customs. 3.
Women--Vanuatu--Ambrym--Social conditions. 4. Christianity--Vanuatu--Ambrym. I. Title.

HN935.A95E75 2007
305.48'67099595--dc22

2007025291

ISBN: 978 0 7546 7209 8

Printed and bound in Great Britain by MPG Books Ltd, Bodmin, Cornwall.

Contents

List of Illustrations and Tables

Fixity, Movement, and Change: An Ambrym Kaleidoscope

Andrew Strathern and Pamela J. Stewart

We are happy to present Annelin Eriksen's work as an original and thoughtful contribution to debates on gendered aspects of social process in the South-Western Pacific, as well as an illuminating ethnography of Ambrym in the wider national and contemporary setting of Vanuatu. Dr. Eriksen's study makes a special further contribution through her use of historical records and her argument of how gendered relations of power and movement have changed over time.

Analyses of process in terms of alternating, competing, or complementary principles as the underlying and guiding factors have a considerable lineage in anthropology. Frazer's magic vs. religion or religion vs. science distinctions are one example, structured in terms of the evolutionary theories of the day. Similarly with Maine's idea of a transition from status to contract in the organization of social life, or Durkheim's mechanical versus organic solidarity; or Tönnies' gemeinschaft versus gesellschaft dichotomy or Levi Strauss's concept of hot and cold societies. Edmund Leach produced a different take on such notions by proposing an oscillation between the gumlao (egalitarian) and gumsao (hierarchical) modes of structure among the Kachin of Burma. His account was ethnographic, local, and historical, as is Eriksen's in the present study. Accounts of social life as structured around gendered oppositions also have a long history. Rodney Needham institutionalized this kind of representational analysis with his dichotomous lists of male and female gendered associations in a number of South-East Asian societies. Arguments have been deployed as to whether such lists properly represent social realities'. Needham was often dealing with societies in which forms of prescribed or preferential marriage vitally influenced the development of gendered symbolism. In Papua New Guinea Highlands contexts gendered relations of antagonism or conflict were often invoked and Mervyn Meggitt (1964) produced a list of oppositions among the Mae Enga modelled on Needham's ways of representing such dichotomies.

Eriksen's discussion, however, belongs to a different trend of analysis, one which relies on a more recent set of distinctions regarding male and female modalities of sociality. What is particularly compelling in her work is that her discussion is both ethnographically and historically grounded, and that her major purpose is not just to display a form or structure, but to display a structured process of historical change resulting from the introduction of Christianity. Her work is thus a contribution to the emergent category of the anthropology of Christianity and to the broader, established character of historical anthropology at large.

Her work has another forerunner. Fredrik Barth, in his *Form and Process in Social Life* (Barth 1981) laid the foundations for a sophisticated study of change by deploying the contrast between 'form' and 'process' as analytical concepts. Eriksen, like Barth, is concerned with how process may affect form over time, and her answer is that in Ambrym the forms of sociality, male and female in gendered value, have altered their relative positions, a female 'communal' form gaining ground against a male 'personified' form. For her then, the 'process' of life and history has led, not to totally altered local forms, but to transformations in the balance between forms. Such an argument is, of course, an abstraction from reality: but such abstractions are useful as tools for thinking about change, even if they are not the only tools for doing so. Theorists in general tend to vary between those who emphasize discontinuity, rupture, and radical change in historical processes, and those who look for hidden continuities, transitions, and gradual alterations. In practice, issues of this kind may be simply empirical ones: at times change is rapid, at others it is not, and radical discontinuities may later be modified by a return to transformed versions of earlier practices. For instance, in the field of Christian missionization, at first the agents of change may propose a radical break with pre-existing practices and beliefs. Later, perhaps two generations later when the grandchildren of the original converts grow up, they become interested again in their ancestral culture and begin reviving it or mingling elements of it with Christian practices. These Christian practices themselves become inflected over time in local or indigenous directions, particularly if the people run their own churches and are not checked on regularly by external authorities.[1] This is only one example of the many possible trajectories of historical change that can occur.

Eriksen herself points out in one passage how a form of dualistic or dichotomous thinking that is widespread in the Pacific Islands, that is the contrast between *kastom* ('custom, tradition') and Christianity, actually conceals the complexities of contemporary circumstances. From one point view, that of evangelistic preachers, it is important to espouse this view, that Christianity should be kept outside of indigenous custom. Yet, from another viewpoint, that of the outside observer, it may appear evident that in popular practice the realms of custom and Christianity are fused or intermingled. At the very least, they impact each other with ramifying consequences. It is the case that where custom becomes institutionalized in the form of specific social roles or offices, a sphere of custom can be defined separately from that of Christianity, or of government at national level. Ideas about sorcery on Ambrym provide an example. Fears of sorcery remain strong.[2] People in the past would flee from an area because of fear of sorcery, so this fear was a cause of migration from one locality to another. Sorcery is also identified as an arena of custom. In one sorcery case that Eriksen reports on, one participant tried to argue that they should all be subject to Christian ideas of 'the truth'. But a local 'custom chief'

---

1   For references on the impact of Christianity in the Pacific see, e.g., our discussion on Christianity in our Series Editors' Preface to *Religion, Anthropology, and Cognitive Science* edited by H. Whitehouse and J. Laidlaw, Durham, N.C: Carolina Academic Press, 2007, p. xv.

2   See P.J. Stewart and A. Strathern, 2004.

(an introduced office incidentally) rebuked this intervention, saying that sorcery was a matter for men to deal with, and in accordance with custom; the church's ways were the ways of women.

The anecdote is telling, and reveals a part of the kernel of Eriksen's overall argument. Social action and realms of social life are gender-tagged, and this tagging becomes implicated in struggles over change and relative power between people. Thus, Eriksen is able to develop her 'table of contrasts' between stereotypes of male and female forms of action and the dominance of one or the other over time. Her stress on the communal aspect of women's activities in the church – a stress which is intrinsic to her overall interpretations of her materials – shows us that to associate Christianity simply with 'individualization' can be misleading. Interestingly, this communal aspect seems to go with an aspect of movement and migration of women at the time of marriage, so female-gendered action seems to have not one, but two modalities: a communal aspect that fixes it to a place, and a migratory aspect that moves it between places. Perhaps these are two poles of a single complex reality or processual sphere of action. If so, it is perhaps indeed the 'fixing' aspect that belongs to Christianity, as expressed in local, female-centered church activities. Above all, it is important to stress that Christianity remains always relational at its core, via the relationship with the divine Trinity. Christian songs elsewhere in the Pacific (e.g. in Papua New Guinea) stress that God is always there for the people, as in the lines:

> Your father can let you down
> Your mother can let you down
> All of the world can let you down
> But Jesus never fails.

The 'movement' aspect has to do with earlier patterns of movement of women at marriage and the setting up of networks of exchange through these patterns, and also with contemporary movements of women as migrant workers to urban areas. Eriksen makes the important observation that migrant female workers tend to send back money as remittances more reliably than do male migrants. This is interesting and in some ways surprising. Elsewhere in the Pacific, males tend to be the predominant migrant workers, and they either send money back or they bring back money and goods for distribution after a tour of contract work, the latter especially if their home area is remote from areas of economic development. The emphasis on the significance of women's migrant earnings in Ambrym has perhaps influenced the development of the practice of *sakkem presen*, which Eriksen intriguingly compares to dowry gifts. *Sakkem presen* gifts are made by a brother to a sister on her marriage. They consist of household utensils, things she may need to set up a new home in a 'modern' fashion: plates, cups, pots and the like, intended for her own domestic use. Previously, Eriksen notes, yams or a small female pig might be given, both categories of things which were living and could reproduce. One could add that the implication was they would reproduce 'locally', in the local ground. She also notes that the new items are 'consumer' items and belong to distant, urban contexts. Yet these contexts, too, are wealth-producing in a new way, if women send remittances back to their kin. *Sakkem presen* is seen, however, as a new kind of national custom belonging to the whole of Vanuatu, not specifically to Ambrym. The ceremonial economy at home depends on the production of pigs and yams, which urban-based women cannot undertake. It is also expensive for those who are at home. Children growing up in towns lose contact with their mother's brothers in the village context. The giving of *sakkem presen* looks like an attempt by brothers to reinforce the tie with their sisters in a new way.

One wonders about the role of money in this context. If women send money back, can it be used to buy yams or pigs? Elsewhere in Pacific Island societies people contribute money to the purchases of pigs for use in exchanges, or money itself enters these exchanges (see, e.g., A. Strathern and P.J. Stewart 1999, P.J. Stewart and A. Strathern 2002a, for a case study of this in the Mount Hagen area of Papua New Guinea). Eriksen refers to Christina Toren's analysis of money in Fiji, how it represents otherness and the outside world, but is brought inside and re-socialized or domesticated by being used to buy kava, which is then shared at drinking ceremonies (Toren 1989). *Sakkem presen* similarly puts money to a social, kinship-based, use. However, it does not fully turn back the circle into distribution as happens in Toren's Fijian example.

A similar partial moment of conversion of value is found in a new tendency in Duna bridewealth practices in the Southern Highlands Province of Papua New Guinea (P.J. Stewart and A. Strathern 2002b; A. Strathern and P.J. Stewart 2004). In the 1990s the kin of a bride tended to demand a higher sum of money to go especially to the mother of the bride for her care in giving birth to and bringing up the girl. The kin of the groom seemed to find these escalated demands something of a burden and they grumbled about them, especially because the demands were usually made at an advanced stage of the final public presentation of bridewealth items. What did this increase signify? As with *sakkem presen*, it referred to the specifics of a particular gendered kin tie, and whereas in the past the emphasis would have been on a demand for a large pig (a reproductive creature), now the demand was for money, which could be used in acts of consumption. The growing importance of consumption and its problematic relationship to the circulation of wealth appears to be a theme in both *sakkem presen* and the Duna case, although the specific contexts differ. Both cases also appear to indicate an increasing recognition of women's agency and claims in kinship contexts. The *agency* of women in situations of alliance between groups or in criss-crossing networks of exchange is a general theme that Eriksen brings out well in her overall study. Such agency does not only belong to the contemporary world of postcolonial change. In Hagen women were seen as vehicles of alliance between groups or between particular men, for example, but they exercised plenty of their own choice and agency in control over pigs, decisions of when and how many pigs to give, and the like, largely because of the work they put into looking after pigs and growing them. Shell valuables were more the realm of men because they came along the 'roads' of exchange and men went and asked for them as gifts from partners. But in another area, Pangia, in the Southern Highlands Province, where a different and more diffused structure of marital ties held, the women of a particular local settlement played a highly visible role at the conclusion of a pig-killing ceremony, carrying pearl shells in netbags in many different directions, to be given to partners. Such gifts were often, but not always, gifts to mother's brothers to ensure the health of their sisters' children. The women moved out en masse, laughing, joking and talking among themselves, shells jingling at their backs, visual embodiments of their own agency as links between people. This custom was called *yonea moriki.*

There are many such ethnographic parallels or comparisons that can be made between Ambrym and features of Papua New Guinea societies. Eriksen points to the alternative selections of paths of kin relations that people can pursue in Ambrym. The same is true for the Duna, particularly because of the importance of cognatic ties in their system of kin relations (P.J. Stewart and A. Strathern 2002b, A. Strathern and P.J. Stewart 2004). The indigenous concept of the road or 'paths' of kin ties is found in the Wahgi area of the Western Highlands of Papua New Guinea, referring largely to forms of marriage (Reay 1959; O'Hanlon 1989). The idea of the 'original place' which is significant in Ambrym is also a deep-seated characteristic of many Austronesian and non-Austronesian speaking people in the Pacific region. Eriksen notes this parallel with the Duna people from our own work (see references in A. Strathern and P.J. Stewart 2004). She goes on to argue that in Ambrym people are iconic of places, because they carry their place-affiliations around with them. The same can apply to descent affiliations. In Duna an agnate of a particular local unit or 'parish' (*rindi*; the term 'parish' indicates that these units of structure were also defined ritually) carries their agnatic affiliation around and retains it while living elsewhere. And the 'placing' of people or their symbolic identification in terms of place occurs in other locality-sensitive contexts outside of the Pacific. In Scotland (another area in which we have worked for many years, see e.g., A. Strathern and P.J. Stewart 2001), for example, a person visiting Dumfries and Galloway may explain that they have ancestral ties with the county of Ayrshire north of Dumfries. The word gets around and someone who meets them will say 'So you're an Ayrshire man'. Their 'placeness' is portable as in Eriksen's example. This is an example among many of Eriksen's creative rethinking of familiar ethnographic themes.

An important comparative topic which is intrinsic to Eriksen's central argument is the problem of gendered forms of leadership. Eriksen argues that male prominence consisted in personifications of power achieved by men in the graded societies, the idea being that in some way particular men stood out among or 'eclipsed' others as well as the communal context on which their prominence was actually founded. Eriksen opposes this to female, egalitarian, communal power. She briefly discusses the Hagen system of 'big-manship' articulated in the competitive exchanges known as *moka*, and relates this to a theory of personification and the process of 'eclipsing' others (for details on *moka* and the Hagen people see A. Strathern 1971 and A. Strathern and P.J. Stewart 2000). Here one might raise a question regarding eclipsing. It is true that big-men do claim personal prestige for themselves in the organizing of *moka*; and in particular in the speech-making that accompanies a *moka* occasion. They also try to obtain pigs from many sources which they can give away in their own name at a *moka*. But on a *moka* occasion the big-men also instantiate their groups as a whole; by using the term 'I' in speeches they often mean 'we', i.e. their own group, so that they simultaneously foreground themselves and their fellow clansmen who are contributing pigs in their own separate names for the occasion. The big-man assembles pigs; but he does not claim they are all his. Thus, no-one's agency is eclipsed. The agency of women as producers of pigs is ceremonially recognized in the *werl* dances which married women perform at such events. These same observations may be applied to suggest a modification to another part of the model of big-manship. 'Big-men' in Hagen do not simply harness the labor of others to the attainment of their personal prestige. If they depend on the labor of others, they can do so only on the basis of reciprocity, not by any authority they have. If they deploy pigs raised by their wives for *moka* exchanges, they can do so only by gaining the wives' support to do so, partially by cultivating partnerships with these wives' own natal kinsfolk. These observations do not directly impinge on Eriksen's own argument, which depends on a semantic distinction between mediated and unmediated exchange and its gendered concomitants. It is important to get details of the kind we have clarified above documented, because they inevitably influence the kinds of theoretical schemes into which data are fitted, including the contrast between 'big-men' and 'great men' that is prevalent in the literature. As a general point here, it is interesting to note that not only does the interpretation of data influence how these data feed into theoretical schemes, but also theoretical schemes influence how the data are interpreted in the first place. Thus, whether a relationship is seen as 'unmediated' or 'mediated' is not a simple matter of observation: it is itself already a product of interpretation. Similarly with concepts of 'assembling' pigs or 'harnessing labor', or whether one person 'contains a relationship' within them, and the like.

In her own carefully constructed argument, Eriksen has made creative use of pieces of theoretical argumentation regarding exchange, gender, and leadership – all classic themes – in order to weave her own ingenious argument about historical change and the processes that give rise to alterations in the dominance of forms in social life. Hers is a work that is founded equally on close ethnographic study and on clear theoretical lines of interpretation. It deserves to have an impact well beyond its immediate area of reference, particularly as a study in historical anthropology and in anthropological research on gender and Christianity, in the Pacific and elsewhere.

Cromie Burn Research Unit, Blacksidend Section, April 2007

References

Barth, F. (1981), *Process and Form in Social Life. Selected essays of Fredrik Barth: Volume I.* (London and Boston: Routledge and Kegan Paul).

Meggitt, M.J. (1964), Male-female relationships in the Highlands of Australian New Guinea, *American Anthropologist*, N.S., 66:4. Part 2: 204–224.

O'Hanlon, M. (1989), *Reading the Skin.* (London: British Museum Publications).

Reay, M. (1959), *The Kuma: Freedom and Conformity in the New Guinea Highlands.* (Melbourne: Melbourne University Press, for the Australian National University).

Stewart, P.J. and Strathern, A. (2000), Introduction: Latencies and Realizations in Millennial Practices. In P.J. Stewart and A. Strathern (eds), Millennial Countdown in New Guinea, *Ethnohistory* Special Issue 47:1:3–27.

Stewart, P.J. and Strathern, A. (2002a), 'Transformations of Monetary Symbols in the Highlands of Papua New Guinea', for a special issue of the journal *L'Homme* on money (Questions de Monnaie), 162 April/June, pp. 137–156.

Stewart, P.J. and Strathern, A. (2002b), *Remaking the World: Myth, Mining and Ritual Change among the Duna of Papua New Guinea*. For Smithsonian Series in Ethnographic Inquiry (Washington, D.C: Smithsonian Institution Press).

Stewart, P.J. and Strathern, A. (2004), *Witchcraft, Sorcery, Rumors, and Gossip*. For New Departures in Anthropology Series (Cambridge: Cambridge University Press).

Strathern, A. (1971), *The Rope of Moka* (Cambridge: Cambridge University Press).

Strathern, A. and Stewart, P.J. (1999), Objects, Relationships, and Meanings: Historical Switches in Currencies in Mount Hagen, Papua New Guinea. In Akin, D. and Robbins, J. (eds), *Money and Modernity: State and Local Currencies in Melanesia*, ASAO (Association for Social Anthropology in Oceania) Monograph Series No. 17, pp. 164–191 (Pittsburgh: University of Pittsburgh Press).

Strathern, A. and Stewart, P.J. (2000), *Arrow Talk: Transaction, Transition, and Contradiction in New Guinea Highlands History* (Kent, Ohio and London: Kent State University Press).

Strathern, A. and Stewart, P.J. (2001), *Minorities and Memories: Survivals and Extinctions in Scotland and Western Europe* (Durham, N.C: Carolina Academic Press).

Strathern, A. and Stewart, P.J. (2004), *Empowering the Past, Confronting the Future, The Duna People of Papua New Guinea*. For Contemporary Anthropology of Religion Series (New York: Palgrave Macmillan).

Toren, C. (1989), Drinking cash: the purification of money through ceremonial. In Bloch, M. and Parry, J. (eds), *Money and the Morality of Exchange*, pp. 142–164 (Cambridge: Cambridge University Press).

Preface

This book is based on seventeen months of fieldwork in Vanuatu during the periods 1995–96, 1999, and in 2000. The aim of the study is to approach an understanding of what I have called the gendered social structures on North Ambrym as they unfold in kinship, marriage, political movements, church movements and in development projects. My basic assumption is that the tension between two contrasting modes of sociality, the one lateral and outward oriented and the other internal and hierarchical, generates social developments. An understanding of social life on Ambrym is premised on seeing how this tension works and how it is gendered. In the first three chapters I relate this problematic to discussions of kinship, marriage and place. Whereas a focus on the descent groups, the *buluims,* as patrilines and a focus on men as *men of the place,* generate an idea of a place-bound sociality, a focus on the alternative ways of relations-making crossing the borders of the *buluims* and a focus on women who marry away from their natal place generate an idea of another form of sociality which is mobile and flexible. In the next chapters I analyze town migration, new ceremonial institutions, church movements and development projects emphasizing this latter mode of sociality. This 'mode of sociality' can be referred to as 'silent'. It is 'silent' both in the sense that, for instance, the church movements which are to a large degree based on women's work, do not emphasize women the way the traditional male institutions such as the male graded society emphasized men. The whole point of the latter institution was to create men with famous names. The names were loudly expressed through significant objectifications of the male prestations during rituals. Women, in the church movements and in other social practices, do not yell out their names.

The female "mode of sociality" is "silent" in another respect as well. Women move and change residence at least once during their lifetimes and on Ambrym this value of women's adaptability is gaining new significance as women migrate to town and marry to other islands. The social significance of this movement is however to some extent unexpressed both in the anthropological literature and in the way people themselves talk about place and movement on Ambrym. Bislama expressions like *"Long Vila kastom i lus"* [B: *Kastom* is lost in Vila/Port Vila], *"Vila i tanem kastom"* [B: Port Vila changes *kastom*] point to the way people feel their island identity as threatened when they move away from their village and their island. These expressions point to the way urban life takes people away from work in the garden and from redistributions within the traditional economy, and express how people feel that the new demands in town, such as wage labour and work migration, give them less time to invest in matters which for their parents and grandparents were of such significance, such as the men's graded society, or amassing food for food redistributions during life cycle ceremonies. In spite of these "disembedding"

(Giddens 1990) mechanisms, a certain degree of connectedness still exists between North Ambrym people in the village and those who have moved to town or to other islands. This connectedness is created and recreated in new ways through what I call the female "mode of sociality", a "silent" movement. One new way of creating connectedness is through the *sakkem presen* ceremony I describe in Chapter 4.

The names of the Ambrym people I refer to here have been changed to some extent. As a general rule I have not changed the names of the people who were aware of how I intended to use the information they gave me. I have changed the names of those people whom I only heard about and who are therefore mentioned without their knowledge. In some historical cases I have also changed some of the names mainly because of the potentially disputed grounds on which stories from the past figure. When I, mainly in Chapter 3, use genealogies and map migration and village relocations, I mention names more as examples of general patterns than as a description of actual movement and genealogies. I have based my analyses on the stories I was given, but there are many other stories that I was not told. The information on which I have based my analysis is therefore not complete (it would be impossible) and thus only partial. This book can therefore not be used as a historical document in any objective sense.

Acknowledgements

This book is a result of funding from the Norwegian Research Council (Norges Forskningsråd; NFR) from 2000 to 2003 and one year's funding from the University of Bergen from 2003 to 2004. I am indebted to both the NFR and the University of Bergen for giving me research grants. The grants have been substantial enough to allow several periods of fieldwork and for me to take my family along. I have thus spent a great deal of time in Vanuatu mainly with people on North Ambrym as well as among people from North Ambrym living or visiting the capital Port Vila. I am indebted to them for their hospitality towards me and my husband as well as, and especially towards, our children. I would like to thank the whole Ranon community, but in particular Billy, his wife Nelly, and their children Rose, George and Ronny. Rose especially has played a major role in how I managed the urban-based part of my fieldwork and she is also an important figure throughout the whole book. I also want to thank Billy's sister Mamu and her husband, Tango, Serah Lissak, a fieldworker for the Cultural Centre, and Elisa from Ranmuhu who helped me conduct a survey in Port Vila in 2000. I am particularly indebted to Kwen from Ranon and Peter Bumseng from Fanrereo for their effort and patience when I struggled with the local language. I would also like to thank the men and women both from Ranon and other villages in Lolihor who took us around in the Ambrym hills and forests to show us abandoned villages and old ceremonial places.

I am also indebted to the staff at the Vanuatu Cultural Centre and its director Ralph Regenvanu for their help and guidance, particularly in the initial phases of the project, and for accepting my project in the first place. I would like to thank the archivist at the National Archives and the women at the Vanuatu Cultural Centre's library for always patiently responding to my requests. I am also indebted to the late Dorothy Shineberg who kindly approached me during the conference "Walking About: Travel, Trade and Movement in Vanuatu" in Canberra in 2000, after I had given my paper on female migrants from Ambrym, and offered to make her database on migrants from Ambrym to New Caledonia available to me, which she subsequently did. I also want to thank Dianna Downing for very efficient and competent editing of the manuscript. Kjell Helge Sjøstrom has assisted me greatly in preparing the maps and figures for this book. Yvonne Wilkie, the archivist at Knox College, Dunedin, New Zealand, provided me with a copy of Rev. Murray's diary written in Ambrym, and for this I am very grateful.

I also want to express my gratitude to Dr. Pamela J. Stewart and Prof. Andrew Strathern who kindly accepted my manuscript for consideration as series editors and for comments on both the initial proposal and the first draft. I also want to thank an anonymous reader provided by Ashgate.

Without the intellectual stimulus of important scholars I have been fortunate to work and discuss with, and who have read and commented on parts and chapters of this book, this work would never have been completed. Professor Edvard Hviding has been my supervisor since I started as a graduate student in 1995, and has since been an important source of inspiration and encouragement. Professor Bruce Kapferer as well has been important for my intellectual development and an inspirational teacher during my time as a PhD student. I also want to thank Professor Joel Robbins, whose work has inspired me, and whose engagement and encouragement, has been vital. I am very grateful for the comments and suggestions he has provided for this book. I also want to thank Dr. Andrew Lattas who contributed useful perspectives for an early draft of Chapter 3 when he visited our department in May 2003. I am also grateful for comments from Prof. Deborah Gewertz and Dr. Lissant Bolton.

I find it important also to thank my family; my parents, Anne Marie and Roy Eriksen, for fostering my interest in the world outside of home and for encouragement and support during my student years and later. Lastly, but not least, I want to thank my husband and fellow anthropologist Knut Rio, who has been my greatest support both through fieldwork and during the process of writing. I thank him for his critical reading and constructive comments. It has been of invaluable help to have a partner in life who is also a partner in anthropology. I also thank our children, Anna, Oline and Ingrid who made me think of other things.

Parts of Chapter 5 have appeared as an article in *Anthropological Theory*, Vol. 6, No. 2, 227–247 (2006), and Chapter 6 has appeared in a slightly different version in *Oceania*, vol 75, No.3 (2005). These are reprinted with permission from the editors.

A Note on Language

I have based my three fieldwork periods mainly on communication in Bislama. Bislama is the Vanuatu version of Neo Melanesian, also called Pidgin. In the first stage of the development of this language it was used for commercial communication. However, it is in no way an "artificial" language. Keesing (1988) has pointed out that the language has developed through different stages. As Pidgin was not only used between traders and local people, but also among local people from different islands, the language started to develop along the grammatical and syntactical lines of the vernacular languages. Bislama is today a language with close similarity to the many languages of the different islands of Vanuatu, and following Independence in 1980 was made into an official language. Bislama is the major language for the urban centres and also a language most people in rural areas speak. On Ambrym I never found it difficult to communicate in Bislama, particularly because, during my 1995 fieldwork, there was a newly wed woman from Pentecost who had just settled in the village, and informal gatherings among women would often take place in Bislama to include the two of us. In 1999 there were a number of people from other islands living in Ranon who relied on Bislama to communicate, for instance some of the teachers at the secondary school. On Ambrym I only met one older woman who did not speak Bislama.

It was probably the easy access to Bislama that made it difficult for me to become a fluent speaker of the local language. During both my field periods in Ranon I made an effort to learn the language, and even arranged for a teacher. Although the teaching was useful and helped me understand many local concepts, I never managed the local language the way I managed Bislama. In addition to my own local teachers I have had much assistance from Paton's dictionary of the Lonwolwol language published in 1971.

Bislama spelling represents the vernacular phonetic values as opposed to the English values so that for instance the word 'fire' in English becomes *fae* in Bislama. For the spelling of the local, North Ambrym language, I have used the following vowels:

u-as in *buluim* – like in English 'bull' or 'super'
o-as in *om* – like the English 'loss'
a-as in *talang* – like the English 'army' or 'after'
e-as in *melon* – like in English 'beggar'
i-as in *tarin* – like English 'kill'

The consonants sounds are much more diverse than my spelling would indicate. I have based myself on a simple spelling using, for instance, only a distinction between *r-* and *rl* to indicate the difference between r sounds. There are however many more r sounds.

In the text I have written Bislama words and words from the local language in *italics* and translated them in brackets indicating Bislama with a capital B in front of the translation and local language by a capital L in front of the translation.

Value of Vanuatu Currency

In 2006 one hundred VATU cost about one USD.

*For my daughters
Anna, Oline and Ingrid*

Chapter 1

Gender, Christianity and Change

Introduction

Sorcery and Christianity

People in the village of Ranon in the northern part of Ambrym were, by the end of 1999, disturbed by a great increase in sorcery (see also Rio 2002b). There had been an increase in the number of deaths, more sickness, and in particular skin infections were not healing as they should. The fruit trees were not producing as much as they usually did, and, the most important indication of sorcery, people were generally much more antagonistic toward each other. It has been reported that the approach of the millennium for many people, in the Pacific and elsewhere, was tied to a fear of what was perceived as a liminal period of transition (see for instance P.J. Stewart and A. Strathern 2000a). In Ranon however, there was little, if any, talk about year 2000 as an important bellwether of change. Rather, the focus here was on the past: what should they do with this sudden increase in a kind of sorcery they considered belonging to the past? People in Ranon have been Christian for almost a century and sorcery is, for them, part of a world they characterize as dangerous and belonging to pre-Christian ancestors.

In order to deal with the sudden and dramatic turn of events in Ranon in 1999 a village court was organized. The whole village and people from neighbouring villages gathered in Ranon's communal square early one morning. The most important and recognized chiefs from the area were all present, sitting together at the end of an oval circle of men, women and children; everyone was there. There had been many rumours, and people were frightened, some even expressed their wish to leave the village completely, as they believed it might be cursed. Now they gathered to learn the facts.

The eldest, most prominent chief in the area gave an opening speech summing up people's anxieties and pointing out that the local development was going in the wrong direction. Several other people spoke as well, and not only the chiefs. They were mostly men who voiced their opinions as to who the sorcerers were. At midday however, when the angry discussion had turned to naming the sorcerers, a brother of one of the accused sorcerers and a member of a relatively new Church known as the 'Holiness', asked everyone present to swear on the Bible that they would only tell the truth. 'We are Christians' he said 'we should follow the rules of the Bible'. This statement implied a sudden shift from discussing 'who was responsible' to discussing 'how to deal with it'. The man from the 'Holiness' church wanted to establish the Church as the framework for the event. However, this was not an easy matter. A man with a reputation for knowledge of *kastom*[1] rose and replied aggressively: 'We are not women. We can make no use of the Bible here'.

This event is indicative of how people on Ambrym see Christianity as embodying a contrasting and alternative logic in relation to a pre-Christian cosmology wherein control of sorcery was more important than nowadays. Moreover, alternative logics such as this are also gendered. The court case was an effort to establish a ground wherein sorcery, as something outside and contrasting the church, could be discussed, but this, as was overtly expressed by the *kastom*-man, was not perceived to be a matter for women. As will become apparent throughout the chapters of this book, Christianity has seriously challenged what we might call the male hegemony on Ambrym, implying the rise of alternative values.

Understanding Cultural Change and New Social Formations

The literature on social and cultural change in Melanesia, especially in relation to Christianity, is growing. Papua New Guinea ethnographers in particular have become more focused and interested in understanding the cultural and social implications of Christianity (see Barker 1992, 1996; Douglas 2002, 2003; Jebens 2005; Robbins 2004; Stewart and Strathern 1997, 2000a,b,c, Robbins, Stewart and Strathern 2001) as well as of changing ideas of personhood, gender and agency (Robbins and Wardlow 2005; Wardlow 2006). This book contributes to this growing and important literature in two distinct ways. Firstly, the book concerns Vanuatu, which provides an interesting comparison to Papua New Guinea, since Vanuatu has a completely different colonial history. Whereas colonialism came very late to certain areas of Papua New Guinea, and the Highlands in particular, Vanuatu has over a hundred years of colonial history and knowledge of Christianity. People in island Melanesia became entangled very early on in relationships and encounters that took them across the sea to new places or created inroads for new ideas and practices (Hviding 1996, 2003). However, in Vanuatu's case, with the English-French Condominium government, the country was colonised by not only one European power, but two, creating a somewhat less efficient colonial power than existed in the 'one-nation' colonies where the hegemony of one power could develop with less interference from other nations. An understanding of changing systems of meaning and forms of social organization must take into consideration this particular colonial history.

Robbins (2004) has recently described the incredible transformations of cultural ideas taking place among the Urapmin of the western highlands of Papua New Guinea. Having had only two decades of exposure to colonial Christianity at the time of their Independence in 1975, the Urapmin converted to a charismatic form of Pentecostal Christianity and became obsessed by ideas of a morally good life according to Christian ideals, controlling their sinfulness. According to Robbins, their encounter with colonialism and Christianity was so dramatic and to some extent shocking – removing them for instance from their pre-colonial position

---

1   *Kastom* is a pan Melanesian concept referring to both traditions as well as the relevance of these traditions in the present. The term will be discussed in Chapter 7.

of importance in the regional ritual system – that they completely changed their perceptions of the world. Through a process Robbins terms 'humiliation' (see also Robbins and Wardlow 2005) the Urapmin changed their worldview radically. My analysis of Christianity in Vanuatu also deals with cultural and social change, but not of the radical kind Robbins's account reveals. Robbins, drawing on Dumont (1980), shows that the dominant cultural values among the Urapmin, that of the 'the relation', became encompassed, and was thus replaced as a core cultural value by a completely new and utterly contrasting value. It was the value of the individual as an autonomous being (especially in the face of God on the last day) that became formative for a new conception of self among the Urapmin.

My analysis draws attention to how an already existing but not dominant cultural value gained in prominence as a result of the mission and the church. I show how Ambrym men and women, not in the face of rapid, humiliating and shocking change, but rather in the course of several decades, reformulated their cultural system. Here I arrive at the second distinct characteristic of my analysis. In understanding the role Christianity plays in Ambrym cultural values and social organization, I have emphasized a perspective on gender. The chapters of this book will outline the double character of many principles of social organization as well as cultural values and ideas. I show how kinship, migration, ceremonies and rituals all reveal two contrasting but complementary forms. One of those forms I have termed male, the other I have termed female. A value hierarchy is therefore always according to a gendered form. Toward the end of this book I show how the traditionally encompassed social form has become primary, and how the male form is losing ground. The new value that gains in prominence is therefore not a completely new introduction, but a social form that has been foregrounded in the encounter with Christianity.

In this book I will outline these two contrasting forms and show how they play out in different parts of Ambrym social life. Before doing so however, I will begin at the beginning with how I encountered Ambrym sociality.

Ranon

My first encounter with Ambrym was late one night in October 1995. My husband, Knut Rio, and I had travelled from the capital Port Vila to the airport in West Ambrym on one of the smallest planes operated by Vanair. It was hot and humid, and the plane was crowded, not only with people, but also with chickens and small piglets. It was heading towards Santo in the northern part of Vanuatu as its final destination, and had already landed on several of the islands between Efate and Ambrym. We were dizzy but relieved when we landed safely on the small clearing between the coconut groves and villages on West Ambrym. My husband had already visited the island the year before when he first travelled to Vanuatu and met with Director Ralph Regenvanu at the Cultural Centre in the capital Port Vila. Before carrying out ethnographic fieldwork in Vanuatu, a research agreement with the Vanuatu Cultural Centre [VCC] has to be worked out. This agreement secures the cooperation between the VCC and the researchers and makes sure that what the researchers learn is reported in the form of a written document in Bislama and returned to the place where the researcher

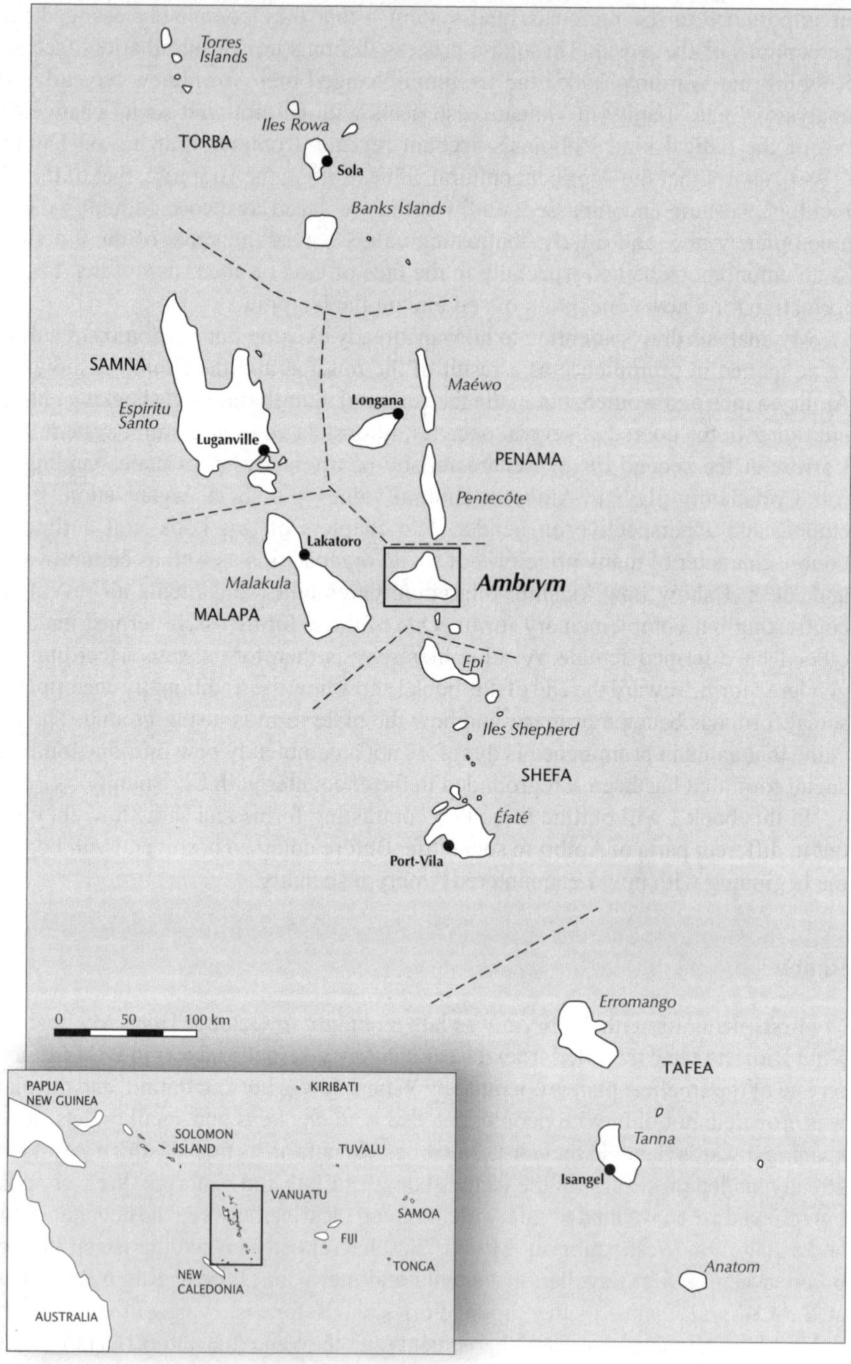

Map 1.1   Vanuatu

stayed. The VCC might also ask the researcher to do some work for the VCC while in the field. For its part, the VCC facilitates the researcher's work as far as possible, by for instance suggesting fieldwork sites particularly relevant to the ethnographer's interest. Regenvanu had recommended Ambrym to us. I was interested in how small-scale societies with intricate structures of social organization have sustained and changed through colonial and postcolonial times. Ambrym seemed the perfect location. Ever since Rivers's (1915) and Deacon's (1927) account of Ambrym kinship, this particular social system has been the subject of anthropological interest (Seligman 1927; Radcliffe Brown 1927; Lane and Lane 1956, 1958; Löffler 1960; Scheffler 1970; Patterson 1976).

As we arrived on Ambrym that afternoon in 1995, it was a comfort to know that one of us had been on the island before and could look for some familiar faces. Knut recognized a smiling man at the outskirts of the airport. He was the north Ambrym chief responsible for managing the community-owned speedboat that connects people in the north to the west. It was already late afternoon and, travelling with an infant, we decided to hurry aboard the boat in order to reach the north before nightfall. By the time we approached the beach in Ranon, however, it was completely dark. We could only hear the excited voices on shore, children laughing and shouting, men talking and dogs barking. We were led through a crowd of yelling children and entered, at the very outskirts of the village, a low-roofed kitchen house. Men and women with children were sitting on mats in front of the fire. We were fed and before

Photo 1.1   Ranon village, seen from the sea

long installed in our own thatch-roofed sleeping house.

We stayed in the household of Billy Bong and his wife Nelly. Billy was a fieldworker[2] for the Cultural Centre, and it was this connection that enabled us to rely on their hospitality during this visit and the years to come. During the first field period we slept in Billy and Nelly's elder son's house. He was married to a woman from the island of Pentecost and was living in Port Vila, and only occasionally needed the house for himself. Later however, we built our own house in the village close to Billy and Nelly's house. During the first period in Ranon from October 1995 to April 1996 I stayed close to the house and always in the village. Caring for an infant while doing fieldwork made me quite familiar with the paths from my house to Nelly's kitchen house, and also to my next door neighbour Serah, who cared for a child of exactly the same age as mine, and to the house of Mamu, who was an experienced grandmother and always knew what to do for fever and children's lack of appetite. Serah, also a fieldworker for the VCC, was helpful whenever I wanted to visit a place or when I heard of a marriage or another ceremony I wanted to observe.

The company of women and my involvement in their daily lives, the gossip and their concerns, made me adopt a female perspective on life in the village. The analysis of this book is very much influenced by the perspective these women presented as we talked about daily concerns.

Movement, Marriage and Women

My initial general interest in studying how small-scale communities have sustained and changed their social organization as the colonial state, the independent nation state, and the global economy pushed them in new directions, was soon influenced by a particular focus on movement, marriage and women. This was so because women were always keen on discussing marriage arrangements. They discussed this among themselves all the time and were always eager to answer my ignorant questions on how and why certain marriages were arranged. I came to realize that an understanding of my initial interest depended on a deeper understanding of how social organization connected to women's agency in movement and marriage. My impression of the vital role women's mobility played was enhanced as I conducted an historical field survey on demography and movement of people in the last generations. As will become apparent in Chapter two and three, women play a crucial role in creating 'roads' for different kinds of movement, and not only roads for people, but roads for social institutions as well. When asking for instance about the first churches and how different villages became Christian, I not only realized the tight connection between demographic movement over the last century and mission history, but also the role women played in these processes. Women, who moved when marrying and brought the church along, revealed a pattern in my historical investigations. It was as if my first interest in women's role in marriage arrangements unravelled, for me, a new

---

2   During the last decades, the Vanuatu Cultural Centre staff has developed a fieldworker's programme. They recruit local fieldworkers willing to voluntarily document customs and language. Initially there were only male fieldworkers, but Lissant Bolton and Jean Toreissei started the female fieldworkers programme in the early 1990s.

dimension of how social life works on Ambrym. I 'found' a female social structure. In this book I try to analyse how this female social structure worked as counter logic to a more immediate, and perhaps more outspoken social structure, a 'male' social structure. In relation to kinship for instance, the focus on place and on patri-lineages, is what I call a male social structure. The female alternative, as I will show in the next chapter, breaks down the monopoly of the patri-lineages in setting the premise for new relationships. Unravelling female agency in relation to movement then also revealed an alternative social logic.

Anthropological analyses of the region have often taken marriage as the point of departure when addressing the relations between the genders (for instance, M. Strathern 1972; Josephides 1985; Gewertz and Errington 1987; Kelly 1993). Women's roles as 'in-between' or 'outside' in relation to male land holding groups have been emphasized. In this book I will show that connection-making and movement are assets that have social recognition and importance within a value hierarchy where landholding is not the primary asset. M. Strathern (1988) has suggested, in referring to the relations between men and women among the Sa speakers on Pentecost, the island north of Ambrym, that 'One could argue that the differentiated spheres of male and female activity afford a framework for the conceptualization of a dual process in social life' (1988, 82). The creation of alternative universes wherein the value hierarchy of the one is reversed in the other, points to such a dual process.

It is important however to point out that when I talk about female and male social structures, I refer to ideal types. In this book I will single out certain values and certain practices that I argue become key elements in this model of a gendered social structure: I show how the value of connectedness, of emphasising the relation more than the personification of the relation, of emphasising the road more than the place, is female gendered. However, I would have no trouble finding women who would be ideal personifications and women who have become icons of their place. My intention in singling out female values is not to argue that no woman can do otherwise and act according to other values. Rather, I argue that these are the values that are defining the 'female'. Women can, however, act according to other ideals. Women can act according to male ideals and thus seek personifications and become more place bound than mobile. It is a fundamental premise for my argument that gender is not only a characteristic of the individual. By this I do not only mean that gender is more than biological sex. It is well known and accepted in feminist theory that gender is different from 'sex' and that gender is 'performed' more than 'born', although the degree is disputed (Butler 1990; Grosz 1990). Paradoxically, even the most constructionist positions in feminist theory seem to focus primarily on gender as an aspect of the body and of the individual. My claim is that we need to recognise the relevance of gender for more than an understanding of individual gender play. More importantly, when gender is seen as fundamentally related to individual properties (whether biological or constructed/performed) this might be characteristic of a cultural construction where the individual plays the role as the dominant value. Within these cultural frames, gender becomes individualised. In cultures that are not organized around the notion of the individual as a fundamental value, gender is not basically an attribute of the individual. In line with a dominant trend in Melanesian anthropology (M. Strathern 1988) I will outline in the following chapters how relations as well as persons are gendered. More than this, gender on Ambrym is the one difference that organizes other differences.

When I discuss male and female social structures, forms and values, I am thus not talking about what all women and all men do.

The Chapters

In Chapter 2 I describe the anthropological history on Ambrym, and thereby present Ambrym kinship as it has been analysed since Rivers first visited the area. In this kinship analysis I emphasize the way kinship on Ambrym can be seen not only as a fundamental structure which forms relationships according to prescriptive ideals based on an agnatic model, but also as a form which can make sense of change and innovation. I show that on the one hand, agnatic connections to place organize the way people think about kinship and marriage, but on the other hand, matri-lateral links open up for alternative ways of reckoning kinship and relating to potential marriage partners. The alternative ways are potential relationships which can be activated if needed. I thus analyse a dynamic between agnatic descent and 'matri-lateral alternatives', as a relationship between actual and potential relationships.

In Chapter 3 I draw the analysis of kinship further and relate it to notions of place and movement, and reveal the same structural principle focused on in Chapter 2: the dynamics between actual and potential. In the same way as women open up for alternative ways of relating to people, women's movement when marrying opens up potential connections and roads into new places for their natal families. When villages historically were relocated as a result of conflict, war, sickness, or missionization, the roads created by the outmarried women were essential. I furthermore show that even though people move and follow women's alternative roads, connection to place and ideas of agnatic origin are still important. It is as if a merging of female mobility and male origin focus creates a notion of a movable place.

In Chapter 4 I continue the focus on movement, marriage and women, and look specifically at movement beyond the island and to the capital. I show how women's town migration and wage labour have affected family structure and kinship organization in town, and I show how the role of women in creating alternative relationships and making connections to new places becomes even more vital in the new urban environment. Then, in Chapter 5, I return to Ambrym and to history in a search for the role of women and female agency during the time when people on North Ambrym became Christian. I argue that mission history is tightly connected to women's movement and that the most efficient missionaries on Ambrym historically where not the white educated missionaries from overseas, but rather Ambrym women who brought along the church as they married into new communities. I continue this focus in Chapter 6 where I return to present-day developments and look at the role of the church on Ambrym today. I show how it has changed gender relations and how women now hold a much more prominent position within the church than they did in the previous ceremonial institutions, such as the men's graded society. On the one hand the church was seen as a new kind of ritual society and part of the men's secret knowledge when it was first established on Ambrym. On the other hand, the church has become something completely different. I argue that women have become prominent in the church, but that the traditional focus on male leadership in the church has not sufficiently explored this. Women have, through different forms of fund raising activity and Christian ceremonies, made the church into an idiom for social belonging. Women have been able to do this because of their established position in kinship and marriage, which makes them connect people and places. This is the premise on which the church operates on Ambrym today.

As a parallel to this interplay between women and church, we find the dynamics between *kastom* and men. Whereas the church creates social communities, *kastom* creates big men. The relationship between church and *kastom* has become a gendered relationship. In Chapters 7 and 8 I include other social movements in the analysis, and compare the men's graded society as it has been described in the literature to newer institutions through the colonial and postcolonial period. In Chapter 7 I analyse the political movements leading up to Independence and base much of my data on my archival sources. I show that the gendered interplay I found between the church and the graded society is also found in relation to other social institutions. Understanding the development of the local council for instance is premised on an understanding of the gendered social structure generating male and female social forms. I show that the local council takes another form than that of the graded society, being more related to the social form of the church. I thus argue in Chapter eight that the development of leadership within the local council is more difficult than the development of *kastom* leaders who operated on the social structure of the male graded society. In chapter nine I sum up my argument and social and cultural change on Ambrym and compare my analysis within and beyond the region.

Theoretical Directions

Within anthropology, and social science in general, different models of sociality have been paradigmatic. The concept of society varies from the classical Durkheimean model of society as either based on organic or mechanical solidarity to a more post structuralist notion of society as a construction. Different social philosophies have of course also marked different concepts of society, from Marxism to rational choice models. Understanding the oscillation between the structured forms of social life and the unpredictable and changing elements of social life remains the basic problematic of social science. One of the more radical theoretical stances in recent decades is the one advocated by Gilles Deleuze and Felix Guattari. In their book *Anti Oedipus* (1983), and their late work *A Thousand Plateaus* (1988), they make a symbiosis of Marxism and Freudianism while at the same time breaking with the theoretical premises for both of these traditions. They reject the Marxist philosophy of history and replace this with the concepts of micro and macro assemblages. Contradictions and oppositions do not create change and progress. Rather, the processes of 'territorialization', 're-territorialization', and 'de-territorialization' of 'codes' are made primary. The processes of re- and de-territorialization are again connected to the two different kinds of social structure which work against each other. The 'arboretic' structures create order and predictability, while the 'rhizomatic' structures work across them in unpredictable manners. The one works vertically while the other works horizontally, trying to de-territorialize the codes of arboretic structures.

In this work, although I make few explicit references to Deleuze and Guattari, I have been influenced by their models and in particular by their notion of two different kinds of social structures working against each other. The gendered social structure on Ambrym, as I will outline in particular in the last part of this book, can be said to be organized around two different axes, one vertical and the other horizontal. I show how these different social forms alternate in different situations, and that the one can be said to be an inversion of the other. Whereas the female social form is focused on creating relations between people and creating community, the male social form inverts the former version by focusing on the ability to distinguish oneself from others and transcend the communal. In the most general sense, the female form creates communities, whereas the male form creates big men. As I go more theoretically into my concluding chapter, the one is however only a variation of the other.

De Coppet (1992) has argued that in modern Western ideology society has become less and less imaginable because the individual, or what he calls the autonomous subject, has been made the ultimate value. Society then seems to be reduced to a collection of individuals, a 'pile of sand' (1992, 60), and, as Kapferer (2005, 1) has pointed out, the social becomes a vacated category. De Coppet (1992), in the Dumontian (1980) tradition, has advocated for a way of conceptualising society, which emphasizes shared values as the main dimension. 'Society' then is based on shared values organized in a 'hierarchy of values' (De Coppet 1992; Dumont 1980). My outline of the two opposing and alternating social forms, are different ways of organizing a hierarchy of values. Analyzing social life on Ambrym in terms of these competing hierarchies of values enables me to conceptualize 'Ambrym society' as something more than a 'collection of individuals'. Rather, 'society' becomes a dynamic which on the one hand is based on a comparable model of value hierarchies and different structuring principles and on the other, enables a specific analytical focus on the ethnographic material which distinguishes the locally specific mechanics of interaction.

Vanuatu, the Ethnographic Context

Geography and general characteristics

Vanuatu, an archipelago consisting of about eighty bigger and smaller islands dispersed over a distance of 850 kilometres in a Y formation (see Map 1.1), is situated east of Australia, north of New Caledonia and south of the Solomon Islands. Vanuatu was the former New Hebrides under the colonial rule of the joint English and French Condominium. The colony was created in 1906, which is fairly late compared to other European colonies in the region. However, de Quiros visited the archipelago as early as the sixteen hundreds. He mistook the islands for the great southern continent and gave the largest northern island the name Tierra Australia Espirito Santo. In 1766 Bougainville sailed from France, circumnavigated Cape

Horn, and in 1768 discovered the islands he named Pentecost and Aurora, the central islands of the archipelago. In 1772 Captain Cook set out on his second journey to the Pacific, and in 1774 he sighted the islands in the archipelago. Cook realised that he had found the southern continent de Quiros had visited. He sailed around the central islands, between Ambae and Maewo, and as Speiser (1923, 8) writes, 'Cook was off the northern tip of Ambrym, and realized from the two columns of smoke rising from the mountains of the islands that Ambrym possessed two active volcanoes'. Captain Cook never anchored on Ambrym, according to his logs, but rather harboured in southern Malekula, in Port Sandwich. Storytellers on Ambrym however, have another version (see also Rio 2002a). Captain Cook anchored on the beach of Ranon, and a man who was descending from the hill village of Fanla on his way to Ranon, discovered a white man on the beach. The man from Fanla, named Roronemal, gave the white man a cycas leaf as a token of peace. Afterwards Roronemal gave Captain Cook a yam and pronounced: *'Am rem li'*, 'This is your yam'. Captain Cook consequently called the island 'Ambrim'.

The colonial period

At the end of the nineteenth century, when European states were controlling the Pacific, and had annexed all the islands, Vanuatu remained outside any sovereign jurisdiction. Great Britain as well as France had economic interests in the archipelago, and both English and French settlers were expanding their land interests on the islands. The British and the French nationals pressured their respective governments to annex the archipelago as a colony, and thereby secure their economic interests. On the British side, it was mainly Australian business interests that were being defended by preventing the French sovereign control in the archipelago. Van Trease writes that it was the French who in 1886 proposed that the two governments should begin negotiations regarding the situation in Vanuatu in order to 'arrive at an arrangement providing for the security of their respective subjects'[3] (1987, 36). In 1906 a Condominium of joint government was agreed upon between Britain and France, establishing a joint court, which had jurisdiction over land matters. All the documents I came across during my work at the National Archives in Port Vila, and those I found in a brief visit to the French colonial archives in Aix en Provence,[4] indicate the difficulty with which the French and the English ruled. The country was divided into three administrative units: the southern district, the central district and the northern district. Both the English and the French had one district agent each in these administrative territories. In Port Vila both the French and the English had their own administrative units: the British and the French residencies, and they had a joint court. However, there were major disagreements between the French and the British residencies on what the joint court had jurisdiction over. According to Van Trease (1987) the French were quite content with the lack of the joint administration's clear demarcations of power. They took advantage of the situation as far as possible

---

3   Van Trease 1987 cites this from British Foreign Office Documents, c.5648, p3.

4   Archives de Outré Mere. I visited the archives in October 2003.

and assisted the French settlers and the SFNH[5] in their acquisition of territories for commercial use. If a planter for instance was convicted in the joint court for abuse of the labour force and of the local population, the execution of the sentence was left to the national courts. If a French settler was found guilty, the French court, and not the joint court, decided the punishment. This of course severely weakened the power of the joint court. The Condominium government never had a firm grip on the situation in the New Hebrides, and at the local level, the district agents had difficulties in administering affairs and arbitrating disagreements between different villages and different chiefs, because the French would side with one party and the British with the other.

Independence

As I will outline in greater detail in Chapter 7, the conflicts between the French and the British residencies continued during the political processes leading up to Independence. The two allied themselves with different factions of the independence movement. The French residency supported a *kastom* oriented anti-colonial movement called the Nagriamel (I will return to this movement in Chapter 7), and of course also the francophone UCNH[6] party, while the British residency can be said to have been more positive in their attitude toward the National Party[7] led by the Anglican pastor Father Walter Lini. The period around Independence clearly divided the population of Vanuatu into an either Francophone or an Anglophone side, and thus polarized the population along Condominium lines (see Van Trease 1987 and Miles 1998). There was much turbulence during the decade before Independence and the first years of its existence. Chiefs were fighting each other for the right to represent their island in the new national assembly. The land that had been alienated during the colonial period was to be repatriated back to its original owners, and the traditional land tenure system was advocated. Van Trease (1987, 31) writes: 'Vanuatu's progress towards Independence was characterized by a series of political crises, which forced the colonial governments to concede step by step, rather than an orderly and planned handing over of instruments of power'. This was of course a result of the fact that there never had been any orderly holding of instruments of power during the joint government.

On Ambrym the period leading up to Independence seems to have been a somewhat traumatic time, and people are almost ashamed to talk about it today. The Australian planter whose family had resided in the village of Ranon for several generations, and who had himself matri-lateral connections to the place, was driven out of the village. He was, according to him, forcefully made to leave without any of his personal possessions. The men from Ranon who had been working most closely with him, also had to leave the village and live elsewhere for a period, because of the hostilities. Today these people have returned to the village but the Australian

---

5   Societe Francaise des Novelles Hebrides, an organization established in order to secure French interest in the archipelago.

6   Union des Communautés des Novelle Hébrides.

7   NHNP.

plantation owner from colonial times still lives in Port Vila. In Chapter 6 I deal with the difficulties with which the alienated land was retrieved by the *kastom* owners and the ongoing problems associated with this.

Today the new nation-state is divided into six administrative units; Malampa, Penama, Sanma, Shefa, Tafea, Torba, and local councils administer the relations between the local and regional level. A national council of chiefs was installed around the time of Independence and operates as an advisory body to the Parliament, in particular on matters relating to *kastom*.

Chapter 2

Kinship, Place and Movement

The Field Locations: Ranon and Port Vila

Ranon village on the western side of North Ambrym has about two hundred inhabitants and is composed of several households, a church, a communal place and the cooperative store. A huge mango tree forms the centre of the village. During my times in Ranon I often sat on a pandanus mat peeling mangos or other fruits for my children while talking to passers-by. Everyone passed by this place as they were returning from the gardens in the afternoon, or coming ashore from a fishing expedition or a trip to another village by boat. From this spot in the village I felt at once situated outside all the hamlets and at the same time I had access to all of them. People stopped as they walked by, and sometimes women in the village, who were for some reason not in the garden or busy doing other work, joined me on the mat. Just below where I sat there was a stone structured grave, the burial site of Tumal, one of the most well respected and highest chiefs in the history of the village. Although Ranon is a Christian village, the relationships to ancestor spirits is still important. These spirits affect not only people's well being, but also happenings in the natural environment, such as the weather and the harvest. When people are sick or the weather too bad, this is often taken as a sign from the ancestors.

Apia, whose yard was closest to the grave, was a direct descendent of Tumal. If there was a problem such as someone was sick or if the sea was too rough, the villagers would ask those who had close genealogical links to the ancestors buried in the village for help. Apia often calmed the sea during my stay in Ranon. He also warned me about the grave, saying that my children should not play around it, as this would upset the ancestor. His connection to the place seemed undisputed, but often in Ranon issues about belonging and original rights to place are problematic. My outline of the village is therefore only based on the things I was told while I was there, and which seemed to be common knowledge.

Sitting on my spot by the Mango tree, with my back towards the sea, I faced Billy and Nelly's yard. Billy is the son of Bongsubu who originally lived in West Ambrym but who moved to Ranon in the fifties in order to work on the plantation. Bongsubu married a woman from Ranon, and they settled in her father's place. Next to them, on my right when I sat underneath the mango tree facing Billy's household, was Aro's yard. Aro, the son of Billy's mother's brother, is regarded as *manples* or 'of the place'. This means that he has a long genealogy connecting him to Ranon. He has three sons. One of them, married with a small child, built a sleeping house next to his father's, sharing the same kitchen house.

Then, as I turned westward, toward the sea from my position by the mango tree, I looked at Tiwor's house. He is also a man considered to be 'of the place'. Beside them, Rawo and his brothers had built their hamlet. They are the sons of one of the most prominent Ranon chiefs in recent times, Chief Worwor. Above them, on my left, I could only just see the houses belonging to Tokon and his brother on the outskirts of the village. They were originally from one of the villages in the interior, from Hawor, and moved to Ranon to work on the plantation some decades ago.

Walking down toward the beach, passing by the cooperative store and Tiwor's house, I would walk straight into Douglas's yard. Douglas lives with his mother, and next to their house is the small house of Douglas's mother's brother who is not married. Douglas built his own private store right on the beach, and was, during our last period in Ranon in 2000, building a guesthouse for tourists on the beach on the outskirts of the village. His younger brother operates the store, because Douglas is always busy travelling to Port Vila or taking care of tourists arriving in the village.

Walking along the beach in the southern direction I would pass the two large school buildings, one of them a blue painted concrete house and the other a smaller wooden house with large verandas. These are remnants from the colonial era when the plantation manager used the latter as his private residence and the former as a warehouse for copra. After independence the wooden house was made into the primary school for all the children from Ranon and the neighbouring villages, and the warehouse was made into a secondary school for children not only from Ambrym, but also from the whole northern region of the archipelago. It is a boarding school and the children from Ranon attending the school also sleep at the dormitory and do not return home in the evening. Every weekend however the children in Ranon return to their parents' houses, often bringing along a school friend who cannot afford to travel home by the cargo ships which pass by at least once a week. During the weekend the village is much more lively than usual, in particular on the beach where the village youth gather after dusk.

Continuing the walk along the beach, a small cluster of thatched roofed houses appeared right behind the secondary school. This was the village of Fantor. About a half-hour walk even further along the beach, passing by a large area of coconut trees, I arrived in the village of Ranvetlam. People in Ranon often walk to Ranvetlam on Sundays to join combined church services. Ranvetlam is about the same size as Ranon and in many ways competes with Ranon as a location for development projects. Walking from Ranvetlam and uphill for another half-hour on a steep path through the coconut groves, I arrived at a small clearing with just a few houses. This was Faramsu village. Ranvetlam and Faramsu are the last villages on the northern part of Ambrym. The area between Ranvetlam and the northern most villages in West Ambrym is called Dotee, which means 'along the shore'.

Back in Ranon, walking the other direction, first along the beach, and then, after about one kilometre, turning uphill through the forest, I found the villages of Fanla, Fanrereo and Lonlilio. The village of Fanla is famous throughout the archipelago for its *kastom* reputation. It is a powerful place, people say, because of the knowledge people in Fanla still have of magic and ancestral rites. If I left Ranon, not from the beach, but rather by following a path uphill behind the village, after just a ten-minute walk, I arrived in Ranbwe, a small village half the size of Ranon on a plateau. Leaving Ranbwe, still following the path uphill for another fifteen minutes, I arrived in the village of Lonbwe. Lonbwe is about the same size as Ranbwe. Most people in these smaller villages come down to Ranon to attend church services or to buy something in the store. The children from Ranbwe and Lonbwe pass through Ranon every morning on their way to school, while their parents usually go to the garden further uphill.

Most people in Ranon and the surrounding villages have gardens a great distance uphill. Later I will go into more detail as to why this is so, but people usually said that the garden has to be far away in order to prevent the pigs, which usually wander unrestricted around in the villages, from destroying the crops. Walking to the gardens usually takes at least an hour of steep uphill climbing, and some gardens are even further away. Generally people in North Ambrym live by what they grow in the garden. People say that store-bought food is weak food, the kind of food that will make the body slow and soft, whereas food grown in the gardens is hard and makes the body strong. Jolly (1991b) has argued that the idea that rice makes you weak and yams make you strong, is not so much related to the fact that rice is soft in itself and a yam is a hard substance, but rather that the rice is not from the home place or from local earth. According to Jolly, food mediates between the body and the land, so food from the garden makes a strong connection between person and place.

Money is usually not spent on buying food for daily consumption, although rice is becoming more popular, but rather to pay for school fees and ceremonies. Money is not plentifully available in the village, and most people will harvest some coconuts for cash cropping when they need money. In addition to cash crops, selling artefacts to tourists who occasionally arrive in Ranon – either on one of the large cruise boats sometimes passing by or on smaller sailing boats – is an important source of money. Some of the young men in the village have also started to arrange guided tours to Fanla and to the famous Ambrym volcano, the Marum. If available money is not spent on school fees or ceremonial costs, such as bridewealth, the money might be used to pay for a journey on the cargo boat passing by on its way to Luganville, the northern capital, or Port Vila, the national capital.

People travel for different reasons. Patterson (2002, 207) has pointed out that 'active volcanoes foster an outward orientation to the world and the presence of Ambrym communities in other islands attest to the recurrent need for refuge that their unruly presence requires'. However, it is not only the physical conditions on the island that make people prone to travel, but also social conditions. Sorcery, as Patterson (2002) also points out, or the fear of becoming the victim not only of sorcery itself, but of accusations of practicing sorcery, have caused a lot of people to flee the island. As I will elaborate upon in Chapter 4, people go to town for a number of reasons: youth in order to go to school, those seeking work, others just for the adventure. Some stay in town permanently; others stay for shorter periods.

People move frequently between Ranon and Port Vila. Not only do people move, but so do bags of copra, pigs, chickens, and garden produce to be sold on the market. Letters and messages go to and from the island. One of the most common ways of sending messages to the village is over the radio. Every evening the radio announces messages from people in town to their relatives on the island informing them about someone coming from town to the island, or requests from people in town to send someone or something with the next cargo boat passing by on its way to Port Vila. Bolton (1999a) pointed out the importance of the radio in the process of nation-making and certainly, for the maintenance of the Ambrym-Port Vila community, the radio was its most important communication link.

The Anthropological History of Ambrym Kinship

When I write about people from North Ambrym, I imply the whole community in Ranon and the other villages, as well as the people who have left the island and now live elsewhere in places such as Port Vila or in the northern town, Luganville. One of the most salient features for understanding the 'tying together' of this society is of course kinship. In the following pages I outline an analytic model for understanding how Ambrym kinship can provide flexibility in the construction of social relations, so that people might move both on and beyond the island, changing their residence temporarily or permanently, while still managing to remain within the Ambrym kinship cosmos.

Ambrym kinship is discussed widely in anthropological literature (Rivers 1915; Deacon 1927; Barnard 1986; Seligman 1927; Radcliffe Brown 1927; Lane and Lane 1956, 1958; Löffler 1960; Scheffler 1970; Patterson 1976). In line with previous anthropological paradigms, kinship on Ambrym was studied as a descent system at the expense of understanding Ambrym kinship on its own premises, or as a system meaningful, not in relation to preconceived models, but to *Ambrym* ideas of sociality. Kinship and descent theory underwent critical review during the seventies and eighties. Carrier and Carrier (1991) have assessed the history of anthropological kinship studies in Melanesia since the fifties, orienting themselves around the opposition between structure and process. They start out with the structuralist notion of an isomorphic relation between category and social segment, implied in Fortes' (1953) unilineal descent models for understanding a social system. This isomorphic relationship implied that there was a one-to-one relation between the structure described in descent categories and the social organization as it actually unfolds. Fortesian structuralism implied that a 'total social structure' existed, objectively observable from the outside. This model for the study of kinship was challenged, firstly by the idea of individual choice, and secondly by the concept of kindred. If these factors should be an element in the analyses, the focus would be on interaction more than on structures. This implied, in other words, a processualist perspective. Scheffler provided in 1965 what Carrier and Carrier call a 'processualist manifesto: structure is but a simulacrum animated by process' (1991, 16). Carrier and Carrier argue that during this critique of African lineage theory, and also of structuralism on which it was based, anthropology gave up on the notion of society. It ignored social structure except as an epiphenomenon of individual's actions, and saw society as a construct that was not present in the 'on the ground' lives of people.

It is Carrier and Carrier's aim to overcome this division between structure and process in their analyses of kinship among the people of Ponam Island. In the same way, I will claim that an understanding of the dynamics of Ambrym kinship demands a perspective that highlights the tension between structures and practices, between the way people talk about kinship and what people do. Moreover, the dynamics between pre-established ideas and social interaction which Carrier and Carrier outline for the

Ponam case have interesting parallels to the Ambrym case. They describe a common Melanesian way of organizing social relations into two matrilineal moieties and several patrilineal groups. The problem they dealt with was: How were these groups organized and how did they cope with problems of multiple membership and the conflicting obligations of their members (Carrier and Carrier 1991, 47)?

As will become apparent in my outline of Ambrym kinship below, there is a similar discrepancy on Ambrym between structure, or the way kinship should be ideally, and the 'on the ground' practice. A person's possibilities in group affiliation are numerous based on a number of overlapping agnatic groups, and thus alternative ways of reckoning kinship can always be found following new 'roads'. Before outlining my own model of how Ambrym kinship can be understood, I will give a brief outline of Ambrym kinship theory the way it has figured in anthropological writings.

The Six Class System

The first ethnographer to write about Ambrym social organization was Rivers. Basing his information on interviews with a man from West Ambrym whom he met at a mission station in south Santo, Rivers (1915) pointed out that Ambrym represented an interesting case because the kinship system contained elements of both matrilineal and patrilineal organization. According to Rivers's evolutionary scheme, matrilineal dual organization was the most primitive form of social organization and characteristic of most Melanesian societies. Ambrym represented a special case because, while descent was patrilineal, in most ceremonies and rituals, the relation to the mother's brother was a common theme. Therefore, Rivers assumed that elements of an earlier matrilineal organization were preserved in ritual life. Not only did the presence of both matri- and patrilineal elements puzzle Rivers, but the Ambrym marriage practise, which prescribed marriage with the father's father's wife, was also anomalous to him. He called the system a gerontocracy, implying that older men monopolized access to women and younger men had to wait until their elders died before they could marry, and thus married their father's father's wife.

T.T. Barnard (1986), a student of Rivers who visited the New Hebrides after Rivers's death, rejected Rivers's evolutionary theories and explained the system of seemingly anomalous marriages as being the result of a class system. Ambrym kinship was based on a matrilineal dual principle where the two moieties intermarried. However, each of the two moieties was divided into three patrilineal groups, resulting in a six-class system. This was the conclusion Bernard Deacon (1927), a student of W.E. Armstrong, came to as well after some weeks of fieldwork on North Ambrym. Deacon's informant explained that there are three tribes called *bwulim*, and that descent in the *bwulim* is patrilineal. However, each *bwulim* is divided into two sides, or lines, such that a man and his father's father and his son's son belong to one side, and his son and his father, etc., belong to the other side. These sides, based on the principle of alternation of generations, are called *batatun*, a word meaning literally 'brother'. The *batatun* is said to be matrilineal, both by T.T Barnard and by Barnard

Deacon, because ego and father's father and son's son share the same mother, i.e., their mothers are from the same place and they call the same women 'mother'.

The term *batatun,* which T.T. Barnard and Bernard Deacon translated as matrimoiety, is not used to refer to a moiety in any explicit sense today on North Ambrym. Most people translate the term as 'brother' and in daily use this is how the concept is used. However, the concept *tahi viung,* literally meaning 'one side of a bunch of coconuts', refers to a group of people of the same *bwulim* but of alternating generations. This concept reveals the idea of two sides and implies a notion of moiety. People will relate to a person and his father's father and son's son in the same manner, as brothers and as *tahi viung.* These are men of the same kind, and they are even interchangeable to a certain degree. A person's son's son might, for instance, represent him in a ceremony, or in payments after his death (see Rio 2002a). The matri-moiety then, is non-localised, and has first and foremost an important ceremonial purpose.

From Structure to 'On the Ground' Practice

Guiart (1951) has criticised Deacon's outline of Ambrym kinship on the premise that there are several different patrilineal groups, *bwulims,* and not only three. I experienced myself that the system is not as tidy as Deacon presented it. There are a number of different *bwulims.* However, I believe it would be useful to make a distinction between a structural level where *bwulims* are classed together according to a principal of three different groups, and an 'on the ground' level. Studying Ambrym kinship as a *system,* focusing on the structuring elements, we find only three *bwulims* on Ambrym (see also Patterson 1976; Rio 2002a): one's own *bwulim,* one's mother's *bwulim* and one's wife's *bwulim.*[1] All the other *bwulims* are classified according to these three categories. This implies that from an ego perspective there are three kinds of people in the world, and all the patrilineal groups are classified according to these three classes of people. These three classes are conceptualised as *gemasul,* which literally means 'us' or 'we few', and then *wuren,* which was translated by Patterson (1976, 98)[2] as the local group from which one's mother came. The third concept is the *mukuen,* which literally means 'chased among' (see Patterson 1976, 101), and refers to the local group from where one gets a spouse and among whom one's presence is taboo.[3] These categories of kin are outlined thoroughly in Mary Patterson's (1976) dissertation based on material from North Ambrym. These three classes of people – the *gemasul,* the *wuren* and the *mukuen* – can be said to represent Deacon's three *bwulims.* Furthermore, the matri-moiety, which both Barnard and Deacon referred to, can be seen as a result of the marriage principle, making the father's father and the son's son occupy the same structural position in the class system, classing the

---

1   Deacon's informant phrased it this way: one's own *bwulim,* one's mother's *bwulim* and one's mother's mother's *bwulim,* which is the place where you get your wife, i.e., wife's *bwulim.*

2   Spelling it *wuruen.*

3   Women marry to the *mukuen* and are of course not tabooed in the presence of her in-laws, and this is a central gender difference which I will return to.

Perspective 1

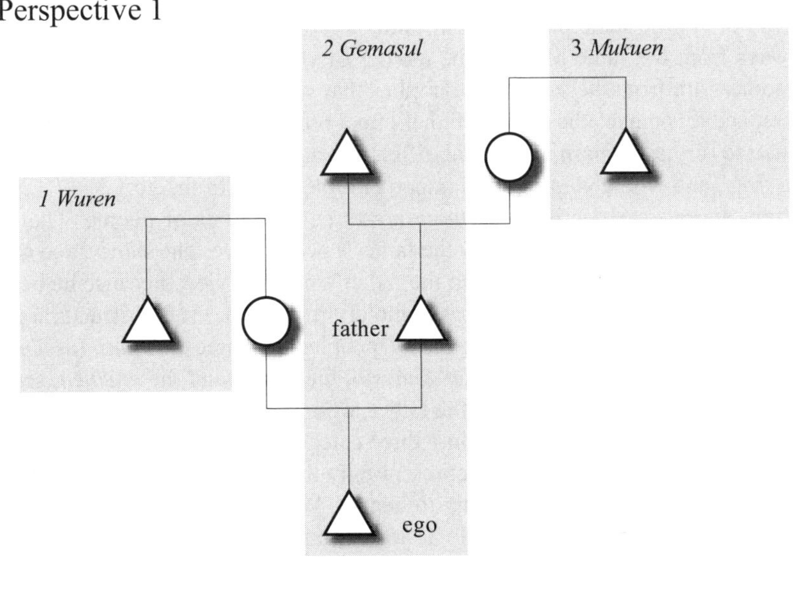

Perspective 2

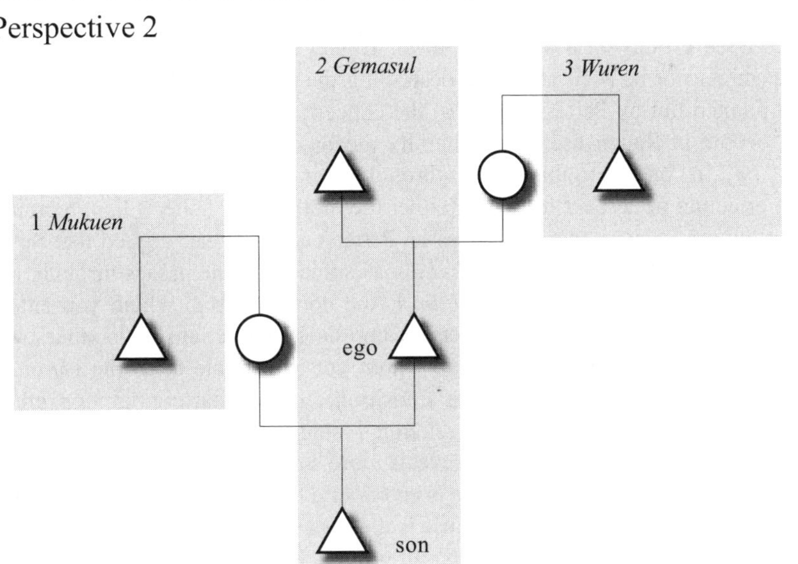

Figure 2.1   The six class system

same local groups as *wuren*, i.e., mother's place. People explained to me that you always *wur*[4] to the same place as your father's father. This means that your mother is always from the same place as the mother of your father's father. The idea that the mothers are from the same place implies that you and your father's father share mother, and this makes the father's father into a brother. In practice this implies that you *wur* to [or have *wuren* in] several different places, both where your own mother came from, and where your father's father's mother came from, etc.

From an ego perspective then there are three categories of people. The ego's perspective is, however, opposed by the father's perspective. The same three groups of people are named differently from the father's point of view, because he belongs to the other side in the generation-based moiety formation. From a structural meta-perspective then, there are six classes of people: the three *bwulims* (as Deacon [1927] would have phrased it) or the *gemasul*, the *wuren* and the *mukuen*, seen by ego, and then another three seen by the father, who belongs to the other matrimoiety. From an ego-perspective there are only three categories of people, but from a meta-perspective these three categories represent only the first moiety. This generational perspective does not differ according to gender. Whether it is a son or a daughter, they would both regard other people as *wuren*, *mukuen* and *gemasul*. Their father however, would have the opposite perspective. His son and daughter's *mukuen* [the place where they would get a spouse] would be his *wuren* [the place where his mother came from].

In other words, it seems as if both T.T Barnard and Bernard Deacon's conclusions that there was a matri-moiety system at the bottom and that these two matri-moieties could be divided into three patrilineal groups – one's own, one's mother's and one's wife's – make sense if the different 'on the ground' *bwulims* are classified according to the three groups on a structural level. However, the concept of the patrilineal group might not be accurate when describing the dynamics of the *bwulim*. As has been pointed out by Patterson (1976) the concept *bwulim*, or *buluim*, which is the term people in Ranon use today, literally means doorway or hole/house [*bwul* or *bulu* / *im*]. In contrast to the usual anthropological conception of (uni) linearity as a strict principle of descent following either the mother's or father's line, recruitment to the *buluim* is more open and flexible. Patterson (1976) has argued that the term 'doorway' implies a notion of the *buluim* as something one passes through, not as something one belongs to. The *buluim* is the doorway from which you enter the village and the specific *im* [house] sets the premises for relationship to others: whom you will relate to as the *mukuen* and whom you will relate to as the *wuren*. One might argue that the *buluim* provides a position, a sort of starting point or reference point when orienting oneself in the relational landscape. I will, however, argue that even though the concept of *buluim* reveals more a notion of a reference point than a notion of a group, the idea that there is an *im*, or a house, from where you start your 'relational journey', and that this house is the house of your father, is comparable to the idea that there is an agnatically based group to which you belong. Furthermore, reducing the *buluim* to something one passes through is problematic, because there are aspects of the *buluim* that are not covered by this concept, in particular aspects

---

4   *Wur* is a verb from the root of the noun *wuren*.

tied to inheritance. In this sense the *buluim* as a relational reference point at a structural level is different from a localised version of the *buluim,* which organizes inheritance and land tenure.

Deacon does not deal with transmission of property and land tenure, but rather occupies himself with the logic of the system, and relationships between classes of people. Patterson (1976, 88) however seems to argue that the *buluim* is not a descent category to which membership adheres. However, she nevertheless (1976, 69) discusses the *buluim* as if it is a group and argues that the *buluim* is not patrilineal, but rather cognatic, in the sense that relations through females are included in the *buluim.* I will claim that we have to make a distinction between structure and 'on the ground' practice. On the one hand the *buluim* is a reference point in the relational cosmos, defining a person's classificatory *wuren* (relations through mother) and *mukuen* (affines), and on the other hand, the *buluim* is a group of which a person is a member and which transmits property rights. 'On the ground', there are a number of different *buluims,* although these *buluims* can be structured into a six-class system. The practical level is relevant when discussing property transmission, because at this point, of course, there is distinction between classificatory kin and persons related through a specific *buluim.* I presume that it is this last aspect of the concept Patterson refers to when she argues that the primary rights to *buluim* property – meaning land and its produce – are transmitted through an agnatic line. She says:

> Any individual may claim membership in a large number of bulufatao [another word for *buluim,* my comment], besides the one associated with the ancestor who founded the parish in which he has primary rights to land by virtue of agnatic descent. (1976, 69)

In other words, although primary property rights, implying use rights to the lands *and* the right to transmit this use-right, follow a patrilineal descent principle, membership in the *buluim* and achievement of secondary rights, including rights to residence and use of the produce from the land, such as fruits, and other produce, are held in a number of *buluims* following matrilateral links.

To sum up the argument so far; on the one hand we have a classificatory level, and on this level kinship relations can be reduced to the principle of three classes of people seen by ego, or six classes of people seen from a meta-perspective. On this level, the *buluim* is like a doorway. It is an entering point to the village, like a reference point on a map giving the three directions: the *gemasul,* the *wuren,* and the *mukuen.* This aspect of the *buluim* gives a person a structural position vis-à-vis others in the village. On the other hand, on an 'on the ground' level, there are many more *buluims,* some of them localised groups, and others dispersed in different households and different villages. They become relevant as categories of people in relation to transmission of property and rights to land.

The Dynamics of Actual and Potential

There is thus a difference in how Ambrym kinship is analyzed, depending on whether the emphasis is placed on structure or process. I argue, along with Carrier and Carrier (1991), that both these perspectives are necessary for an understanding of Ambrym kinship. I will now focus on the flexibility of the 'on the ground' organization of kinship, and what I call the dynamics between actual relationships ánd potential relationships. On Ambrym, every relationship has alternative forms, or rather, a relationship is a realization of one out of several potential forms. A husband-wife relationship is a realization of one form, and not the only one possible, and classificatory brothers might become affinally related if a marriage cuts across the 'brotherhood' and the new affinal relationship is a realization of an alternative form.

This oscillation between potential and actual relationships can be compared to the dynamics between what Hirsch (1995) calls the potential and the actual landscape. The geographical landscape treated by Hirsch can be seen as an analogue to the landscape of the social relations in Ambrym. Hirsch has developed a model for the study of landscape as a cultural process based on the dynamics between two poles of experience. The first pole is what Hirsch calls 'the foreground' which 'corresponds to what we would understand as the context and form of everyday, unreflexive forms of experience' (1995, 4). The other pole, the background, refers to the opposite, the experience beyond the everyday. The foreground corresponds to the actuality, while the background is the potential. The background, or the potential landscape is, according to Hirsch, more easily conceptualised from an 'outside perspective', in the sense that those living in a place and interacting with the landscape in their everyday lives are not sufficiently distanced from it to perceive it as it potentially can be.

Hirsch likens this to the difference between image and representation. The representation of the landscape demands the outside gaze, in the sense that it is a de-centred non-subjective representation of the landscape, like a map. The difference between the inside image based on everyday practical relation to the landscape, and the potential outside representation of it, is like the difference between the insider's orientation in the landscape, which is centred on experience and preferences for routes, etc., and that of the outsider who navigates according to a map with a number of potential routes, but without any practical knowledge of these.

In the case of Ambrym, this difference would be found between the structural level where a 'relational map' reveals all possible relations on the one hand, and the

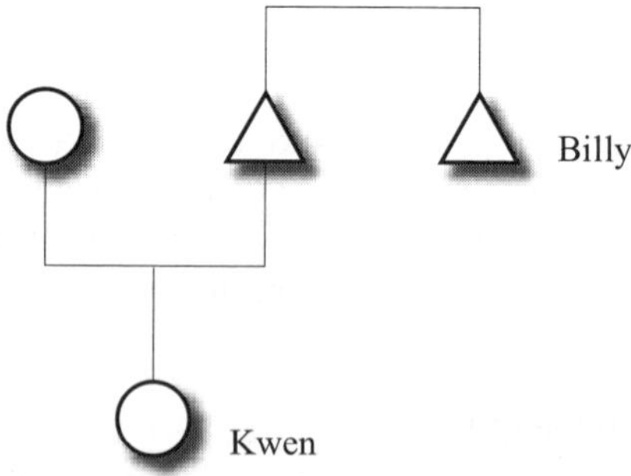

Figure 2.2   Kwen's relationship to Billy, alternative 1

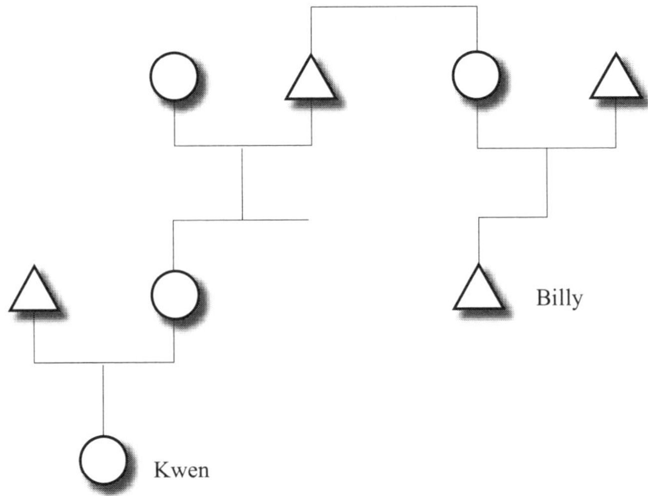

Figure 2.3   Kwen's relationship to Billy, alternative 2

actual practice on the other. A relational map is formed through a meta-perspective where the structural principles of the three classes of people are considered without any 'preference of routes', without any dominating 'on the ground' practice. The map might reveal several other alternatives than the actual practice. When one of my informants in Ranon, a woman named Kwen, in an attempt to explain to me how kinship relations could be altered, listed every possible way she could relate to our host Billy, she made such a relational map. In the figures below I have drawn two of the alternative ways in which she can relate to her neighbour Billy. Figure 2.2 shows that Kwen's father and Billy are classificatory brothers, and that Kwen is Billy's classificatory daughter. Figure 2.3 shows that by following the line through her mother, Billy is her classificatory mother's father's sister's son. This 'relational map' is in a certain sense a contrast to real life where she prefers one relation above the other. This map is a distanced or an objective view of her relationship with Billy, but in everyday life she talked to Billy as a father following her link through her father.

Carrier and Carrier (1991) pointed out in the case of Ponam that whenever they asked someone what they call so-and-so, the person answered 'Through what link? Through my father or my mother or someone else'? (1991, 30). This is also the case on Ambrym. Although there is an established 'on the ground' practice which is usually based on following the links through the father, especially if residence in virilocal, there are a number of potential links to follow through other people. By tracing genealogies through one's mother instead of through one's father, another relational scenario might emerge and open up alternative 'roads' to use when relating to someone. On Ambrym, as well as in Ponam and much of Melanesia, the concepts for relationships are expressed in terms of 'roads', or, *hal* [L: path, road].

As Hirsch argues, the 'insider' is able to have an 'outside' representation of the potential (relational) landscape, as Kwen did when she made the map. These two poles implicate each other and it is the dialectics between them that create the (relational) landscape as a cultural process, according to Hirsch. Perceptions of the structural level then require a detached perspective, or, one might say that the gaze is lifted from the 'on the ground' level to a more structural level, and it is the oscillation between these two levels that creates the dynamics of the Ambrym kinship system and opens up the possibility of alterations of relations between people.

These kinds of relational alterations are perhaps their most creative when people get married. Kenny from Ranbwe for instance wanted to marry Rosy from Ranon. Rosy was his father's sister's daughter, and thereby his potential mother-in-law. In other words, she was classified as a taboo person because her daughter would be marriageable to him. In order for their marriage to be arranged, he changed the relational landscape in the sense that he opened a closed or tabooed 'road' between them, by changing the *singaut* [B: the term he used for her]. He changed the term he used for her from *metauno* [L: mother of wife] to *wehen* [L: wife, woman]. By paying compensation to Rosy's father for the change in relational codes, he changed the relationship between them and he could marry her. His act of payment changed what was potential into what became a new actuality. Potentiality is perceivable at the level of kinship as a classificatory system at the structural level. There are always a number of ways in which one can relate to a person. There is firstly an established 'on the ground' practice, and then, at the level of potential kinship, there are a number of alternatives.

Before seeing Rosy as a potential wife, Kenny followed his relations to Rosy through his father, because this line was 'more strong'. The relationship between Kenny's father and Rosy's mother as classificatory brother and sister was stronger, because children, as I outlined, usually follow relations through their father if residence is virilocal. In the transformation from actual to potential however, when the 'on-the-ground' practice encounters other possibilities at the structural level, a matrilateral link is often followed. The matrilateral link opens up to allow alternative relationships. When Kenny changed his relationship to Rosy, it was done by following the relational scenario that was opened by using his mother and her position in the relational cosmos as his point of departure. In Kwen's case, described above, it is also the matrilateral link that emerges as an alternative road into Billy's

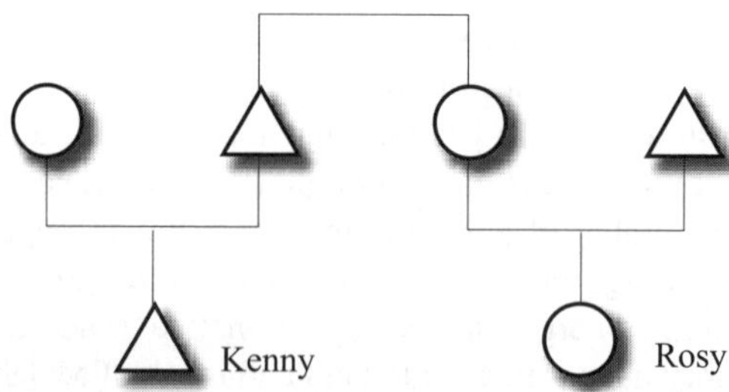

Figure 2.4   Kenny and Rosy, following the link through Kenny's father

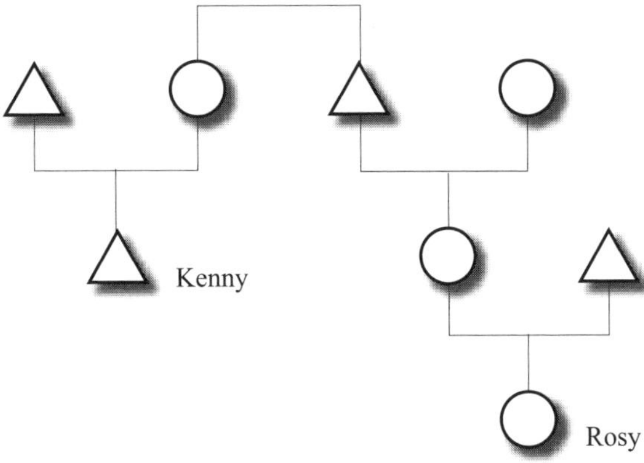

Figure 2.5   Kenny and Rosy, following the link through Kenny's mother

place. The matrilateral relationships are often transformative because they imply another perspective than the patrilineal perspective one usually follows.

The history of alternative navigations in kinship relations creates a system which is incoherent, in the sense that the kinship system never fits and exactly matches the matrilateral relation codes and the patrilateral relational codes. During my first period in Ranon I was naïve enough to believe that a coherent system of relationships operated in practice, so that when for instance Billy told me that Tiwor was his mother's brother, I deduced that Tiwor was the mother's brother of Billy's sister Mamu as well. However, I learnt that Tiwor was Mamu's husband's brother, and therefore classified as marriageable to Mamu. When Tiwor's wife gave birth to twins the year before, Mamu wanted to adopt one of them, since she had only one son who was already grown up. She therefore had to change her relational codes so that Tiwor's children would become her classificatory children. She therefore changed the codes between them, making Tiwor's children adoptable. I realized that there are so many relational crisscrossings, because people have not followed the fixed patrilineal codes, and a kinship diagram is only a partial and a personal diagram. There is, however, a ground rule: the relational codes from the father are usually followed. The matrilateral codes emerge as one alternative perspective, or a potential perspective. When Kenny married he lifted his gaze from the ordinary everyday relationships to the structural level and found another way of classifying Rosy. This case shows how the dynamics of kinship work at two levels: kinship as it is perceived from an ego-perspective in daily interaction, and kinship as it potentially can be viewed if the perspective is lifted to another level where the matrilateral relationships can provide alternative relational 'roads'.

It should be pointed out, however, that this does not mean that the individual is free to choose what kind of relationship he or she wants to establish. These changes take place within a structured universe. Firstly, if changes of relational terms are to be made, one must first find another suitable road to follow. There must be a legitimate opening for this relationship through someone else. Very often this alternative road is opened through the mother's *buluim*. Secondly, the six-class system provides the ground rules implying that once the new relational term is established (towards a specific person), a number of other relationships are changed as well, because the position in the system has been changed.

By analyzing the marriage of Kenny and Rosy – the merging of the two levels of kinship – the potential and the actual relations become visible. Kinship alterations also affect where one resides, where one might move, and who one must avoid – in essence how one operates in the landscape. Before Kenny changed his relational codes to Rosy, he could not visit her house nor walk the same path as her, because she was a tabooed person. When they married this changed and new paths opened. The very act of walking between villages always involves a conception of a foregrounded landscape. Walking certain paths and avoiding others confirms this landscape. The path that is followed creates the actual landscape. Walking is like an act of speech (De Certeau 1984). Walking and speaking are both practices that build upon predefined structures, but these structures can never predict acts, and acts innovate structures. Kenny's sudden shift in 'direction' and relational map also changed the actual landscape, the available and the tabooed paths. Walking is a 'space of enunciation' as De Certeau poetically phrases it (1984, 99). The de- subjective place becomes subjective space through the enunciating act of walking. Walking 'implies relations among differentiated positions, that is, among pragmatic "contracts" in the form of movements (just as verbal enunciation is an allocution)' (1984, 98). The path one walks becomes the taboo path of others because of one's own act of walking. Analyzing kinship relations in terms of landscape, paths, and acts of walking is relevant for an understanding of Ambrym kinship, not only as metaphor, but also because kinship has very physical manifestations in the landscape.

From Kinship to Place

This dynamic between actual and potential relationships makes people flexible not only in relation to marriage, but also in relation to residence. Extensive movement of residence does take place, a concept I will return to in the next chapter. However, in spite of this openness of the system, people never seem to be in doubt as to where they have their origin or *stamba* [B: stump of tree] as it is called in Bislama. People would point to persons and say: this man or that woman is not *really* from such and such place. I found this surprising in some cases, because I knew, after tracking genealogies, that these particular persons had long genealogies relating them to this specific place. On one hand then the flexibility of the kinship organization gives people opportunities to move and change residence, yet on the other hand, there seems to be an idea of a first and original place, to which you never lose your attachment and which is based on agnatic links.

This original place is usually expressed as *neng harl. Harl* is usually translated as *nasara*, a Bislama word meaning 'ceremonial ground'. *Harl*, or *nasara*, becomes a key concept for understanding Ambrym ideas of attachment to place and how this affects social organization. It is particularly interesting that when asking people on

Ambrym what the term *buluim* means, people often translate it into *harl* or *nasara*. This connection between *buluim* and *harl* was quite surprising to me, and at first I saw it as a simplification they used in order to help me understand the concept more easily, because the *harl* had a physical manifestation whereas the *buluim* was more of an abstract concept. However, I believe that this definition of the concept, moving it from the domain of kinship and descent to its relation to place, was a useful and appropriate translation. This 'conceptual shift' opens up other dimensions of Ambrym social organization.

All of the villages I visited in North Ambrym had a ceremonial ground, a *harl*. I had the impression that the *harl* was a public area where ceremonies such as the distribution of New Yam and other public events, such as weddings and initiation ceremonies for boys and puberty ceremonies for girls, were performed. In addition to this kind of *harl*, I also heard about other kinds of ceremonial grounds, which were not accessible to everyone, and particularly inaccessible to me as a woman. These were ceremonial grounds of a more private character for men who had entered the graded society. This division between two kinds of ceremonial grounds became more apparent to me when I did a survey of old village sites in North Ambrym. The guides often began their presentation of the old sites by pointing to a *harl* and emphasizing that the actual village where the people have their sleeping houses were separated and shielded from the *harl*. They explained that there are two different kinds of *harl*. There is a taboo *harl* and a non-taboo *harl*. The taboo *harl* outside the village was connected to the men's graded society and hidden from women and uninitiated men and boys. On these taboo *harls,* men who had taken grades in the men's graded society, the *mage*, erected their insignia and performed the initiation ceremonies. A ceremonial ground for the *mage* ceremony usually contained a circular stone alter where pigs were killed, and then the symbols of men who had climbed the *mage*, either the three fern figures marking the lower grades in the hierarchy or the big, erected stones marking the four top grades. Next to the taboo *harl* there was usually a men's house.

These *harls* signify the place from where one originates. The important rites and ceremonies constituting the relational person are conducted on the *harls*. People, who perform kinship ceremonies together on the same *harl*, therefore also share a structural position in the relational landscape. However, the idea that there is a connection between the *harl* and the specific *buluim*, and that the *harl* somehow is an icon of the *buluim* and its place of origin, does not make sense from the perspective of modern villages such as Ranon. As a result of the colonial economy and the plantation in Ranon, people with different *buluim* affiliations settled in the same village using the same *harl*. The village *harl* of this modern village then cannot be said to refer to any one *buluim*. However, the village organization in the interior of Ambrym is different. Here we see a pattern, which more easily connects the *buluim* and the *harl*. Patterson (1976) for instance, argues that the *buluim* is partly locality focused and connected to one 'parish', which she calls the *buluim* territory. When walking from the northern tip of Ambrym, from Olal or Magam, and southwards through the interior, there are villages that are localised *buluim* settlements and consist of usually two or three households centred on a *harl*. The typical pattern (see Figure 2.6) might be a household of an elderly man and his wife, another house with his son and the wife and

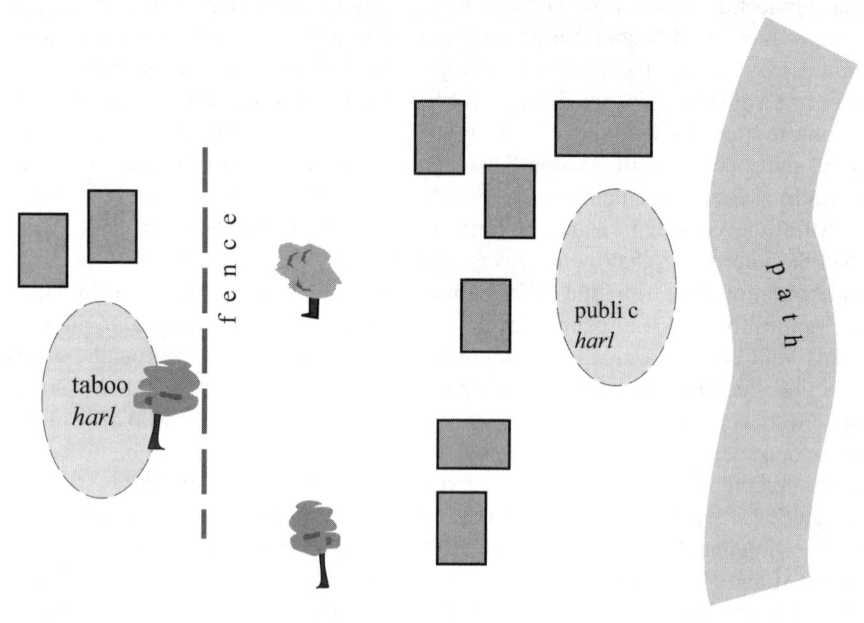

Figure 2.6　　Traditional village

children and then perhaps another son and his children. There might be one or several kitchen houses, and the taboo *harl* is typically situated just outside the living quarters, hidden in the bush, fenced in and protected from the female gaze.

Felix Speiser visited Ambrym in 1915, collecting information on material culture as well as customs. After his tour he wrote the volume *Ethnografische Materialen aus den Neuen Hebriden und den Banks-inseln* (1923). Speiser had the impression that the structure of the coastal village was changing and he wrote, 'Thus on the coast almost the only major settlements to be found now are in the forms of mission villages whose layout has however been modernized and no longer retains much of the original village structure,' (1923[96], 86). He comments that in Olal, the village on the northern tip of the island, as well as in the south of the island, the village structure is characterized by many small and independent villages 'which are adjacent to one another without any border being drawn between them. If there are any differences at all between the villages it is that their houses are oriented more or less to their own men's club houses (...).' (1923[96], 86). The clubhouse is presumably a men's house on the *harl*. According to Speiser then, the typical village structure on Ambrym in 1915, with the exception of course of the mission villages, consisted of houses around a *harl*. When people on Ambrym today translate *buluim* using the term *harl*, this is based on a strong conception of the *harl* as an icon of the *buluim,* because the original village structure was based on a localised *buluim* centred on a *harl*.

Persons and Places

I opened this chapter by saying that an understanding of kinship on Ambrym must provide for an understanding of how this relational system can provide for flexibility for people who move not only on the island but also beyond the island, as for instance the urban migrants. I have shown how the transformation from potential to actual relationships takes place by using alternative roads of relations, often maternal links. However, land rights are not so flexible, and inheritance is a matter of actual *buluim* relationship more than potential *buluim* relationships. On the one hand, the Ambrym kinship system provides for flexibility and alternative ways of relating to people, but on the other, there is a strong connection between people and a specific *buluim* territory that is unalterable. This has created a situation where people change residences often, but always emphasize where they are from and their connections to this particular place. Guiart has pointed out for the neighbouring island of Santo that:

> ...one notices that very few people live where their fathers used to live and, even when they do, their father tends to have come from elsewhere. Thus each head of family is almost always living on land, which he does not own. His land is some way away and he goes to it from time to time to pick the fruit from the trees (especially coconuts). Every dwelling, therefore, involves bargaining and a verbal agreement with the custom owner, who himself may be living a very long way away, dependent on the good will of third party (Guiart cited in Van Trease 1987, 7).

Guiart's description of settlement patterns on Santo might well have been a description of Ambrym. Movement from settlement to settlement takes place both on the individual level, in the sense that a person leaves his natal settlement and moves to another, as well as on the collective level, in the sense that a whole village community relocates. However, the attachment to the original *harl* remains. This aspect of the *harl* is related to the notion of origin, which on Ambrym is expressed by the concept of *tangbarite* [L: the very beginning, or the first origin].

Rio (2002a) has discussed the Ambrym concept *tangbarite*. He points out that people on Ambrym are obsessively concerned with the origin of things. People trace histories, genealogies, objects, etc., back to their beginning, and so also with place. People refer to themselves as being a man or a woman of somewhere. For instance '*Tarin Ranon*', implies that one is originally from Ranon village, even if he or she lives elsewhere. People sometimes refer to themselves by villages that are empty and left-behind settlements, or a village where they themselves have never lived. Perhaps no one has lived there for five to ten generations. One's place, in the sense of *tangbarite* [L: where I come from, originate], is conceptualised as one's *harl*, a specific localized place (which might be a mythological place where the first ancestors were created).

This idea of a first and original place is also found in other parts of Melanesia. P.J. Stewart and A. Strathern (2004) have described the Duna of Papau New Guinea and their notion of *auwa rindi* meaning 'ancestral place'. However, on Ambrym the notion of one's place is not restricted to only this localized mythological place, the *tangbarite*. Here, one's place, in the sense of *harl*, is portable. It is as if a person's place is specific (comparable to the on-the-ground level of the *buluim*) and related to an actual geographical location (which is where your land rights are), but at the same time it is first and foremost represented *in persons,* and thereby also portable. People are not only from a place, but they are iconic of their place. If a person has a long genealogy connecting him or her to a place, or a *harl* – for instance the village Willit – this person *is* Willit [*hemia wan man Willit,*[5] B: this a Willit man], as if the *harl* becomes that particular person's essence. When moving, this person remains *harl* Willit, even though the movement might be to another island and the physical village of Willit no longer exists. When people say that the *harl,* or the ceremonial ground in the village, is analogue to the category *buluim,* they direct attention to the way persons are places. A person that is Willit, for instance a long time after the village of Willit, or the *harl* of Willit, ceased to exist physically, will move the place along his or her route.

On the one hand, this original place of Willit refers to an on-the-ground *buluim* association and is decisive for where the land rights are localised, making the *man Willit* walk a great distance every time he wants to tend his garden. However, on the other hand, the *man Willit* brings Willit along the road, so that the route that once started in Willit is brought further by the *man Willit'*s movements. His descendants will have a longer route to relate to. Following new potential relationships, the *man Willit* moves and, through generations, a long route starting in Willit is formed. In the next chapter I will go into more detail about these stories of movement and how they relate to people's notion of place. I here want to emphasize that the dynamics between actual and potential *buluim* relationships that make people's choice of residence flexible does not create chaos with random rules. The flexibility provided by allowing for alternative roads into new places, builds on the idea that persons bring along their place. This notion of place, being at once an original locality and also extending when people move, is the organizational logic which people relate to. People move and change residence frequently, but it is not as if every new settlement on any new *harl,* is a beginning from scratch. The movement of past generations and the original *harl* form a route to which people relate. When I talked to Billy's sons in Port Vila about their place, they emphasized that they were originally from West Ambrym, but that their place now was North Ambrym, and there is no contradiction here. Billy's residency in Ranon is based on the flexibility in the kinship system that allows him to follow matrilateral links though his mother and cultivate garden areas that belonged to her. Bongsubu, Billy's father, who came from West Ambrym to find work on the plantation in Ranon and married a Ranon woman, has land in West Ambrym, which is used by someone else who has their original rights somewhere else.

In order to understand social organization on Ambrym, kinship must be related to ideas of place and movement. People see relationships as formed through places, and relationship between persons might be talked about in terms of relationship between places. A statement that a certain person moved from Ranon to Fantor village is

---

5   The merging of man and place is expressed in the Bislama by the expression 'Man Willit'. In Bislama one talks about persons as being places, for instance 'Woman Ambrym', or 'Man Ranon'.

also a statement of who this person is related to and why this person has moved. A movement from Ranon to Fantor implies, as I will return to in Chapter 6, that one moved to Ranon as a plantation worker and after independence (and the closing of the plantation business) when land rights were disputed there, moved on and settled in the newly established Fantor village. Social relationships are talked about in terms of movement between places; places are coding relationships. Deleuze and Guattari (1983) outline the workings of what they call *the social machine* as the coding of flows. The mechanism of the Ambrym social machine is place. All flow on Ambrym – the flow of persons, of food, of words, of movement – is structured according to the idea of place. In other words, sociality is conceptualised through territoriality.

The Distributed Place

In the colonial period, when movements accelerated and village compositions changed character, and when the plantations covered areas where before one used to make gardens, the role of origin stories became essential. Only a few people today live in the area of their *harl*. The sense of place then, developed through this practice of moving residence, becomes a sort of distributed place, comparable to Gell's (1998) concept of the distributed person. The concept of the 'distributed person' directs attention to the way the essence of a person is not bounded. In the same manner I want to emphasize that on Ambrym, place [B: *ples,* L: *harl*] has a distributed essence as well.

In his outline of an anthropological theory of art, Gell takes an anti-aesthetic stance, arguing that '… works of art …, have to be treated, in the context of an anthropological theory, as person-like, that is, sources of, and targets for, social agency' (1998, 96). He further argues that representations of things are part of the things themselves, the same way smoke is both a representation of and part of fire. The notion of distributed personhood stems from the conception that: '… persons may be distributed, all their parts are not physically attached, but are distributed around the ambience …' (1998, 106). This is also how the social agency of the art object becomes the prime locus for anthropological research, according to Gell. The social life of entities with social agency, whether art objects or persons, are perceivable through the concept of distribution. A person is not a bounded entity, but aspects of the person – for instance relational parts of the persons or other artificial qualities – are present in many different places at the same time.

In a parallel manner, place on Ambrym is not conceived of as only present in *one* location, but rather extends from this one location into a number of other locations. The historical village relocations and the origin stories recounted in the next chapter give an impression of how place on Ambrym is distributed through routes, at the same time as it is rooted.

Chapter 3

Origin Routes: Historical and Contemporary Relocations on Ambrym

White (1991) described his first encounter with rural villagers on Santa Isabel in the Solomon Islands as an encounter with narratives of 'beginnings'. About the excursions he was taken on to see places people associate with the pre-Christian life, White (1991, 30) states:

> While not apparent to me at the time, that tour and the running exegesis accompanying it afforded an opportunity for enacting understandings of self, community, and history…

In the same manner, people on Ambrym are keen to tell stories of beginnings and movements, and during our first fieldwork in 1995 Knut Rio and I conducted a survey of old village sites as part of our voluntary work for the Vanuatu Cultural Centre in collaboration with the local fieldworkers, Billy Bong and James Hanghang Tainmal. We continued this project during our 1999 fieldwork-period, and this time we also recorded people's stories of where they came from and why the old villages were deserted. We walked around the North Ambrym hills and were taken to abandoned places and sacred areas. As we explored the Ambrym hills and forests, crossing creeks and looking for marks of abandoned settlements, we tried to map how people had moved, and in the process we also recorded the way people talked about place and movement. In this chapter I build mainly on this material, but in order to give more historical depth to my mapping of past village relocations, I have added to my own collection of stories the descriptions of conflicts between villages written by the missionary Charles Murray in his diary of 1887.[1] They contribute to an understanding of why people relocated and moved so frequently during the colonial period.

In the preceding chapter I argued that flexibility in kinship organization, as it opens opportunities for movement and change of residence, does not create total chaos when the notion of a first and original place, which is also a portable place, is seen to structure this flexibility. If place is brought along and not left behind, place still provides a structural position from which relationships are formed. My aim in this chapter is to delineate in greater detail the logic of place and movement through an analysis of historical relocations. Furthermore, I will point out that movement into new settlements is usually mediated through women. This gendered dimension of place and movement is highlighted toward the end of this chapter and continued in the next one.

---

1   Charles Murray's diary was sent to me with the help of Yvonne Wilkie, an archivist of the Presbyterian Library, Knox College, Dunedin, New Zealand.

Historical Village Relocations

It has been pointed out before that hamlet residence in this region is mobile (Bolton 1999b; Rodman 1987), with hamlets and villages disappearing and reappearing in new constellations. Bonnemaison (1994, 22) argued, 'space in traditional Melanesian society is not perceived by its divisions, nor by its limits, but by relations along the route'. As I will demonstrate, people have moved from settlement to settlement in the past as well as today, and they conceptualise their place as much in terms of 'routes' as 'roots'. Not only does 'routes connect roots' (Miles 1998, 12), but routes are roots. In this chapter I will try to create an image of how these past and present movements have created a social as well as a geographical landscape of complex and intertwined 'origin routes'.

Elsewhere I have listed the detailed movement from each of the villages in the interior of the Lolihor area of North Ambrym (Eriksen 2005a), and I will here only mention the main lines in the movement. The information we collected can be divided into movements within two main areas: one in the interior south of Ranon and one in the interior north of Ranon. Although some movements cross this division, there seems to be a concentration of movement within certain areas. My general impression is that when whole villages relocated, the movement was rather short, and new settlements were created in the area. Accounts of village relocations within a relatively short time span, such as the last three or four generations, tell of movements that don't seem to have involved large distances. Personal origin stories however, which I will return to below, involve movement over greater distance both in time and space.

In the area north of Ranon, the Lolihor area, there are today ten major villages: Ramvetlam, Faramsu, Lonbwe, Ranbwe, Fantor, Fanhumhul, Ranon, Fanrereo, Lonlilio, and Fanla. Some generations ago there were about thirty villages in the same area. The only remnants of those villages today are the many *namele*[2] which were planted on the ceremonial grounds, and which still grow on these *harls*, or the overgrown stone circles people used for killing pigs. The quantity of villages then has clearly decreased, and people endlessly point this out as they walk past old signs of past settlements. As noted in the previous chapter, village structure dramatically changed on Ambrym during the colonial period. There are a number of reasons for this. As a result of the plantation economy, mission history and work migration, people today live in larger villages of perhaps ten to twenty households, whereas in the past villages consisted of one *buluim* centred on a *harl*, and one village contained perhaps three or four households. People moved closer to where they could find work, especially during the colonial period. Closer proximity to the mission station and church was also one of the reasons why people created larger villages during this period. Although one *buluim* was located in the vicinity of where Ranon is today, this village, with its present form and size, is one of the most recently established villages on North Ambrym as a result of the plantation and mission.

---

2   Cycad (Cycas Circinnalis) is used in grade taking ceremonies in all of the northern islands. It is sometimes also called *pistri* (peace tree) in Bislama (Crowly 1995).

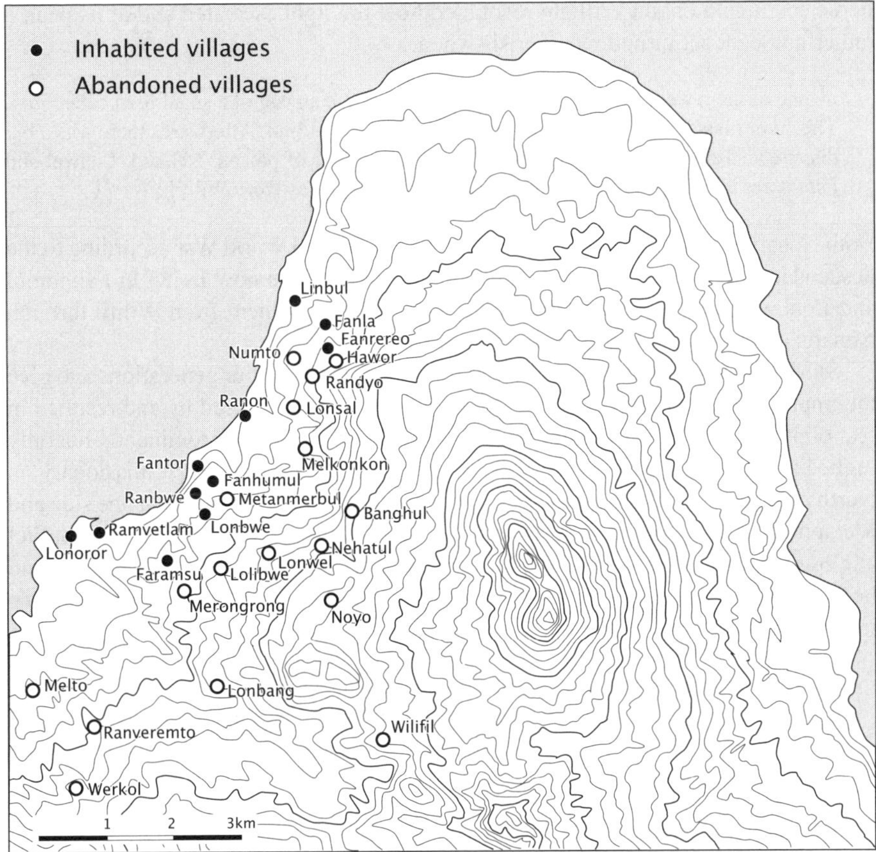

Map 3.1   Villages, North Ambrym

A picture of village patterns in the last century must take this change into account. The many small villages gradually became fewer but larger villages. However, the stories about the abandoned village sites and the ancestors who lived there remain important and the knowledge about who came out of where distinguishes people and their land rights in the larger present-day villages. These stories also give an impression of why people relocated. Although people who moved away from old village sites often ended up in the larger villages on the coast, like Ranon, after perhaps one or two intermediary locations, the reasons why people left, especially when they relocated collectively, are seldom attributed to a search for something new. Rather, people were forced to leave.

For instance, one of the oldest settlements we obtained information about, Wilifil, was abandoned after a warlike event. Wilifil seems to have been a large village with two *harls,* and consequently two *buluims*. Both elder Anis from Ranbwe and Lenkon William from Fantor, who descend from each one of these two *buluims*, have heard the story of a fight between the two *harls* or *buluims* over the rights to the village and its resources. Two men, Magebumrir and Balnaim, representing the two *harls*, were fierce enemies. Lenkon William recounted how the fight escalated and at its peak a rather innocent act turned into a crisis when…

> … one of them went down to the creek where he found an egg of a small fowl called *toto*. The other man saw him carry the egg away and yelled at him. Afterwards there was a big dispute and everyone ran away from the village in fear of poison. Nehatul, Lonwel and Fantor are all villages founded by the people running away from Wilifil.[3]

Both Nehatul and Lonwel were empty before the Second World War according to the descendants from these two villages. The descendants are now living in Fanhumul and Lonbwe close to Ranon and their origin route takes them from Wilifil through Nehatul or Lonwel and to their present location.

Stories like this about the movement of villages three or four generations ago give the impression that conflicts and quarrels often were both caused by and resulted in fear of poison/black magic. Another such conflict which figures prominently not only in the history people on Ambrym tell, but also in the diary of the first missionary on North Ambrym, Charles Murray, is the conflict between Merongrong on one side and Metanmerbul and Lonbang on the other. Charles Murray experienced this conflict at close hand when he tried to establish a Presbyterian mission close to Ranon, and he writes in his diary of January 1887 after a visit to the village of Lonbang, in the interior east of Ramvetlam:

> [visited Lonbang] to see what the men are storming about. They with some other villages have gathered into a league to assassinate Malmalmelun, the chief of Metanmerbul and declare general war on the people of that village and also on Ranon, Numto and Lonsal (entry in diary 12 Jan 1887).

Two days later he writes the following:

> In the afternoon set out in the company of my courageous teacher Amos for the dreadful village of Lonbang. We could get no guide to come, so we set out alone. We trudged on till we came to the plantation where we surprised them. … a great many people were on the plantation…with their muskets on hand…seeing who we were laid them aside and came to shake hands and welcome us …They started to speak about the fighting.
>
> – Why, Lasher, do you want to fight? I said,
> – We don't want to fight but the people of Metanmerbul, Ranon, Linbul, Nomto, Banghul, and Fanla want to fight us.
> – They don't want to fight you, I said. They are all afraid of you.
> – Why, they said, did the Metanmerbul people kill the chief of Merongrong with poison …?

Later he visits the village of Lolibwe and hears the story of how the chief there had mediated in the conflict between the Merongrong and the Metanmerbul people, and

---

3   It was mentioned by other people listening to this story that the egg might be a metaphor for women. The act that provoked the crisis might then have been the act of 'stealing' a woman.

on behalf of the Merongrong people he had given a branch of a special tree called *ra mwel* to the Metanmerbul people as a sign of peace.

Throughout his diary Murray refers to the conflict between the Metanmerbul people and their allies on one side and the Merongrong people and their allies on the other. In particular the people on the northern side feared the people of Lonbang for their powerful *abio*, or poison/black magic. Murray comments in his diary that he seldom could get a guide to Lonbang. In my survey of these villages, the same conflicts seem to be emphasized. The people who live in the present-day village of Faramsu are the descendants of those who once lived in Merongrong. Before this, the people in Merongrong were runaways from Linbul and the fugitives from the village of Farara, where the first plantation owner, Francois Rossi, had chased people off their land.

When talking about Merongrong today people are very eager to point out that Merongrong was the site of the first church on North Ambrym. A returned plantation worker who resettled in Merongrong established a congregation here. Whether this was before or after Murray's time is difficult to say. It might, however, have been the cause of the conflict between Merongrong and Metanmerbul. In a survey made by the Presbyterian missionaries in 1916 Metanmerbul was registered as a place with no Christians, while Merongrong was listed as a Christian place with no 'heathens' (Miller 1989, 170–171). In 1916, non-Christians greatly outnumbered the Christians, and most of the villages had both. The very clear association between Merongrong and Christianity and Metanmerbul and 'heathenism' might have been the root of the conflict. The descendants of those who lived in Metanmerbul and Lonbang all moved in the same direction, and so did the descendants of those who lived in Merongrong and their allies.

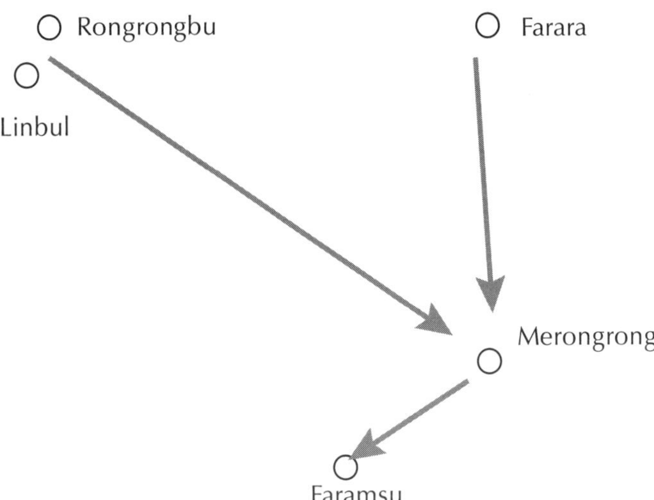

Map 3.2   **Movement to the present-day village Faramsu**

The conflict between Merongrong and Metanmerbul is typical of the kind of tensions that made people move and resettle in the latter half of the nineteenth century. Those living in the present-day village of Faramsu are well aware of whose routes go back where. Having origin routes back to Merongrong is a strong statement about one's Christian roots. The most important aspect of the origin routes however, is tied to land and the use of different garden areas in abandoned villages.

Origin Routes and Rights to Land: Lenkon William's Origin Route

Lenkon William now lives in Fantor, a newly established village close to Ranon. His long origin route and dispersed rights to land and trees exemplify the complex relation between people and place on North Ambrym. Lenkon William's ancestors lived in Wilifil. After the dispute between Lenkon William's ancestor, Balnaim and his enemy Magebumnir, Lenkon William's ancestors fled and resettled in Noyo. Lenkon William thinks that this movement from Wilifil to Noyo must have happened quite a long time ago, and even before there was any graded society on Ambrym,[4] because there are no *namale* or stones used for the grade-taking ceremonies found in the location of Wilifil. After a while, Noyo also became the 'place for trouble', and another dispute made people flee from Noyo. Kintor Apia from Ranbwe has heard the story of why people fled: one of the men living in the village wanted revenge for the poisoning death of a relative, and he had,

> …climbed a mountain, carrying a wood, with which he had dug a hole in the ground. He had then called the water, and it had started streaming through the holes towards the village. The people of the village had to run for their lives, and they all fled in different directions ['*Oli run olbout, oli run wan wan*'].

Lenkon William's ancestors then settled in Metanmerbul, and this movement must have happened at the end of the 19th century, a few years after the first trader and the first missionary had settled in Ranon. After a while people abandoned Metanmerbul. I have not heard any stories that explain the reason why the people in Metanmerbul moved, but the constant conflict between Metanmerbul and Merongrong, described in Murray's diary, might have been one of the causes. The people who moved away from Metanmerbul resettled in Ranbwe and in Ranon. By this time there was a plantation in Ranon and wage labour was available. Today Lenkon William has a complex origin route taking him from Wilifil through Noyo and Metanmerbul, then through Ranbwe to his present location in Fantor. When he works his gardens, he sometimes walks the whole distance to Wilifil where he has his original rights to grounds. Wilifil is his *tangbarite* [L: place of origin]. Lenkon has other garden areas along his route, some closer to Noyo and some closer to Metanmerbul. In these areas he also has rights to trees his ancestors planted, and goes to harvest them from time to time. Lenkon William is a 'man Wilifil' and through his ancestors' movements Wilifil has been extended into new areas:

---

4   It was said on Ambrym that the graded society originally came from Malekula and was imported to Ambrym. More on this in Chapter 8.

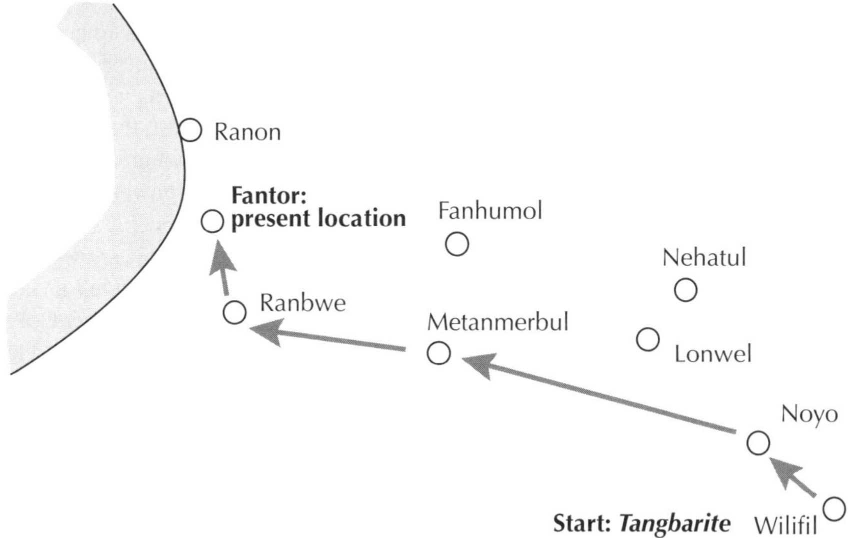

Map 3.3   Lenkon William's origin route

Ambrym Origin Stories

This history of previous localities is visible to people when they walk around in the Ambrym hills, visit neighbouring villages, or are on their way to the garden. *Harls* of previous generations are talked about and remembered as people walk past the old ceremonial places. People will explain that this is their old *harl*, but the people here had to flee because of *posen* [B: poison; sorcery], or the place was deserted because their neighbours killed them. These places are now part of the bush [L: *bobor*, lit. 'place gone stuck'], overgrown and empty of people, but some hidden marks in the landscape, a stone grave, a rotten house post or a small creek where water used to run, reveal the sites of previous villages. The fertile soil and the rapidly growing forest have long ago claimed the clearings as part of the bush landscape, as is usual in this part of the world. White (1991, 32), on his excursions in the forests of Santa Isabel in the Solomon Islands, explains in a similar manner that 'what seemed to me like continuous undifferentiated forest was for my hosts an elaborate patchwork of significant named places, each harbouring its stories of persons and spirits associated with that place'.

Fox has developed the concept of topogeny, 'the recitation of an ordered sequence of place names' which 'figure prominently in Austronesian populations' and '…represents a projected externalization of memories that can be lived in as well as talked about' (1997, 8). The Ambrym origin stories create topogenies, which people use as a mnemonic process in which the landscape represents the past *harl* as well as a map of present-day social relations. The many topogenies of Ambrym, as the origin stories I will present, follow the migration of people from their original *harl*, in the interior and often at the volcanic centre on the island, through the landscape and towards their present location. When walking the tracks, passing through the old places, or when avoiding an old ceremonial ground because of the potency still believed to be attached to it, people recount the past and in this way transmit knowledge of the origin routes and the landscape, as it is socially constructed, to their children. In the seemingly undifferentiated forest, the remnants of potent men from the past lay buried in ceremonial grounds, now unrecognizable to the stranger's eye. Not only the foreign eye is unable to see these powerful places, but the knowledge of them is also unequally distributed among the people on North Ambrym. The knowledge of who lived where is to some extent secret knowledge only accessible to the right people. Sometimes when we asked people to tell us the story of a place, they would be very reluctant, because it was not *their* place. Only those people who have 'routes' connecting them to a place, have the right to tell the story, and they cannot tell the story to whoever they want, because only some people are meant to know. Some people on Ambrym have nevertheless told us the stories that were not so secret.

John Rawo's Origin Route

John Rawo is one of those men in Ranon who descended from a significant line of chiefs and men with high grades in the men's graded society. He was however always emphasizing that he was originally from somewhere else:

> My family comes [*i kamaut*] from Hawo at Dip point.[5] One man alone 'pulled' his canoe to this place [i.e., Ranon, my comment]. The people in Ranon asked him to come ashore. He came ashore on Longmaribagakon, close to where Ranon is today. The name of this man was YumYum. The people who lived here had reached the *melun*[6] in the *mage.*[7] Then, he as well started to kill pigs, and he got the name Melun Sawo. He married and settled in Metamli. He had only one child, Sawo [the name means 'from Hawo', my comment]. Sawo married a woman from Ranveremto [above Ranvetlam, my comment], and the two of them had Tangwor Melun who married in Metamli, and then the two of them had Malnaim. This big name [Mal[8]naim] he got when he killed pigs. His other name was Rawo. He married three women; one gave birth to Mageli, who married Tata in Fanla. He was also a *mal.* The other woman he married was a woman from West, and she gave birth to Worwor. Because of poison his uncle [MB] in Nehatul took care of him, and then when he was a bit bigger, one of his fathers in Randyo took care of him. Then he came down to the plantation [Ranon, my comment].[9]

YumYum first arrives in Ranon and he comes alone. The personal origin stories very often have this form. One person for some reason leaves alone and looks for

---

5   Hawo at Dip point is on the steep rocky cliffs before reaching the beaches on West Ambrym.

6   One of the highest grades in the men's graded society.

7   *Mage* is the local name of the *namange,* the men's graded society.

8   *Mal* as a prefix or suffix means that this person has reached the highest grade in the men's graded society.

9   See Eriksen 2005a for the continuation of this story.

a new place; he meets a woman, whom he marries, and their children again move on. YumYum arrives in Ranon, but he does not settle here. His route takes a circuit through Metamli, Nehathul and Randyo before Rawo's route enters Ranon. Yumyum was originally from Dip point in West Ambrym making Rawo's origin route cross the entire island.

The discourse of past and present villages is characterized by the temporal character of these settlements. The first and original place, the *tangbarite*, is often talked about as 'comming out of' [B: kam aut long], and subsequent settlements are often talked about as '*histary blong me i kam tru long …*' [B: my history goes through …]. Not only past settlements are talked about as 'going through' but also present-day settlements. The emphasis is always on the temporary character of any settlement. Aro, for instance, living in Ranon and being one of the few men who are regarded as *of the place* because his *buluim* was located here before the plantation, said '*Famili histari blong mifala i kam tru long Ranon …*' [B:our family history goes through Ranon]. He does not imply that the movement has ended, although they have the longest record of generations present in this location.

Moving Place Beyond the Island

The topogenies above are restricted to the island, but movements of place were not necessarily restricted to Ambrym. Historical movements could also involve crossing the sea to another island. The first time I became aware of this was when I was walking around in one of the smaller squatter areas outside of the capital Port Vila, in an area called Tebakor. I was looking for an Ambrym man I knew was living there. I knew that he was from one of the old deserted village locations above the hills from Ranon, a village called Randyu. I walked passed the temporary houses mostly inhabited by people from Tanna, south in the archipelago. I asked a woman who was sitting on a mat beside a wooden post with a sign saying 'Mango from Tanna for sale', if she knew about an elderly North Ambrym man named Lenkon Kintor living in the neighbourhood. 'He lives in Randyu', she replied and pointed up a steep hill. The hill reminded me of the exhausting climb from Ranon towards the deserted places of Randyu, Nomto and Hawor (which finally leads you to the present-day villages of Fanla and Fanrereo as well). I wondered what she meant by saying that he lives in Randyu, because my idea of Randyu was, of course, a geographical location physically located in the North Ambrym landscape. I did not ask her however, and continued walking in the direction she had pointed. As I reached the top of the hill, I first noticed a concrete wall on which was printed 'Randyu store'.

A young man who was just closing the store approached me and I asked him again for Lenkon Kintor. He led me through a settlement of four or five temporary houses built around a well. Inside one of the houses I finally met Lenkon Kintor. After introducing myself, I asked him if he could tell me about Randyu. '*Randyu, hemia nao*' [Randyu is here] he said and smilingly pointed towards the store. He told me that he had lived in Port Vila for fifty years, and he had now bought this small piece of land from the *kastom* owner from Efate, and he had called this area

Photo 3.1   Lenkon Kintor and Randyu store

Photo 3.2   Visiting Randyu in Port Vila

'Randyu'. Lenkon Kintor had moved his place on the hilltop of the North Ambrym coast to the hilltop outside the centre of Port Vila.

This is not the only story I heard about movements of place beyond the island. On North Ambrym I often heard people say that they had genealogical connections to South Pentecost, the island north of Ambrym. 'I have my place in South Pentecost', people would say, and imply that this is where they originate.

The Origin in South Pentecost

Chief Tokon in Ranon told the story of how his ancestor had arrived at the shores of North Ambrym. This is a summary of this story translated from Bislama:

> I am from [*kam aut long*] Hawor, but I am not exactly from Hawor. My relatives come from Pentecost. We are from the south of Pentecost, from Big Sea. We are from this place. There was a man. His name was Bila. Bila was at Panbetayal, Big Sea. He made a miracle. He did as God when he created man. He made the ground. Then he put some vines in the sand. The sun burnt it and made it strong. He realized that he would make men. He formed the legs, the hands, etc., and he made twelve of them. His last work was not so good. Then, one day he stood up and preached. He told them the news and everyone stood up and was alive. They stood up. They were as they should. Eleven men were as they should, but the last one was not good. He had too many sores and was disabled. This man they called Kakar. Because in our language, we say that if you have sore, you 'kare'. This is why they called him Kakar. All the others got married, but he was the only one who tried and tried without success. He tried and tried, and then he thought he should try some magic. He made himself some medicine.[10] He stayed in his house. The rest of the family in Panbetayal stayed further up, but Kakar stayed down. If you go to Pentecost, you can still see his *Nakamal*.[11] They put him down there because he was the last man and he smelled. The sores smelled. They put him down by the sea. The rest of the family stayed up in the bush. … Karkar started to make himself some medicine. I believe it was because he wanted to marry. He saw that all his brothers were married and then he wanted to marry as well. This was why he started to make himself this kind of medicine. He did not know whether or not it would work. Then two girls came down to the sea. When they had fetched water, they wanted to go back. Then he made rain, and he put some medicine on his door as well. Then he called out to them. He saw that they were soaking wet as they were going back. He called out: 'Come inside'. When the two came inside he made the rain stop. When he had made the rain stop, he asked the two to leave. The two did not want to go. He realised that his magic worked. Time passed. He married the two girls. They [the ones in the village his brother's/the girl's family, my comment] got angry. They chased him away. They made a float of wild cane and sent Karkar away on it. He floated away and came ashore on Linbul. You know, in the past they ate each other, and when Karkar arrived they wanted to eat him. Then they thought about it and decided: 'No, we must take care of him'. Then Karkar stayed here. … Time passed and they became brothers. When they gave him women they sent him to Hawor. This is how we join the Hawor people. They sent him to Hawor. He married a woman from Rorongbu. The woman from Rorongbu was called Papawe. Okay, the two were married and came to stay in Hawor.

---

10 In Bislama the term 'medicine' also connotes magical remedies.

11 Ceremonial house.

> The woman from Rorongbu gave birth to three children. I will tell the story of the ones whom we descend from. … We became a big family on Ambrym. One group moved to Fanrereo, that is brother Sail and his sons, another group is Pastor Ruben and his family who now live in Erakor village on Efate, and then Alvin and his sons in Ranon.[12]

Again this is a story of a man who on his own arrives on the shores of North Ambrym. This man was an outsider not only because he was from South Pentecost, but also because of his monstrous looks. The 'rubbish man' is a common theme in myths and folktales from Melanesia (Wagner 2001; Lattas 2004). This is a man with a repugnant exterior; with sores on his skin, he smells, walks with a limp, etc. No one wants to marry him, but in the end he turns the order of things upside down, and ends up as the hero of the story. This trickster person often has magical abilities, as a 'chosen one'. In this story Karkar and his brothers are created as if they are the first humans. They were not, however, created by God, as in the Christian God, because, as the storytellers say, Bila, who created Karkar and his brothers, are *as* God. In many of these origin stories local cultural heroes are presented alongside the Christian God, as either existing before he arrived or being similar to Him.

Bila performed a miracle and created Karkar and his brothers out of the earth of Pentecost. This is a strong statement about where their place is. Karkar however was chased away twice. First he was not included in the community among his brothers. He was not welcome to live with the others because of his appearance. Then, he was chased off the island because he married women from the village. On Pentecost he was not welcome because of his difference. On Ambrym however, they did not even comment on his looks. Pentecost is presented on the one hand as the place of origin, but on the other as an unfriendly place, having no room for Karkar. Ambrym is the safe harbour. This story is perhaps not only a story revealing Tokon's, the storyteller's, origin route, but also a story of why he does not want to return.

It is interesting that marriage opens a road for Karkar into the Ambrym settlement. If ideas about land tenure and inheritance are viewed strictly in terms of agnatic descent, then none of Karkar's descendants should have any rights to ground on Ambrym. However, Tokon has ground in Fanrereo, because this was where 'his group', descending from Karkar, settled. As I have argued in the previous chapter, rights to land follow an actual *buluim* attachment. As one moves however, and becomes part of new *buluims*, rights become diffused and dispersed. On the one hand, rights to ground from left-behind *harls* remain as long as one still gardens in these areas, but on the other hand, rights to new ground are also achieved when staying and using new ground. This matter is always under considerable dispute, and always a matter of negotiation. In particular cases where people have used matrilateral or affinal links to attach themselves to a *buluim*, rights to ground are insecure. For instance, after a period of a number of land disputes in the village court in Ranon, the idea of strict patrilineal rights was strongly advocated, in particular after a decision made by the national court on an Ambrym case favoured patrilineal descent. Although none of the disputes concerned Tokon directly, once during this turbulent period he remarked, in a half-ironic and half-depressed tone, that he thought

---

12 See Eriksen 2005a for the full-length story and Tokon's genealogy from Karkar.

he should perhaps just move back to Pentecost, where his rights to ground would be undisputed. At other times, he said that he would move back to Hawor, where Karkar settled on Ambrym, because here no one disputed his rights.

Although the basic idea of inheritance to ground rights follows the principles of *buluim* membership, no case is straightforward. There are always a number of persons claiming rights to the same piece of land, and it happens that people unexpectedly argue for rights to places and legitimize their claims by genealogies no one had thought of, or a story people had forgotten. This happened once during our stay in Ranon in 1999.

Origin Stories and Land Rights

Ranon, the site of the mission station and the plantation, is inhabited by a number of people who are not *manples* [B: men of the place]. There is one man however, who up until 1999 was regarded by everyone as the original owner of rights to ground in Ranon. This is David Aro. In 1999 Peter, an old man from town, showed up and claimed the rights to most of the ground in Ranon. This man who, according to Aro's defenders in Ranon, had lived in town for at least fifty years without visiting the island, was David's father's brother. However, David's father was born during David's father's father's first marriage, whereas Peter was born during the second marriage.[13] David was on good terms with the people living in Ranon, and had never claimed any rent from people who did not have rights to the ground on which they lived. Peter, however, was determined to claim rent from the many people who were living on what he perceived to be his ground. Village courts were held, and negotiations were made, but the case seemed unsolvable. Then suddenly a third party showed up from a neighbouring village, bringing along the story of his origin route, showing that his ancestors had actually been the ones who had first settled in Ranon. This man, who was from Fanhumul, a small settlement south of Ranon, had been annoyed with the people in Ranon and was tired of all the fighting. He decided to make an end to the disputes by telling the story of his origin. He was originally from Ranon village, in a settlement that was then called Lonmaribangakon. However, his ancestors had, because of a quarrel or conflict, moved to the place of Banghul. Later some of the people in Banghul had settled in Fanhumol. Ranon, however, was his *tangbarite* [L:origin].

People were overwhelmed by this sudden turn of events, but somehow relieved that the case might be solved, and no rent needed to be paid.[14] This case shows that no one securely holds land. Rodman (1987) in her discussion of landholding rights in Longana on Ambae in the northern part of the archipelago, comments:

> Socially, a landholder is not alone in exercising rights to a piece of land, as he may be, for example, in owning a canoe. He is rather a pre-eminent right holder for the time being, the tallest tree in the forest of growing competitors (1987, 39).

---

13   See also Rio (2002a, 337–46), for a detailed discussion and a genealogical map.

14   I later learned that the case is not yet over, as Peter's descendents want to try the case in the national court.

Access to land follows the idea of origin routes, and bits and pieces of land are used in different areas. I will claim that this is related to the idea that locality only reflects place at a specific moment, and that access to past localities, or land-areas left behind, is not expressed by moving back, but by reviving the awareness of the topogeny. Although movements back along the origin route do happen, people usually do not, but rather emphasize their topogeny or origin route by creating new settlements and extending the route. For instance, about a decade ago, a new village settlement was created next to Ranon, the village of Fantor. As I will expand upon later (in Chapter 6), the establishment of this new village and the recent breakaway from the Presbyterian Church and establishment of a new one, the Church of Holiness in this village, must be related to population movements in the area during the last hundred years. People who live together in composite villages, like Ranon, dealt with a large number of conflicts over land after Independence. There was no agreement on who had rights to land where. However, there was considerable agreement on how one should go about justifying claims based on the topogeny. One might say that people shared place, or origin route, but not present locality. However, instead of moving back to the original *buluim* locality, and thereby making the connection to the *harl* physically visible by living in the *harl* locality, people moved forward and established new village settlements emphasizing the shared origin route. People had their origin in another *harl,* and were not 'man Ranon'. They therefore resettled in a new village, the village of Fantor. The past was connected to the future of land claims by moving. No one of those living in Fantor today has genealogical connections to Ranon, but to villages in the interior of Ambrym, in areas now deserted. So, in other words, the topogeny was revived, by moving locality, and connections to past places were made.

The Mythological Origin of Hawor

Hawor is one of the places always mentioned in stories from the past, or when someone recounts their genealogy. Hawor was quite a large settlement at the end of the 1800s, but was gradually depopulated towards 1950. It was located uphill north of Ranon.

Hawor village was a feared and powerful place according to the story told by Lenkon Kintor who recalls the conflicts between Hawor and its neighbours. Randyu, Numto and Hawor had been fighting; 'Hawor won territory and just one man from Randyu was still left. He was the only one alive. He lived because he hid in Fanla. He moved to Hawor, as the fighting ended…'. The three *harls* surrounding Hawor were abandoned as Hawor won territory. People in Hawor also controlled the volcano.[15] We have recorded different versions of the origin story of Hawor. One told by Bongnebu (see Rio 2002a, 51), and another told by his classificatory brother, Chief Bongranli. Bongranli's version seems to be more detailed and includes names of old village sites and ceremonial grounds:

---

15   See Eriksen 2005a for a detailed outline of the mythological connection between Hawor and the volcano.

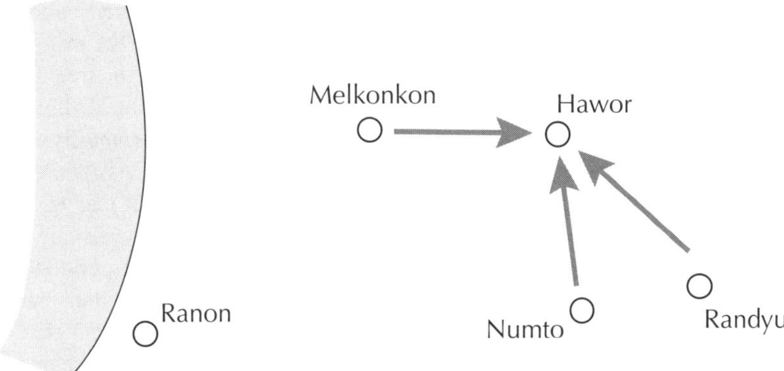

Map 3.4   **Roads into Hawor**

We, the people of Hawor, originated from a tree. The tree growing in Hawor stood upright like a [hu]man. It was like a woman. The big trunk of the tree stood upright, but like a woman. It had breasts. A man came out of it. A child came out of the tree. The child was breastfed from the tree. The child got bigger; it now climbed the oak tree in order to sleep as the small birds did. He made a bow and an arrow in order to shoot birds. God came to create the villages. When he arrived in Ambrym, he called out the name of the village as he created it. When he arrived in our place, Hawor, he saw the small boy shooting birds. He told the small boy: "I am creating men and I am creating villages, but you are already here. I think you are a spirit of the place." He then called out the name of the place: Longbulumar [hole of ancestor spirits]. In our language we call it "helan bulutmar" which means "called out ancestor hole". It is only a small area of Hawor. The name is a bit different. It is a sacred name. It is a *kastom* name because of the man who was there, who was shooting birds. Because God was creating everything, but he saw this man who came out of the tree and was already there. He grew up, and he shot birds in the oak tree. This man, who made our history, our line, multiplied in Hawor. The family grew. The older ones went away to work in a small bush in Hawor. They called it Ranilibju. They made a garden. When it was time to make garden, everyone made a garden. They made the village and the ceremonial ground [*nasara*]. They called the *nasara* Anrakon. This was our *nasara*. They made another one and they called this one Fantubueng.

The people of Hawor are here presented as originating from the ground, being the fruit of the earth. A female tree gives birth to a boy and breastfeeds him. The place Hawor is represented as a tree. The metaphor is significant because it represents place as something rooted on the one hand, but as something which is growing on the other. It has been pointed out by others (Patterson 2002; Weiner 1991) that the tree does not necessarily always connote rootedness and stasis, as is the most common way of metaphorically perceiving the tree, but the tree might also be analogous to movement. The tree in this particular origin myth can be said to be moving, or growing, in two respects; firstly the branches stretch away from the roots, and secondly it multiplies by giving birth to a boy.

In the same way people from Hawor are rooted here but they are also moving away to new village settlements. However, they do not really cut their connections because it is place itself that is growing, in the sense that place is the origin route. Although the roots have very specific locations in specific places, the tree develops through movement, just as people representing these places are never bound, but moving. The pigeons that the boy shoots are contrasting the tree; the flying birds underline the rootedness of the tree. The statement that the tree is like a female characterizes the place as something that gives birth to people, but just as children grow up and move away, so do the people of the place. The story reveals how people of Hawor created other places. The family grew, it is stated, and populated new places where they made gardens and ceremonial places. However, the relation to the place, or to the mother, is of an unalienable character. It is the ultimate origin. The story of the tree giving birth to a boy who multiplies and creates new places visualizes the way origin roots become origin routes.

The idea is that by tracing the history of relationships, the true nature of these becomes apparent. The ability to tell stories and trace the routes back in time legitimizes claims to ground rights. After finishing his story of Hawor's origin, Bongranli lists eight generations of agnatic links[16] and then makes an important point:

> Only we originate in Hawor. All the others came to stay with us. All the others came from a different place. Their ancestors came from other places. They came to stay with us. We became one family in Hawor. This is our history.

Although people today always like to picture themselves as the original dwellers in a location, and thereby legitimize claims to land, there was a general agreement that some people were originally from Hawor, whereas others had joined them later. For instance, when Tokon told the story of his origin in South Pentecost and of Karkar who married a woman from Rorongbu (recounted earlier in this chapter), he ended by telling how Karkar and his wife had moved to Hawor and saying 'this is how we joined the Hawor people'.

Movement as Female: The *Metehal*

I argued in the previous chapter that the link between actual and potential relationships is often matrilateral. As a ground rule one usually follows the relational codes of one's father, but if for some reason the relational code has to be changed, for instance in order to transform someone from unmarriageable to marriageable, this is often done through matrilateral links. In the same manner, when the old villages were deserted it was the links through the mobile women that they followed as they settled in new places. Chief Bongranli in Ranon tells about these changes:

> When we lived in Hawor, when the church had arrived, all the family was spread around in different villages. Because of the church, people became involved in work [for the

---

16	See Eriksen 2005a, Appendix, for this genealogy.

church, i.e., mission, my comment] other places. They became elders. They were involved in worship and made sure others were christened. We were only two brothers, of one mother. Mother died and we stayed with grandfather. We remained in Hawor, but there was no one else. They came out [from the interior, from Hawor, my comment] in order to join the church. They stayed with family elsewhere. ... What did we do? We moved down to Fanla. Then my grandfather died. A father's sister had come down to live in Ranon [i.e., was married in Ranon, my comment]. We joined the family in Ranon. This is why I came to stay in Ranon.

Bongranli and his brother followed 'the road' of their father's sisters and arrived in Ranon. On Ambrym they say that women are like roads or paths. The concept *hal*, meaning path, is important for understanding what it entails to be a woman, particularly a sister, *metehal*. The Ambrym term *hal*, has, through referential expansion, become a complex cultural category. In its most literal sense the term *hal* refers to paths between the hamlets and villages, as well as paths between the hamlet and the garden. The concept *metehal*, refers to daughters and sisters, and builds on the concept *hal* in a metaphorical sense. The concept literally means 'the end of the road', or as an informant explained it to me, the end that makes the road, like the front of an arrow, also called *mete*. Women are like paths between the hamlets because it is through them that social linkages are made. For instance, when doing the survey of village relocations it became apparent that movements from old settlements into new ones are usually through connecting women. The movement from Randyo and Nomto to Hawor (see Map 3.4) for instance was based on affinal links through out-marrying sisters. When the fighting between Hawor and the neighbours ended, the people who sought refuge in Hawor could do this because of affinal ties.[17] When Nomto and Randyu were deserted, these sisters in Hawor opened roads into this settlement for their natal kin. Having friendly links in these settlements must have been essential during this turbulent time when fighting ultimately made the men of villages like Nomto and Randyo flee and seek refuge. Women who marry into new places remain essential connections for their relatives who might need refuge in the future.

Also, on a more general level women are regarded as those who make connections and inclusions. This gendered way of dealing with others has also been described by McDougall (2003). She has outlined how women in Ranongga in the Solomon Islands are responsible for caring for outsiders and incorporating those who arrive from elsewhere into the group. This point can be made historically for the case of Ambrym women as well. As we have seen, the personalized origin stories often reflect the links to new places in greater detail than do accounts of whole villages that were deserted:

---

17 In the village survey (see Appendix in Eriksen 2005a) I have listed the genealogical connections to Hawor, Randyu and Nomto (see genealogy 2 and 3), and these show that there were women from Randyu and Nomto who married men in Hawor and settled here.

Connecting Women: Magenog's Story

Magenog, living in Ranvetlam village, has given an account of the history of his *buluim* and outlined the movement through four different settlements over twelve generations. His story is revealing in respect to the connection between women and movement:

> Madlarlar lived in the place of the volcano. He had no woman. He wondered what he should do about this. After a while he noticed a woman walking around quite near him. Madlarlar used a wood to do some magic, and he hid inside this wood. He talked to the woman and she followed him. He asked the woman, 'Where is your place? This is my place'. The woman told him that she was also of the place. …. The man said he had a house on his *nasara*, and the woman said that her house was the house of her mother. The man wanted that the two of them should go and see the mother of the woman, but the woman did not want to. Then the two of them married. Afterwards they went to the mother, and they gave her some food.
>
> The woman gave birth to three children, first two boys and lastly a girl. When the children were approaching adulthood, the elder of the sons ran away with his sister. This incestuous relation was scandalous and the father, in anger, lit a torch of wild cane and burnt and killed his wife's mother. It was then revealed that the wife's mother was a snake. When the ashes fired up, the man's wife realized that he [her husband] had burnt her mother. She took her children and said, 'Your father has burnt my mother. This is not a good thing. I do not feel good. Let us go home'. When she reached the houses, she found all the men inside the men's house where they were eating. She then made a sound as if she was calling for the pigs and by this act she turned the men and women of the place into pigs.
>
> The elder son was after a while found in the bush and his father and mother brought him along to a new place, Werkol. The son had no wife now, but his father owned a specific kind of magic that attracted women as well as pigs. He told his son that when he died, the son should cut his gut open and remove his kidney. By using the kidney he attracted pigs in plenty. He could climb the men's graded society, and he could pay for a wife. He put a red hibiscus flower behind his son's ear, and he [the son, my comment] found a woman in Lonbang whom he married. His son Sanebu was born, but the place [Werkol, my comment] was no longer 'good', and they moved to Ranveremto. Here Sanubu's son Wanbane was born, and he again had a son here called Toktokmal, and as he married he settled with his wife in Lonoror. Here Rogrogmal was born, who had a son Bongmelun, who again had a son Malmelun, who was the father of Malten, who had a son Bongmelun, [who was the father of the storyteller, Magenog, my comment].

The story is related to Magenog's power as a man of *kastom* today, and it reveals the genealogy of his magical knowledge. Magenog is renowned for his magical abilities and in particular for his power in attracting women and pigs. He has married several wives, and has, at the age of at least 75 years, married a young woman and they already have several children together. This ability to have children is again related to his magical capacity for attracting wealth and making things grow [L: *tal*]. Magenog's 'origin route' reflects his reproductive abilities.

However, this story is significant in other respects. This story is about movement on different levels. First, it recounts a long history of movement in the North Ambrym landscape from the volcano in the interior through Werkol, Ranveremto, Lonoror and to the storyteller's present location in Ranvetlam. It is also a story of a movement from an original state of nature into one of sociality as a result of an encounter with the snake. In this respect it resembles the story of Adam and Eve in the Christian tradition. Adam and Eve were also in an original state of nature when faced with the challenge of the snake. In the same way as Adam and Eve are thrown out of paradise and into the pains of sociality when the snake deceives them, Madlarlar is deceived by the snake's daughter. Madlarlar however is completely alone without the power to reproduce, and here this myth is significantly different from the biblical myth. Furthermore, the snake in this story is female. It is the daughter of a female snake who deceives Madlarlar. Madlarlar thought he had married a human, but he had married a snake in the form of a human. Madlarlar lived in total solitude before he discovers that his, until then, male place is inhabited by a woman. It is the snake, in the form of a woman that leads him away from a state of nature and into, on the one hand, reproduction and sociality, but on the other, the pains of sociality with its implication of keeping order in the relational cosmos by avoiding sibling marriages. Both Madlarlar and the snake lived in an original state of nature. The snake in one sense is the way out of this state, but at the same time, the presence of the snake represents the return to this original state; his son and daughter running off together.

The story seems to reveal that the way out of solitude and stagnation is through women. Women create roads out of places both geographically as well as socially. However, the story also conveys how easy it is to fall back to a state of stagnation and un-productivity. The brother-sister relationship is the foundation for sociality, but only if the sisters marry away. The sister must leave the place and travel in another direction. Holding onto sisters is the road back to the original state. At this point in the story, when the brother and sister have run off together, it is revealed that the mother of Madlarlar's wife is a snake. Madlarlar does not know that the woman he marries descends from a snake, and the snake is revealed because of the incestuous relationship. The storyteller explicitly connects the scandalous relationship with the pre-social state of the snake, and proceeds to kill it. Madlarlar thus disrupts the mother-daughter bond twice. He disrupts it first when he marries the woman and takes her away from the mother snake, and then again when he kills the mother snake after the incestuous relationship has been revealed. Madlarlar takes the woman away from her mother in order to domesticate her, first by marrying her and then, in order to prevent a return to the state of nature, he kills the snake once and for all. By this he powerfully signals that a return to nature, as the siblings have done, is unacceptable. The disruption of the mother–daughter bond is thus the cause of the movement from the state of nature into sociality.

The snake is a common way to refer to ancestors on Ambrym, and snakes around the old *harls* are signs of the powers the ancestors who once lived there still possess over the place. The snake also signifies a transformative power because the snake sheds its skin and renews itself from within. The snake in the myth evokes the transformative and moving capacities of women and opposes the rootedness of men of the place. The fact that the snake in this story is a mother snake is significant because it points to the way women, and in particular mothers, are transformative by their reproductive abilities. In this story the mother snake and her daughter transform from nature to society, perhaps the most powerful transformation of all. The daughter of the snake also transforms the men in the men's house into pigs. By this act she reverses the previous transformation by turning the society back into a state of nature. Women, as snakes, have transformative powers - they can return society back to a state of nature by not marrying away, and they can create society by moving away from their place and into new relationships.

Women on the Move

Bolton (1999b) has argued that women's relationship to place in Vanuatu generally and in Ambae, an island in the northern part of Vanuatu, in particular, is often phrased in terms of garden metaphors. The female cultural fieldworkers from various islands have reported to Bolton that they use expressions of setting root and growing in every possible place to describe the relationship between women and place. Women move at marriage and their relationship to place is a matter of affiliation and not of birth. Women always move and change place, as if they are being re-planted. Furthermore, Bolton argues that a woman is usually regarded as someone who has to 'go before you and open the way there for you' (1999b, 49). In other words, movement into new places is a gendered practise. Movement is female.

In this chapter I have exemplified the way place moves on Ambrym, and shown how people have routes in the landscape crossing large parts of the island. I have connected the movement into new areas and the creation of new settlements to the moving of women. Although men have moved as well, coming alone in their canoes to the shores of Ambrym, they are not able to establish a new place without entering through a connecting woman. Both Karkar and John Rawo's ancestor found women who could open the road for them before they settled. Sisters are more common roads, and in particular the village relocations after missionization and the establishment of the plantation, show how sisters provided roads into new villages. In the next chapter I will look more specifically at movement beyond the island. Traditionally these longer journeys have been male practices and the literature, with some exceptions (see Jolly 1987), has focused on men's travels. I will show however that although men have dominated these longer journeys in the past, women's movements beyond the island today are becoming more significant, and although these movements are also significant in terms of 'opening the road' into new places, the movement from village to town also has other implications.

Chapter 4

Women on the Move

Ambrym Women Beyond the Village

This chapter looks more specifically at movement beyond the island and how this affects the social institutions described in the previous chapters. It explores what happens to relations of kinship and marriage and to notions of place and elaborates on the implications for social organization as women expand their routes.

Mary Patterson (2002, 207) has pointed out: 'there is a greater proportion of the population from Ambrym living elsewhere than of any other island, with the exception of Paama and the Shepard Islands'. This is not only due to the active volcano, which through history has forced the people of Ambrym to cross the sea and inhabit other islands, but is related to a number of factors, some of which I will discuss in this chapter. My focus will be specifically on women's movement.

Men's movement beyond the island in the colonial periods, as well as to some extent in the pre-colonial period, has been documented to some extent (Layard 1942; Bonnemaison 1985, 1994; Patterson 2002). Bonnemaison has outlined traditional forms of mobility on Tanna, at the southern end of Vanuatu where men travelled on exchange journeys, during warfare, in order to seek refuge, and on initiation journeys. Ambrym men did the same, travelling for instance, to Malekula in order to buy rights in the men's graded society. However, we know little of women's journeys in the pre-colonial periods, except that they probably moved when they married. The same is the case for labour journeys during the colonial period. There are historical documents on men's labour journeys to Queensland and to Fiji (Scarr 1967; Corris 1970; Price and Baker 1976; Siegel 1985), but women's labour journeys are not well documented. Dorothy Shineberg has, however, compiled a register of people from the different islands of Vanuatu who arrived in New Caledonia to work during the colonial period, and she made her database available to me. Based on Shineberg's material, as well as works by Scarr 1967, Corris 1970, Price and Baker 1976, and Siegel 1985, we can tally the number of people who travelled from Ambrym to Queensland, Fiji and New Caledonia in the latter part of the 1800s.

As we see from Table 4.1, very few women participated in the labour journeys. Jolly has described the few who did as the 'forgotten women' (Jolly 1987, 136), the women who left for plantations in Queensland, Fiji, or to work in New Caledonia. She has argued that these women have tended to be portrayed as less than 'proper' women, as prostitutes or women who were chased away from their village. The material Shineberg (in author's files) has collected shows that the women who left the island often had labour contracts and were not accidental runaways. Of the 25 records registered by Shineberg, eight women arrived in New Caledonia with servant contracts. These women worked for Europeans, and were probably quite

Table 4.1   Figures of female work migration in the colonial period

Number of labourers from Ambrym to Fiji (see Siegel, 1985)	<u>1864–1900</u> **337** 331 male 6 female	1.2% of total number of labourers in Fiji in this period
Number of labourers from Ambrym to Queensland (Price and Barker, 1976)	<u>1863–1898</u> **3464** Gender unspecified	5.6% of total number of labourers to Queensland in this period
Shineberg database:	<u>after 1887</u>	
Number of migrants to New Caledonia	362	
male	337	
female	25	

young when they arrived. One of the girls registered by Shineberg was only 14 years old. Five of the women had no contract when they arrived. These women might have accompanied their husbands who most likely had been recruited for the mines. The rest of the women had labour contracts in other places, but only one of them at the mines. There were thus women who left as wives, but also women who left alone.

I argued in the previous chapter that women on Ambrym open paths into new places, because women change place and move when they marry. Sisters who have married out become entry points into new places. Bonnemaison (1985) has pointed out that on Tanna women are said to be like birds, descending only where they see good fruit. Men, on the other hand, are like the trees, rooted in places. What happens when the 'birds' fly further away and descend on other islands? Theories of modernity often dwell upon the processes whereby 'traditional' or 'pre-modern' societies become 'disembedded' (Giddens 1990). Relations are made across greater distances and according to new principles. I do not label the institutions of Ambrym sociality described in the previous chapters 'traditional' or 'pre-modern', and it is of course a matter of discussion whether the processes I am to describe here, are disembedding mechanisms, but it is this process of bringing the local principles of sociality beyond the island and its consequences that I am interested in.

Female Town Migration Today

Today large numbers of people move to towns. When employment was no longer available on the plantation in Ranon, people moved to one of the two capitals of

Vanuatu, Port Vila in the south or Luganville in the north. In his study of population movements in the Solomon Islands, Chapman used the concepts circulation and migration. He argues that the pattern most prominent in South Pacific societies is circulation. This implies that people move temporarily, either in order to trade, to visit, or to work, but will return home. Migration, on the other hand, involves changing a long-standing place of residence. The general view of urban migration in Vanuatu has been that it is mainly circular and that only a hard core of the urban population remains stable. Bonnemaison, for instance, has talked about 'the frequent renewal of the migrant population as people come and go' (1985, 58) when describing the urban population in the capital of Vanuatu, Port Vila.

In 2000 I carried out a survey of the North Ambrym people from the area called Lolihor[1] who were living in Port Vila. I asked about gender, about reasons for coming and the length of their stay. I gave a questionnaire to 210 people from Lolihor living in Port Vila, and I found that about half of them had lived there for over ten years, and only about a quarter of them had lived there for less then a year. Relating this data to the study made by Bonnemaison (1985), it seems as if the people coming from the villages to the capital have to a greater degree now become urban settlers rather than temporary visitors. Moreover, women form a major group of those relocating to town. I found that of the 210 people from the Lolihor area on Ambrym in Port Vila in the period April–October 2000, 87 were women. This is over 40 percent of the population from this area in town. Margaret Jolly (1995), after her fieldwork in the seventies, reported that in South Pentecost, about an hour's boat trip from the northern tip of Ambrym, men monopolised access to money, as well as to foreign ideas and values, and inhibited contact between 'their' women and the outside world, particularly by preventing the women from learning Bislama. The men claimed that women's exposure to the outside world would turn them into prostitutes (Jolly 1995, 89). Today, this is not at all the case in North Ambrym. Women's travel to town is highly accepted and even appreciated. Why do women travel now, and what are the implications of this?

While conducting the survey in Port Vila, a North Ambrym woman who had lived in Port Vila for the previous ten years helped me visit all the Ambrym people from the Lolihor region she knew about. We asked the people we met to fill out a questionnaire, but we also had informal talks with them about their experiences with town life and their reasons for leaving the village. I have learnt that the women leaving the island do this mainly for three reasons. Firstly, one leaves in order to obtain wage labour. This might be on a short-term or a long-term basis. Sometimes women meet men in town whom they marry, which leads to the second reason for leaving the island: one leaves in order to get married somewhere else. But inter-island marriage is sometimes problematic, and the difficulties arising from the encounter between different *kastoms*[2] might result in a more permanent stay in Port Vila rather than a return to one of the villages, either on Ambrym or on the husband's island.

---

1   Lolihor is the area between Ramvetlam and Linbul in North Ambrym. See Chapter 3 for maps.

2   Differences between islands are usually talked about in terms of differences between *kastom. Kastom blong olgeta i diffren* [B: their kastom is different].

Jenny was one of the Ambrym women I visited frequently in Port Vila, because she usually spent her days at home and worked during the nights at the hotels in town. She told me that she had tried the first year of her marriage to live with her husband on his island Tanna. After the birth of her first child however, she became seriously ill and almost died. She claimed that it was *kastom* from Tanna that had made her ill. More specifically, it was black magic performed by the family of the girl whom her husband should have married had it not been for his encounter with Jenny on Ambrym when he worked on one of the cargo ships regularly passing by Ranon. When they moved away from Tanna and entered more neutral ground in town, she recovered and has been in good health ever since. She will never return to Tanna, she said, but pointed out that Ambrym is not a place for them either since Ambrym *kastom* would be dangerous to her husband in the same manner as Tanna *kastom* had almost destroyed her.

The third reason for women leaving the island is to help out those who have already gone, for instance by providing childcare. Mothers often leave the village in order to help daughters or daughters-in-law with their children while they work in Port Vila. Not only mothers do this, but sisters and cousins do so as well. Mothers who come in order to help their daughters in town often stay for short periods. When young girls come, however, this often initiates a longer stay in town. Teenage girls are suited to the task of taking care of the children while the mothers work, and are always welcome in the household in town. After a while however, these girls often decide to try something else and start looking for a job where they get better pay, and then new girls from the village arrive to take their place. Helping out relatives in town is a very common reason young girls leave the village.

Bonnemaison (1985) has pointed out that young bachelors represent a particularly large group of those living temporarily in town. Likewise, the table below (Table 4.2) shows clearly that young unmarried women often spend some months or some years in town working before marrying. Of the 87 women from the Lolihor area of North Ambrym living in Port Vila in the period between April and October 2000, 29 of them were unmarried women.

Table 4.2   Marital status of N-Ambrym women in Port Vila 2000

	married	not married	sum
male	66	57	123
female	58	29	87
sum	124	86	210

The largest group of women in town in 2000 were, however, married women. There were 58 married women from the Lolihor area of Ambrym in Port Vila between April and October of 2000. Married women are becoming a major part of the urban population, which implies that families – married couples with children – are particularly well represented in the urban population. This is an expression of the fact that the stable nucleus of the urban population has grown. Furthermore, women in town are becoming important for opening pathways for their relatives, not only by providing them with a bed and a meal while they are in town, but also by connecting them to people from other islands. Ambrym women living in town are often married to men from other islands, and have a wide network of relatives and friends. I will illustrate the typical female urban resident by giving a short account of the movement of Rose, an Ambrym woman in her thirties living in Port Vila.

Rose's Journeys

Rose moved from Ranon to Port Vila in her teens, in order to stay with her aunt (father's sister) Jenny who, as I briefly outlined above, had married a man from Tanna and lived in Port Vila because of the couple's mutual intolerance for each other's *kastom*. Here they had to buy food and pay school fees, and both of them had to work long hours. Rose arrived from the village in order to help her aunt take care of the children. They lived in a temporary house made of corrugated iron in a squatter area outside the commercial centre, called Tebakor. When the youngest children started school, Rose got a job in a Chinese store and moved into a neighbouring house with her two classificatory sisters (father's brother's daughters). These women held different jobs in town. At this time Rose was pregnant, but her boyfriend had deserted her and married another woman. She gave birth to the child in Port Vila hospital, and her mother arrived from the island to take care of the child while Rose worked. After a while it was decided that Rose's mother should take the child back to the island. Rose continued working, and after some years she adopted another child from a colleague, a woman from Ambae. Her mother again arrived in Port Vila and brought this child back to Ambrym. Some years later Rose met a man, originally from the island Tongoa in central Vanuatu, in Port Vila whom she married, and the two children, now both going to school, moved back to Port Vila in order to live with their mother. They now live in an area called Fresh Wota, where they have bought their own ground and where they hope to build a permanent house.

Rose has moved from Ambrym to Tebakor, to Olin and finally to Fresh Wota. During this process, she has become an important connection between town and village for her family, by sending her children back to the island in order for them to engage in relations with their kin, and by providing a natural lodging place whenever her youngest brother, still living in Ranon, or her father or father's sister or other relatives visit Port Vila. Moreover, Rose has become a promoter for North Ambrym business in Port Vila. People on Ambrym wanting to sell kava, ginger, yams or other garden produce at the vegetable market in Port Vila, send their produce to her, and she transmits it to an appropriate seller on the market, and then transfers the money back to Ambrym. She also paid a young man on Ambrym to work a garden plot for her on her father's ground. He sent the crops to Port Vila with one of the passing ships. The prices for yams in particular were very good. Rose was a *woman Ambrym* making a viable road between Ambrym and Port Vila, thus expanding Ambrym to town. Likewise, Jenny, Rose's father's sister who is married to a man from Tanna and whose house was Rose's first entry point into Port Vila, has, in spite of her dramatic encounter with Tanna people herself, made connections between her Ambrym relatives and her husband's relatives. Her husband's brother rents out houses in Tebakor and a number of people from Ranon have stayed there, including Rose and her cousin sisters. In Tebakor, in the midst of people from Tanna, there is a small temporary shelter in which one can always find people from Ranon. Jenny has opened the small Tanna enclave in town to Ambrym migrants.

The Female Headed Households in Vila

The structure of the urban household is different from the household on Ambrym. It is only in town that young women live together and earn their own money. The women who live together in town, like Rose and her sisters while living in Tebakor and Olin, shared their money internally within the households. If one of the women earned more than the others, like one of Rose's sisters who worked at a hotel casino, she would pay for many of the meals and make a greater contribution to the payment of rent. The social relations these women were part of not only involved people from Ambrym, but from other islands as well. These people might be connected to the Ambrym women through work or they might be neighbours. Rose worked in one of the Chinese stores in town with a woman from Ambae and a woman from Pentecost. Working hours from seven o'clock in the morning to half past seven in the evening implies that Rose spent a lot of time with these women. Rose and her colleagues had lunch between twelve and two o'clock in the afternoon, and ate together just across the street from the store where a woman from Paama cooked their meals. The friendship between Rose and the women she worked with developed into kinship when Rose adopted the daughter of the woman from Ambae. She introduced me to the Ambae woman as *sista blong me* [B: my sister]. On Ambrym, children are only adopted among sisters. The woman from Ambae later married, and moved back to Ambae, and the contact consequently was harder to maintain.

Rose and her sisters joked and laughed about the fact that four young women lived together without husbands or fathers. They said that, had it been on Ambrym they would not have had the nerve to live alone. There is too much sorcery on Ambrym, they said, which would make it dangerous for women to live on their own. They said that women, when they were without the company of fathers or brothers or husbands, were vulnerable to sorcery. In town however, no sorcery was strong enough to get a grip on them, and they only laughed when considering the sorcery from Efate. Women from Ambrym seemed only to fear Ambrym sorcery.

Sometimes relatives from Ambrym arrived and stayed in the women's house in Tebakor or Olin. When she lived in Tebakor I met Rose's mother's brother at her house. He was in Port Vila in order to sell ginger at the market. Rose's father arrived sometimes with kava to sell, and Rose's brother lived there temporarily when going to school there. Although her salary was not more than 15,000 vatu a month (about US $140), she and the other women would pay all their relatives' expenses when they were in town, and sometimes even pay for their tickets home on one of the cargo ships. Women in town are expected to share their income and supply their families with a place to stay.

New Ceremonial Institutions: The *Sakkem Presen* Ceremony

As I have shown, women are moving today in great numbers both between villages and between islands, and they are creating roads for both people and products. I will now look more specifically at some of the implications of these new roads. I will start by describing a new marriage ceremony called, in Bislama, *sakkem presen,* and then connect the development of this new ceremony to the new form of female mobility. In this ceremony the bride receives presents from her family, mainly large quantities of consumer goods like saucepans, plates, cups, or large pieces of calico. Some of these presents are put into a chest or a suitcase. I was puzzled when I first observed this ceremony, because it resembles a handing over of dowry to a bride from her family, and this practice coexists with the practice of paying 'bride price'. I have read detailed anthropological descriptions of marriage practices on Ambrym (such as Mary Patterson's work from 1976 and other anthropological accounts from the area, like Margaret Jolly's work from the neighbouring island Pentecost published in 1995) but the present ceremony is not mentioned at all in their work. I think this is due to the ceremony's relatively recent character. People told me that it was not older than perhaps thirty years.

The *sakkem presen* ceremony is a major event, and the family of the bride, in particular her mother, will start preparing it weeks before the wedding. In the weddings I have attended, the bride's mother asks the bride's brothers to buy a chest or a very big suitcase, and she starts filling this with valuables. Although the mothers I watched and talked to during these preparations, all were eager to show me the traditional woven mats they were making, the chest was filled mainly with calico from the local store. The mothers also enclosed an envelope with some money, usually around 10,000–15,000 vatu (US \$100–140), which is an average month's pay in urban Vanuatu. During the last week before the wedding, the mother's sisters and father's sisters came to help the mother fill up the chest. Weddings offer an occasion for the mother of the bride to spend time with her sisters who have married away, perhaps even to other islands, and who return to lend a hand during the wedding preparations. They spend perhaps a week together in an atmosphere of joy and expectation. I took part in a couple of these events in 2000 and every night was like a celebration. The women prepared *laplap* [B: traditional ground oven-baked pudding] and special seasonal treats. On the day of the wedding, people on the girl's side prepared their gifts before going to church. The present ceremony usually took place just after the church ceremony. However, sometimes it is arranged before the wedding if, for instance, the girl is to marry someone who is not from Ambrym. In a present ceremony in Fanrereo in 2000, a Fanrereo girl received presents from her relatives about a week before the wedding took place in Port Vila.

The bride is decorated during these present ceremonies in pretty dresses, often two or three dresses on top of each other, and sometimes decorated handkerchiefs are pinned around the dress to 'flash' her as they put it. Her hair is powdered white and

Photo 4.1   Present ceremony for a Fanrereo bride who was to marry a man in Port Vila the following week

she is scented with deodorant spray, usually finishing two or three bottles. Then the presents are handed over while relatives stand around crying and kissing the bride.

When the present ceremony is finished, and usually after the church service, the bride returns to her place and is again decorated. The bride's father's sisters cover the bride with a red pandanus mat and lead her along the path to the husband's place. This mat is only lifted when the payment for the bride has been received. They also often carry with them a nicely decorated pudding for the bride to share with her new family.

One of the more spectacular present ceremonies I attended on Ambrym was during a wedding ceremony in Ramvetlam in June 1999. The bride, a woman from Lonbwe, was to marry a man from Ranvetlam. The present ceremony started just after church service. The church had been crowded during the ceremony, and there were a lot of people gathered outside on the lawn in front of the church. As the bride and groom walked down the church steps, two of the bride's father's sisters held a branch of a tree decorated with flowers above their heads, and they walked towards the ceremonial ground of the groom's place.

As they arrived, the bride was placed beside her husband on a mat and the present ceremony could begin. The groom's sisters stood behind the couple holding boxes of Johnson's baby powder. The bride's brothers placed a suitcase in front of the bride and the mother and father's sisters tied up the couple with calico and hung flowers and plastic flower garlands around them. While doing this, the groom's sisters threw baby powder and sprayed them as well with deodorant. During the whole ceremony the couple sat tied together with their heads silently bowed down, as if they were being attacked. People said they felt ashamed.

Photo 4.2   A bride from Fanrereo has been decorated by her aunts (FS) and they are now covering her with the red mat. Ambrym 1999

**Photo 4.3   The bride and the groom in the Ramvetlam wedding on their way
to the present ceremony**

The mother and father's sisters cried and kissed the couple and as they retreated, other people started giving presents. It was said that all those on the girl's side gave presents, mainly the bride's brothers from her natal place, and also classificatory mothers and father's sisters. The bride's father's sister's daughters were in an ambivalent position because they, according to the Ambrym classificatory system, belong to both the bride's side and the groom's side. They are daughters of the bride's father's sister, and also of the groom's father's sister's son's (potential) wife. Their position during ceremonies like this was consequently quite flexible and attachment to place and other practical circumstances seemed to be the decisive factors for whether they chose to be on the bride's side and give presents, or on the groom's side and contribute to the 'bride price'[3] [B: *payem woman*]. The presents given by the brothers are often the most valuable – the chest, mattresses, garden tools, calico, saucepans and such – and men often complain that they are ruined by their sisters' weddings. Classificatory relatives of the bride give smaller presents like soap, small pieces of calico or some money.

Rose's wedding

Nowadays inter-island marriages are becoming more and more common. In Ranon women have married men from several of the different islands of Vanuatu, and of

---

3   I use the term 'bride price' because this concept is used by people themselves in Bislama. Furthermore, the concept of 'paying' [B: *payem*] is crucial for the Ambrym idea of transferring rights, both in persons and in artefacts as well as in places.

Photo 4.4   Present ceremony, Ramvetlam wedding, June 1999

all the weddings I have recorded, only half of them were marriages between couples from Ambrym. During an urban inter-island marriage, the ceremony usually takes place some days before the church ceremony and with only the family of the Ambrym bride present. Rose's marriage was such an urban inter-island marriage.

Rose, who had lived and worked in a Chinese store in the capital Port Vila for about ten years, had kept in contact with her relatives on Ambrym by regularly sending money, and her family members from Ambrym visiting Port Vila would naturally sleep and eat at her place. During the last year she had been living with a man named Tonkin from the island Tongoa. Their wedding had been planned for a long time, and Rose's father and mother had visited Tonkin's family on Tongoa in order to negotiate about the bride payment and plan the marriage ceremony. The week before the wedding, Rose's family, her mother, her father and father's brothers, as well as her own brothers and their wives, arrived in Port Vila. They all stayed in the house of one of Rose's brothers, and they all brought along enormous amounts of yam, taro, banana and other garden produce, as well as pigs, from Ambrym. Every night the women prepared large meals for Rose and her family. Rose lived with her brother during this week, and Tonkin stayed with his family at the other end of town. The day before the wedding ceremony was of particular interest. The mother of the bride had announced that this was the day of the *sakkem presen* ceremony. Early in the morning this day the women started to prepare food. In front of Rose's brother's place in Olin a large table made for the occasion was covered with plastic tablecloths. Modern dishes like mixed salad with tomatoes, meat in curry and white bread were put on the table. At noon Rose's colleagues and friends from the store in which she worked came to visit during their lunch breaks. They all brought along presents, mainly plates and cups and glasses. Their visit was short and as they left, more traditional food was prepared. Rose's brother had bought a bullock which was slaughtered and large parts of it placed on top of several puddings and cooked in the earth oven.

At dusk a number of people from Ambrym living in Port Vila arrived, and the present ceremony started. It was similar to those I had experienced on Ambrym, but only Rose was sitting on the mat, without the company of her future husband. She was given an enormous number of gifts, the same kind as those usually given on Ambrym, only in much larger quantities. The main present was the chest. On Ambrym I had mainly seen suitcases being filled up with valuables. For this marriage however, Rose's brothers had ordered a hand-made chest from a carpenter. It was painted glossy red and filled with calico, mats, bed sheets and pillowcases. She also received gardening tools, pillows, several mattresses, and many plastic containers of various kinds to use for such things as washing clothes, bathing babies or storing food. I tried to count everything given and estimate the probable value, and arrived at the incredible sum of 100,000 vatu[4] (which is almost one year's income for Rose). There was a mountain of gifts, and Rose herself cried during the whole ceremony. When people had finished giving gifts, the *laplap* [B: traditional puddings] were served.

The next day was the day of the wedding ceremony, which began in the church. Rose was decorated with a western style wedding dress. She had also sewn pink dresses for her daughter and classificatory daughters who were bridesmaids. After the priest's speech and the couple's 'yes', they were taken for a drive around the streets of Vila in decorated taxies hired for the purpose. People waved and cheered as they drove by. The tour ended at Tonkin's family's place, where they were served lemonade and biscuits as a string band played cheerfully in the background. This was, however, not the end of the ceremony, and Rose and her family did not stay long. As they arrived back at Rose's brother's house, a traditional *laplap* meal was served. Rose's mother had prepared a special *laplap* which was not eaten but given to Rose. She was taking it along to her new home in order to share it with her new family there. It was a yam *laplap*, nicely decorated and it would ease Rose's arrival in her new home, according to her mother when she gave it to her husband's mother as an arrival gift.

After the meal, people started to prepare for the final part of the ceremony which included following Rose to her new home and the receipt of the payment for the bride [B: *payem woman*]. Before leaving however, the father's sisters said goodbye by performing a special ceremony, which involved decorating the bride. They said that this ceremony was *kastom blong ol man Paama* [B: the *kastom* of those from Paama]. It was, in other words, neither an Ambrym *kastom*, nor a *kastom* from Tongoa. I was

---

4   The list of presents: one large chest filled to the top with calico and mats, bed sheets and pillow cases. Then there were two spades, ten dresses of the 'Mother Hubbard' style, twenty large plastic containers, five mattresses, bedcovers, smaller plastic containers and plates and cups, money, and soap. The value of the chest was 20,000 vatu; one mattress costs 10,000 vatu in the stores. The dresses were worth 1,000 vatu each sold on the market, the bedcovers between 500 and 1,000 vatu each. The price for the plastic containers varies according to size, but they were all worth between 500 and 2,000 vatu.

Photo 4.5 **Tonkin and Rose after their church wedding. Rose's mother, Nelly, in the background carrying her small grandchild**

Photo 4.6 **Wedding laplap**

Photo 4.7   **Rose's aunts (FS) are decorating Rose; spraying her with scented deodorant after having put several dresses on top of each other. Rose is holding a handkerchief up to her face. Rose's mother is standing next to her, also crying. Beside Rose's mother, two of Rose's mother's sisters are also expressing their grief**

not given any specific reason why they performed this *kastom* other than 'it is a good *kastom*'. There were five father's sisters present and they all dressed Rose in one dress each of the 'Mother Hubbard' style,[5] one on top of the other. Afterwards they powdered her hair white and sprayed her with deodorant spray. Next to Rose, her mother and her mother's sisters were standing in a row crying and loudly expressing their grief over losing Rose. The father's sisters cried as well and hugged her, and Rose herself cried during the whole procedure.

In order to move all of Rose's presents, her brother borrowed a truck. It was an impressive sight, the truck filled with gifts and cars and minibuses filled with relatives as if in a motor parade on the way to Tonkin's place. About a hundred metres from Tonkin's family's place, the truck and the cars stopped and people started to walk, carrying all the presents. The string band started to play as they entered Tonkin's place. The yard in front of the small corrugated iron house inside the squatter area was decorated and transformed into a ceremonial ground and the string band music created a joyful atmosphere in which everybody started dancing and singing. Rose was at the front covered by a red pandanus mat. Tonkin's father, accompanied by some other men, met the parade in the front yard and gave Rose's father an envelope, which, I later learnt, contained the 'bride price' in the amount of 60,000 vatu.

---

5   The 'mother Hubbard' dress is a special dress made all over Vanuatu in almost the same style, with some variation, and always using flashy colourful material.

Photo 4.8   Rose's presents on the truck as the crowd is entering Tonkin's yard

Sakkem Presen and Comparative Prestations

It is common in Melanesian contexts for gifts to flow both ways between the bride's place and the groom's place. Andrew Strathern (1980) has pointed out that for the Melpa in the Highlands of New Guinea, people do not give gifts or pay for the bride in order to marry, but the contrary: they marry in order to give gifts. Among the Melpa, as on Ambrym as well as most places in Melanesia, the payment of the bride is only one of several prestations. The relation between a woman and her husband on the one hand and her brother and his wife on the other, is one of continuing reciprocity, and this circle begins at marriage. Sisters are very important for men on North Ambrym. Whenever a man holds a ceremony of a kind, be it a circumcision ceremony for his son or funerals and wedding ceremonies, he has to rely on contributions from his married sisters. They give him pigs and yams, which the brother will use as payment during the ceremony.

Traditionally there are no ceremonial prestations directly between a man and his sister. A spouse or their children usually mediate prestations. The children pay their mother's brother in a number of ceremonies: Young boys pay their mother's brother during the circumcision ceremony, the *malyel*. On North Ambrym boys are no longer circumcised during the ceremony, but in the clinic on Ambrym or in the hospital in Port Vila. The ceremony, however, is still important but the focus is not the physical circumcision and the period in seclusion with preparation of special food for the boy to eat, but rather, it is the ceremony where food is paid to the boy's mother's side.

During my last stay in Ranon in 1999 my husband[6] and I observed and participated in the preparations and the performance of a *malyel* ceremony. Most people try to arrange for a *malyel* for their boys. It is talked about as shameful if the *malyel* has not been performed. Couples who do not arrange for their son's *malyel* are considered lazy and without knowledge of the importance of the relationship between a child and the mother's brother.

The payment for the bride during a marriage is comparable to the payment of pigs and yams to the mother's brother during a circumcision ceremony. The payment of 'bride price' compensates a man for the loss of his sister, and the payment during *malyel* in a similar way compensates for the loss of the same woman, but now through her children. In a similar manner to the way the bride is covered with a red mat on her way to the groom's place, the novice in the *malyel* ceremony is covered with a red mat by the mother's brother in the period of seclusion before the circumcision (see Rio 2002a; Patterson 1976). For a *malyel* ceremony the parents of the boy to be circumcised gather pigs and yams and other garden produce in large quantities to be paid to the boy's mother's brother on the day of the ceremony. The productive relation between the husband and wife must be credited to the wife's brother who sent his sister away in the first place. Rio (2002a) has argued that through a *malyel* ceremony the father of the boy labours; he produces food, gathers capital and displays it all on behalf of his son in order to reveal the relation between the boy and his mother's brother. The road that was opened through the marriage of the boy's mother is kept open by the father's contribution to the mother's brother on behalf of his son. The prestation then goes from the married couple, the sister and her husband, through the child, and to the brother.

In a parallel manner, the *yengfah* ceremony for girls compensates the mother's brother for the loss of his sister through the payments of the female child. *Yengfah,* which means 'shining red', is a ceremony where girls pay their mother's brother's wife for gifts she receives during the ceremony. This ceremony is performed at the time when she starts her periods for the first time, and it is thus also a payment for the right to spill the blood she has received from her mother's place. I never observed a *yengfah* ceremony myself, but I have heard a number of accounts of how they are performed. In the *yengfah* ceremony, the young woman is first decorated by the mother's brother's wife.[7] She puts an arm bangle made of the trochus shell[8] around the girl's wrist and a band of beads[9] around her neck. She then paints the face, the eyes and the left side of the hair of the girl red. The red colour refers to the payment of blood that this ceremony centres on. The girl pays back her blood to her mother's side, represented by her mother's brother's wife. The mother's side is seen to be on a person's left side, and the painting of only the left side of the head is an overt expression of where the blood comes from. The mother's brother's wife then fastens pandanus rings around the girl's legs and finally flashy colourful feathers in her hair.

---

6   See Rio 2002a for a detailed description and analysis of this particular ceremony.
7   The mother's brother's wife is also the father's sister and called *ina*.
8   The arm ring of the trochus shell is called *belamalo*.
9   The band of beads is called *waije*.

When the decoration is finished the mother's brother's wife gives the girl a mirror. For every item fastened on the girl, she pays her mother's brother's wife money. In the past it was yams and pigs that were given to the mother's side, but today it is usually money that is paid. In a ceremony which had taken place just before my first arrival in Ranon in 1995, the mother's side had been paid 1000vt for each item fastened on the girl, as well as for the mirror, and then finally a pig had been killed by the girl's father on behalf of his daughter and given to the mother's brother.

A comparison between payments at marriage and payments during *malyel* and *yengfah* reveal many similarities. Firstly, and most obviously, the payment goes in the same directions. It is a transaction between the sister and her brother, which at marriage goes from the sister's husband to her brother (and father) as the 'bride price', and at *malyel* through her son and her husband and at *yengfah* through her daughter and her husband. These prestations are all seen as compensations to the brother for the loss of his sister and her children. These ceremonies are centred on the repayment of the eternal debt the marriage of a woman creates. The husband is responsible for always compensating this debt. The relationship to the place of the woman is seen to be life-giving, and neglecting this eternal debt can be catastrophic and lead to illness and death.

Furthermore, both *yengfah* and *malyel* include present ceremonies. In the *yengfah* ceremony the girl is decorated by the mother brother's wife, but the *malyel*-present ceremony is more like the *sakkem presen* ceremony at marriage. After the payment of yams and pigs during the *malyel*, the boy is given presents in a similar fashion as the bride during her present ceremony. The boy sits with his mother on a mat and the relatives, mainly his mother's brother's wives, powder him and give him mats, calico, soap, and money. The present ceremony is also actually part of the death ceremony. When a person dies, the father's sisters will cover the dead person's body with presents of the same kind, mainly mats and calico.

Although in all these ceremonies the payments are directed to the place of the mother's brother in order to pay back the debts a woman created as she left this place, there are also presents going from the mother's brother's place as recognition of the path that remains open between the two places, a woman's native place and her husband's place. In this respect, the *sakkem presen* at marriage are not so different from present ceremonies in other life cycle ceremonies. However, there are some differences that I will point out and which I see as social consequences of the new contexts the mobile Ambrym women become part of as they move further away from the island, and take part in wage labour and the monetary economy.

The innovative aspects of the present ceremony during marriages are firstly, the explicit focus on the brother-sister relation. During both *malyel* and other ceremonies, those who give presents are mainly mother's brothers' wives and the presents are directed to the sister's children. In other words the presents are mediated through other relations and are not direct presents from a brother to his sister, but rather from his wife to her child. During the *sakkem presen* at marriage however, brothers give presents directly to their sisters. Secondly, this relation is not classificatory in the sense that all her brothers from her village give presents, which is the case for the other relatives who give presents,[10] but only her brothers from her natal household. Lastly, the present a brother will give his sister upon marriage by far exceeds the value of the gifts given at other present ceremonies.

What Makes *Sakkem Presen* Different?

Why does the brother now feel the need to give his sister presents on marriage and why has the present ceremony at weddings escalated in size? When I asked people about the *sakkem presen* ceremony, it was usually pointed out that it started in the sixties. Different people have told me that earlier the only things given to the bride were either a yam or a small female pig that accompanied her to her husband's place. People on Ambrym will use the word *seueran*, which means 'sending out', when referring to the yams or pig given in the past. Sometimes they will use this term for the modern ceremony as well, but usually they use the Bislama word *presen* also when speaking their own language. The traditional *seueran* gift, of a pig or a yam, is still practiced, but usually only in cases where the marriage concerns two from Ambrym, and the gift is usually given just before the payment of the bride. People are eager to point out that in the old ceremony the female pig and the yam were not to be consumed. On the contrary, they should grow. The pig should breed and the yam be planted, and in this way bring wealth to the new household. When talking about the modern ceremony in comparison with the older one, people usually point out that the gifts given today cannot grow [*tal*] in the same manner. The modern gifts are consumer items and usable objects. To some extent I see these kinds of statements about the quality of the new kinds of presents as opposed to the more traditional ones as emphasizing a kind of break with past practices. The idea that the new kinds of presents are not to be planted or grow and reproduce might even be indicative of the quality of the social relations these presents refer to. As I will discuss in greater detail below, women now move further away from their natal kin, and relations are harder to maintain. The modern present ceremony represents something new, and a new kind of social universe where the urban environment plays a larger role. People also referred to it as *kastom* of Vanuatu as opposed to *kastom* of Ambrym, implying that this was a national marriage practice, and not so much a local tradition. People told me that all over Vanuatu they have this *sakkem presen* ceremony at weddings. Some informants have told me that the chest is *kastom* in the Schefa[11] region in central Vanuatu, and that it has spread around the country.

In order to achieve an understanding of why this new wedding ceremony has developed among the North Ambrym people, I will outline different simultaneous processes taking place. I think that this new marriage payment in North Ambrym is a result of a process where practises, or *kastoms,* from other islands spread quickly due

---

10   The mother's sisters and mother's brothers' wives are not only the sisters of her own mother and the wives of her mother's brother from her place, but classificatory relatives coming from the whole area.

11   Regional term for the Shepard group and Efate.

to the growing circulation of people. However this argument is incomplete. There are other changes taking place that make this new present ceremony hook easily onto the Ambrym marriage practices. My hypothesis is that the new ceremony is connected to changing kinship practises, and in particular changes in the brother-sister relationship, as a result of town migration and wage labour. Bolton (1999b, 54) has argued 'Urban growth is effecting significant shifts in kinship arrangements …' in Vanuatu. The *sakkem presen* ceremony is one of those very visible shifts in kinship arrangements due to town migration and its implications.

Women's Wage Labour

Young unmarried women living in Port Vila are expected to send part of their wages back to the island and usually they do this to a much larger extent than their male counterparts. It is often said that families cannot rely on young men for financial help. Young men only share their money with other young men, it is said, and then they usually spend it on alcohol or kava. Young wage earning women on the other hand are a much more reliable source of financial help. This money is needed on the island to pay for school fees, material needs of the family, kinship ceremonies and sometimes for a family member's trip to town. Rose, described earlier in the chapter, was the only reliable source of money for her family on the island. I often got the impression that her mother and father considered her an endless source of money and whenever they needed gardening tools or economic help of any kind, they would telephone her and she would arrange for their needs.

When asked why they give so many presents to the bride, some people emphasized that sisters are becoming more and more economically important to their natal family because they contribute so much of their salary. When Rose married, for instance, her family pointed out that Rose had helped them a great deal through the years, and at her marriage they would show their gratitude. The 'bride price' Tonkin's family paid was also relatively low compared to the national standard which is 80,000,[12] and the average which is considerably higher. This reflects, according to her family, that Rose had 'paid for herself' by contributing so much to her family while working in Port Vila.

If the present ceremony at weddings is a result of the introduction of women into wage labour, then those women who have not worked in town at all should receive no presents. This is not the case. However, a comparison between the ceremony for a woman who has lived in Port Vila for a long time and contributed a lot of money back to her natal family and the ceremony for a woman who has not worked in Port Vila, but stayed on the island, shows that there is a connection between wage labour and the present ceremony. The size of the presents to the woman who has lived and worked in Vila is often double those given to women who have stayed on the island. Furthermore, there seems to be a difference between the coastal villages, such as Ranon, the site of the colonial plantation, and the 'bush villages' in the interior.

---

12 The National Council of Chiefs, the Malvatumauri, set this standard in order to control the inflation of the 'bride price'.

Older women have told me that the *sakkem presen* ceremony started in the coastal areas, and that when they were young, people in the 'bush villages' did not have such a ceremony. One might then argue that the coastal villages, such as Ranon, have given women access to wage labour earlier, and also, of course, access to the commodities sold in the plantation store.

A New Family Structure

However, women's introduction into wage labour and their new financial position vis-à-vis their natal household is only one of the processes to be considered, and which I will argue is part of the total picture. Another important element is the new independent family developing in town. When discussing the introduction of the *sakkem presen* ceremony with some Ambrym people, it was pointed out that the presents given are meant to create a new independent household. A woman receives everything a household needs, particularly cooking equipment: saucepans, plates, cups, and similar things. One Ambrym woman told me that before, there was no need to give such things because everything was shared. A newly wed woman would have natural access to her husband's mother's cooking equipment,[13] and there was no need for her to bring it into her new home. Today however, when moving to town it is expected that in the long run a family should get their own house. They might live with relatives for a while, but not as a permanent solution.

Furthermore, being able to pay for the expenses required to provide for a family in town weakens one's ability to take part in the ceremonial economy on Ambrym. Involvement in the ceremonial economy is very expensive, and it is particularly expensive for those who do not have the opportunity to grow their own yams and raise their own pigs. Buying yams on the market in Port Vila for instance is extremely expensive. One yam might be priced 1,000 vatu or more, depending on the size. Buying yams to pay for a *malyel* ceremony for boys in town is often impossible. Several people from North Ambrym in Port Vila expressed their frustrations and their shame for not having had the opportunity to pay for their sons' *malyel* ceremony.

A life in town often implies that the ceremonial economy on Ambrym becomes more distant and that the circle of reciprocity between a sister and her brother in the different life cycle ceremonies becomes difficult to maintain. Rose's father's sister, Jenny, who was married to a man from Tanna and living in Tebakor outside the commercial centre of Port Vila, had not arranged for her sons' *malyel* ceremonies or her daughters' *yengfah*. In addition to the financial difficulties that most North Ambrym people in town experienced, she was also 'caught between two *kastom*s'. Her children were Tanna children now, she explained, and should perform *kastom*s from Tanna. She nevertheless sent one of her daughters back to Ambrym to live with a classificatory mother, so that she could get to know Ambrym *kastom*. On the island the classificatory mother paid for this girl's *yengfah*. Jenny's remaining daughters and sons in town however, did not get involved in the ceremonial economy.

---

13 In the past the women did not of course use saucepans and plates and cups, but they nevertheless had cooking equipment, such as bamboo canes for cooking and *laplap* stones.

It is hard for women living in Port Vila to keep up the ceremonial payments to the brothers on Ambrym even though they were married to men from Ambrym. The most immediate problem for people in town is the cost of entering the ceremonial economy. Several Ambrym women in Port Vila pointed out to me that in their households they prioritized the payment of school fees over paying the children's mother's brother for ceremonies such as a *malyel*.

When ceremonies like these are not performed, and when the distance to the mother's brother's place broadens, people say that the children do not learn to respect and love their mother's brother as they would on the island. The children are cut off from this relationship and cannot rely on him for help to the same extent as those who have kept up the relation through pig killings and food distributions. They say that the children growing up in town have not paid their debts to the mother's brother.[14] As the continuing reciprocity between a sister and her brother is cut off because payments from a sister's children to her brother are not performed, this is symptomatic of a new family structure with more emphasis on the nuclear, independent family.

In town then, as well as when women marry to other islands, the ceremonial focus on the relation between a woman and her husband on the one hand and her brother and his wife on the other, is difficult to maintain. *Malyel* and *yengfah* ceremonies are performed less frequently. The new focus on the relation between brother and sister, which the present ceremony during weddings represents, might be replacing these older ceremonies to a certain extent. The expenses for a *sakkem presen* ceremony are much lower than, for instance, for a *malyel* ceremony. In the latter, huge amounts of yams and many pigs must be gathered in order to pay all the child's mother's brothers, not only from the natal households, but also classificatory mother's brothers in the village. The father of the boy might rely on contributions from classificatory brothers, but this is premised on his earlier contributions to their ceremonies. A man in town might not have been able to contribute to others' ceremonies and is then unable to rely on their help either. All major life cycle payments on Ambrym are based on the principle of generalized reciprocity within an extended group of agnates. Both 'bride price' payments, payments at *malyel* and *yengfah*, as well as death payments are based on contributions from a number of classificatory kin. When a man is gathering money for the 'bride price', relatives not only from his own patrilineal group, his *buluim*, but also from a number of *buluims*, will contribute. Although the greatest burden of collecting the money, the pigs, and the yams rests on the shoulders of the groom and his *buluim* brothers and their father and he always has to 'flatten his money' as it is expressed, the essential assistance arrives from those places where they themselves have previously contributed to ceremonial prestations. If one has not participated in the ceremonial economy on the island, and has not oneself contributed to other's ceremonies, it is hard to arrange for one's own ceremony, such as a *malyel* or a *yengfah*. The *sakkem presen* ceremony might be seen as a substitute.

---

14 People say that these children *kaun long mama*. *Kaun* is a verb referring to having debts, or having an 'account' [account = *kaun*], which must be repaid, and in this case the children have not repaid their mother.

Buying presents is a one-time affair. When a brother buys a chest or a suitcase for his sister, this is only for her, and it is only this one time.

When the *malyel* and *yengfah* are no longer performed, because involvement in this kind of ceremonial economy relies on access to pigs and yams and continued contributions to others' ceremonies, the new present ceremony can be seen to fill the empty ceremonial space between a woman and her brother. The new gift between a man and his sister can be seen as an effort to sustain the reciprocity in this relationship in a ceremony that is more feasible. It is an attempt to keep up the relation to a sister who has become distant, both geographically and ceremonially, when the cost of entering the ceremonial economy on the island is too high.

However, the new ceremony is objectifying this relationship to a greater extent than before. It is now a direct gift between a man and his sister, whereas before it would go via the son or daughter and be directed toward the sister's husband (see Figure 4.1). Because of the rule of classificatory sister exchange, the sister's husband would be the mother's brother of a man's child. The pigs and yams would go from a man to

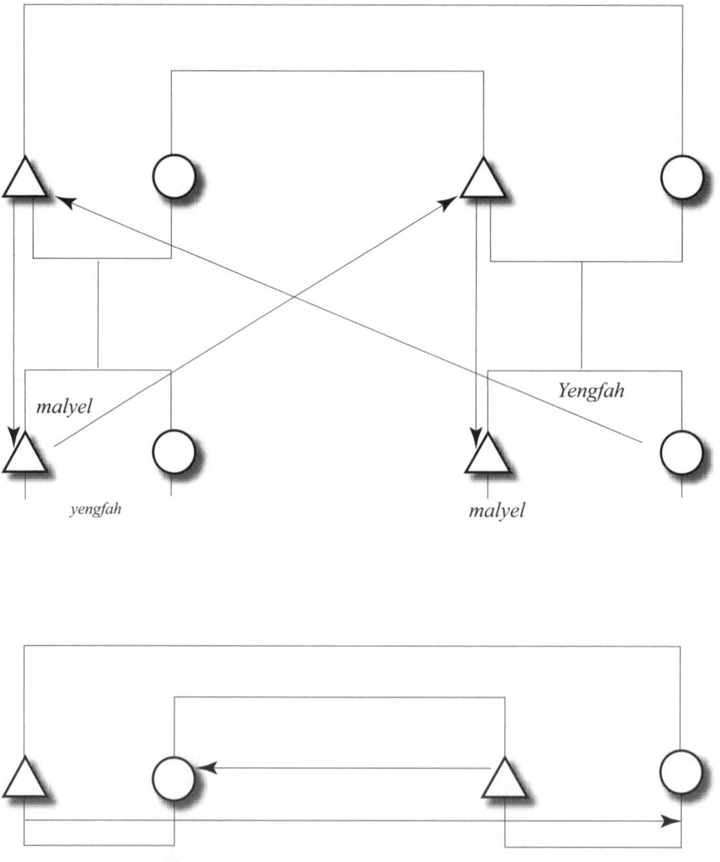

Figure 4.1   The new gift relation

his child, who would pay his mother's brother. Perhaps the new and direct focus on the relation between a man and his sister is caused by the processes described above, whereby a woman contributes more explicitly to the natal household as a result of migration and wage labour, and she thereby receives the counter gift directly without the mediating relations of children and husband.

Changing *Kastom*

The North Ambrym community in Port Vila is quite large; in 2000 I estimated there were 210 adults from the Lolihor area in the town. Judging from the recent population census, this is between 15 and 20 percent of the population from this area (NPS; Statistics Office 2000). One should think there would be frequent social relations between these people. Perhaps a woman would make closer contact with her cousin brothers, so that her children would learn to know the important relationship to the mother's brother. However, during my fieldwork among Ambrym people in Port Vila I realised that the contrary is often the case. The North Ambrym people living in Port Vila are spread around in different areas, and do not seek to live together in town. On the contrary, it is often the case that people moving away from Ambrym do this because of conflicts in the villages, or what they themselves call 'too much talk' [B: *tumas toktok*], which is often closely related to the fear of black magic, and this must be related to the reasons why they left the island. People who move to Port Vila very often move away from not only the island, but also from their kinsmen due to gossip, jealousy and ultimately the fear of *abio*, or black magic attacks (see also Rio 2002b). In Port Vila they do not seek the relatives of those whom the conflict concerns, and perhaps they will seek places where no other people from their area live. This was the case for some of the people I met in town. They lived in areas with people only from other islands. I asked some of the North Ambrym people about their relations to other people from North Ambrym living in Port Vila. They replied that there are families from neighbouring areas of their own place on Ambrym whom they seldom or never visit, but who they might run into at the market or in the streets in town, and then they might talk a bit. The fact that people are from the same village or from the same area on North Ambrym does not in itself imply that these people are closely connected in town. An incident during my stay in Port Vila characterizes this phenomenon.

A woman from West Ambrym died, and it is expected that when a person on the island dies, there should be a ceremony in Port Vila similar to the one they have on the island, because not many people can afford to go back to the island 'to cry'.[15] The woman's son in Port Vila, having little money to provide food for everyone who would come to cry for the dead, was unable to hold the ceremony. It was decided

---

15 When people attend funerals they refer to it as 'going there to cry' [*go blong krae*]. They cry in order to show respect and grief on behalf of the place of the mother of the deceased. The life that is lost is always seen to belong to the place of the mother. People from the place where the diseased was living, the brothers (if it is a man) or sons of the deceased pay those who come and cry for their effort by giving them food after crying, often rice and laplap and pork.

that a classificatory brother of the deceased woman should assist them, but because of lack of contact between the different relatives, and also because of the failing ability to cooperate, as one informant phrased it, the classificatory brother held the ceremony himself without the involvement of those who, according to *kastom*, should have been in charge. A woman's brother is not from the place of the woman (because she has married away). During this ceremony a number of people told me that it was only in Port Vila that a woman's brother could arrange for a ceremony like this. On the island, it is always a woman's husband and sons who are in charge of the death ceremony. One man phrased it like this: *Vila i tanem kastom*, implying that Vila turns *kastom* upside down.

Sakkem Presen and Dowry

The new *sakkem presen* ceremony, however, represents a rather dramatic turn of *kastom*. The economic character of the things given is different from the usual Ambrym prestations.

The *sakkem presen* ceremony has important similarities with dowry. Goody (1973), in his classical analysis of dowry and 'bride price' societies, has pointed out that it is characteristic of the dowry that it should remain with the girl as her capital in her new home. This is clearly the case with the things given during the *sakkem presen* ceremony. For instance, in Rose's case, described earlier in the chapter, Tonkin's presence was not at all required. Goody further notes that dowry is based on resources from the family, and not what he calls 'societal funds'. 'Bride price' is, according to Goody, traditionally based on such societal funds, and this is also the case on Ambrym. As I have outlined, on Ambrym a man who wants to pay for a wife, will, together with his father, use all their relations to places where they themselves once contributed to build the 'bride price' – yams, pigs or money – in order to receive back what was once contributed. In this sense, 'bride price' on Ambrym is based on a societal fund. The resources in the fund circulate so that everyone can make 'bride price' payments when necessary. The same principles are at work during *malyel* and *yengfah* ceremonies.

Goody explains that the societal fund is characteristic of societies with a low degree of stratification as, for instance, in African agriculture societies. This is in contrast to Eurasian societies where the degree of stratification is much higher, and where one does not pay 'bride price' at all, but rather practices dowry. Dowry is the opposite of the societal fund because it does not circulate, but is tied to the family and transferred from one generation to the next or from parents to daughter (Goody 1973, 17).

What about the things given during the present ceremony? These gifts seem to be of two kinds. The burden of buying the chest, the garden tools, the mattresses, and other items rests on the shoulders of members of the girl's natal household, and in particular her brother. Those gifts, which are bought by her natal family, are to remain with her in her new home as her capital, and are not to be distributed. In this sense it is quite contrary to the 'bride price', which is collected among many and shared among many. The bride's presents are in many respects the contrast to the societal fund and resemble the familial fund, which is characteristic of the dowry. Those smaller presents given by classificatory kinsmen, on the other hand, she may distribute parts of if she wishes. These presents might be said to have more the character of generalised reciprocity. Usually the bride will share parts of these smaller presents with her husband's brother's wives, who are her classificatory sisters. My interest here however is on the gifts going to a woman from her natal family.

As I have pointed out, the *sakkem presen* ceremony can be seen as a replacement of a ceremonial connection between sister and brother. The classical Eurasian dowry, on the other hand, can be considered as a form of inheritance and is thus quite different. Goody argues that dowry is tied to women's property rights and is part of societies where kinship is bilateral and property follows women as it does men. Dowry is connected to alliance between families and a premise for hypergamy. Having a big dowry is important for getting a desirable son-in-law and making a good alliance. This is not the case in the *sakkem presen* ceremony. The focus in this ceremony is not on the relation between the parents of the bride and the groom and his family. Rather it is, as my descriptions show, focused on the relation between parents and brothers on the one hand and the bride on the other. This is clearly then not a matter of alliance. However, a comparison with dowry societies is useful in other respects because it helps focus on the emerging class structures in urban areas.

Emerging Class Structures

I have shown in the preceding chapters that moving, creating roads and connections into new places, is a female gendered quality. Historically, women's movement at marriage has been important for the social dynamics of the local village structure. However, when women's mobility is stretched, and when this mobility connects them to new contexts where salaries and payments of bills are more pressing than kinship obligations, this leads to an accumulation of capital within the family to a larger extent than before. In Port Vila the focus is to a lesser extent on the kinship network based on generalised reciprocity, and to a greater extent on the economic needs of the nuclear family. When a family lives in town and is involved in wage-labour and has children in schools, it needs to protect the capital from flowing out. The wages of the working parents do not generally exceed the everyday economic needs of the family. When resources do not flow so easily between households and families, differences based on economic capacity emerge. The new present ceremony might be symptomatic of economic changes: from a distributive economy based primarily on generalized exchange developing into an economy based on an increasing degree of familial funds.

Gewertz and Errington (1999) have argued that class structures are emerging in the towns of Papua New Guinea as an effect of the capitalist economy. Kinship obligations are difficult to maintain, especially across class distinctions. Dinner auctions at Rotary clubs are easier to relate to for the growing urban middle classes than are demanding kinship obligations and gift giving: 'the Wewak Rotary Club provided a template for the formation of a middle class sociality: it was a sociality of the unentailed but voluntarily concerned. It was a sociality of neighbours, not of kin'

(1999, 40). Charity auctions are replacing the kinship-based prestations with more 'unentailed' relations. The *sakkem presen* is not 'unentailed' in the same manner, but it is only an obligation toward one sister and not an obligation to a wide network of relatives. The new payment between the brother and the sister, which is based on familial funds more than societal funds, makes the entailment more feasible for urban residents. Involvement in large networks of generalized exchange does not take place in town like it does on the island. For people living in town other concerns are more immediate, in particular for those of the aspiring middle classes. However, the processes of accumulation and development of familial funds found clearly among the urban middle classes, are also taking place among those living in the squatter settlements, but to a lesser degree.

Gewertz and Errington claim that for New Guinea this division between those sharing and those who accumulate points to the development of a class structure. Accumulation has become morally justified, particularly for the middle-class individual. They claim that the difference between the middle class and those in urban squatter areas, as well as those in the villages, has become one of kind more than of degree. This is partly the case in Vanuatu as well. The development of the present ceremony based on familial funds is part of this process of differentiation. There is a very noticeable difference between presents given in the village, presents given in urban squatter settlements, and presents given in an urban middle-class context. The size and quality of the presents differ according to the economic capacity of the family.

The Return of the Ambrym Gift

I argued in Chapter 2 that place on Ambrym is not regarded as bound, but extending, and that a person to a certain extent *is* place, representing the ceremonial place (*harl*). I continued this argument in Chapter 3 and showed how movement of place, or extension of place, is gendered. Women are always the entry points into new settlements. To what extent do these premises still hold in the case of urban migration?

The Ambrym people in town are not creating a satellite community there. They do not live together in one area as if they collectively relocated. Rather, they all moved on their own, for their own reasons and live by themselves in new independent families. The stable nucleus of the Ambrym population has grown and they do not return so often to the island. In this context it seems that the role of the *metehal*[16] is different but still vital. I showed in Chapter 3 that women, and in particular sisters, were the connecting points into new settlements. In the colonial period women from the villages in the interior who had married to Ranon directed the movement for the brothers and brothers' children to the commercial centre and plantation in Ranon. It is by looking at the way women in Port Vila connect people from Ambrym and beyond that one can discover how it is still possible to maintain relations to the island and become involved in a new sort of ceremonial economy. This economy

---

16   *Metehal*-sister: *Hal* refers to path and the concept signifies the way sisters open new roads as they marry away. See Chapters 2 and 3.

is based on the one hand on the principles of Ambrym kinship by being focused on the reciprocity of the brother-sister relationship. On the other hand, it is taking new forms, being more shaped by the presence of the capitalist economy. It is nevertheless by focusing on the way women, under new circumstances, create roads in and out of places and involve their relatives along the way that the dynamics of the Ambrym-Port Vila community is perceivable. The new *sakkem presen* ceremony is one such way in which sisters and brothers are getting involved and relationships back to the island are sustained. This new kind of ceremonial economy is a conjuncture of capitalist structures on the one hand and Ambrym principles of kinship and marriage on the other. Firstly, the new ceremony is connected to the changing role of women, as they have become involved in town migration and wage labour. Secondly, the present ceremony is indicative of a new social differentiation with an increasing emphasis on 'familial funds'. Even though the *sakkem presen* ceremony is creating a new gift relation between a brother and his sister in a time when this relation is more difficult to maintain, new premises like town migration and economic differentiation structure the ceremony.

Toren (1989) has likewise described how money has become part of ceremonial life in Fiji. Money has come to represent everything that is not Fijian – interdependence, outsiders with no sense of kinship, lack of order, and the profit-based motif – whereas the Fijian morality is based on kinship, generosity and gift relations. Toren shows how money goes through something like a ceremonial laundering. Very simplified, she argues that through a kava drinking ceremony where kava is bought for other people with money (and never for oneself), money comes to represent the gift relations within the traditional kinship cosmos. One might say that in a similar way this new Ambrym gift-ceremony is encompassing the commodity economy. The present ceremony represents a new kind of gift marked by the commodity economy, both in the sense that it involves products bought by money, and in the sense that the premises for buying the gifts are an increasing notion of private property and familial funds. This is unlike the' bride price' on Ambrym, a balanced and direct exchange between the father of the bride and her husband that eclipses the generalised reciprocity on which it is funded. The societal fund is momentarily forgotten in the direct transaction of the 'bride price'. During the new present ceremony the opposite is happening. During the *sakkem presen* ceremony the commodity economy and the growing capitalist forces are momentarily forgotten as the commodity products are transformed into another Ambrym gift that restores the circle of reciprocity between the brother and sister.

Chapter 5

The Loud and the Silent Stories: Female Agency and Mission History[1]

Extending Female Agency to the Church

I have in the previous chapters showed that women have triggered movements between settlements historically and continue to make roads into town today. In Chapter 2 I argued that the transformation of relationships, or changes in the codes so to speak, often takes place by shifting from patrilineal to matrilateral 'roads', as when Kenny made Rosy marriageable by relating to her through his mother instead of through his father (see p. 37–38). This gendered transformative capacity was also highlighted in Chapter 3, where I pointed out that extension of 'routes' and creation of new settlements rely on women as entry points. It is this female mode of sociality that I investigate further in this chapter. I do this by analysing mission history and the first Christian movements on the island. As will become apparent, an understanding of Christianity on Ambrym, at least as a social movement, is dependent upon seeing how gendered values are played against each other. Female capacities, such as mobility, connection-making and transformation, stand in contrast to the male capacities of representing place and people.

When analyzing the history of Christianity on Ambrym, there are two stories to consider, and these stories are differently gendered. The first one is perhaps the most conventional and the better-known story of how men of political and ritual importance turned away from the church, resisted it and created a counter movement known as the *kastom* movement. However, in order to understand how the church finally got a foothold a hundred years ago, and how it has transformed, grown and developed into the most important social institution on the island today, we need an analysis that considers another story, a more silent and unknown story: a story about unexpected agency.

Literature on the relationship between church and local communities in island-Melanesia tends to portray a stark contrast between *kastom* and Christianity (Keesing and Tonkinson 1982; Lindstrom and White 1993; Jolly 1992) that, in my opinion, is based on the first of these stories about the agency of resistance to the church displayed by some chiefs in the encounter with missionaries and the church. The first story I call the 'loud story' because of its visibility not only in anthropological

---

1   This chapter has also appeared, in a different and less ethnographically detailed version, as an article in *Anthropological Theory*, vol.6, nr. 2, 2006.

literature on Christianity in Melanesia, but also because of its audibility in the local narratives about the church. In this chapter I consider these stories and I relate them to the anthropological writings on the topic, but in the process I also outline the second story that in many respects contrasts the first one. This story I call the 'silent story'. It is silent because one has to look for it. It is not the story that is volunteered when people tell accounts from the past. It is thus silent, both for people themselves and for the anthropologist. I will start this analysis with a presentation of different historical accounts. Some of these illustrate the 'loud' story; others illustrate the 'silent' one.

How Magekon Purchased the SDA Church

Linbul, a village north of Ranon in North Ambrym, is today predominantly an SDA (Seventh Day Adventist) village. An Ambrym pastor in the SDA church, a man in his fifties, told me the story of how the SDA church was established on Ambrym. The pastor himself was born and raised in Linbul, and had worked for some years as the local pastor there, but in later years he had moved to the capital Port Vila were he still worked as the pastor of an SDA congregation. I met him in Port Vila, and he told me the story of his grandfather and how the SDA church was introduced to his village.

He was keen to point out to me that it was not as if the missionaries had brought the church. Rather, it was his grandfather who had established the church some seventy or eighty years ago. During the first years of the 1920s congregations were established in several of the villages in Lolihor. Merongrong[2] had a church, and there was another church in Melkonkon.[3] These churches were probably the first ones established in Lolihor, and they pre-date the mission-station that was built in Ranon in the 1880s by the missionary brothers Charles and William Murray. Linbul, one of the larger villages at the time, did not yet have a church, according the pastor.

The pastor's grandfather, Magekon, set out on a journey to the western part of the island. Magekon was a man of great reputation and respect. He had climbed grades in the *mage*[4] and he had been one of the prominent men in his village, Linbul, for some time. He witnessed the building of a Presbyterian mission-station in Ranon, and he observed how some of the men, also of the graded society, joined the mission, at least for a while. When he went on his journey to West Ambrym, he had one purpose in mind, according to the pastor. He wanted a church. The churches in Ranon, Melkonkon and Merongrong were Presbyterian, and he wanted another church. He had heard about the SDA church in West Ambrym and wanted to purchase the SDA church from Lonwe village in West Ambrym. This was the first village to build an SDA church on the island. He brought along large male pigs that he had raised for use in ceremonial exchange in the *mage*, and as he arrived in Lonwe he staged an

---

2   See maps in Chapter 3.

3   See maps in Chapter 3.

4   *Mage* refers to the men's graded society. It is called *Namange* in Bislama and there are variants of this kind of hierarchical society in many of the northern islands of Vanuatu. Further discussions of the *mage* appear in Chapters 6, 7, and 8.

exchange ceremony in which he offered his pigs to one of the local big men. As they received his pigs, he paid for his rights to the SDA church.

This way of actively seeking the church rather than being a host for an overseas missionary has been described by McDougall (2003) who outlined how a certain chief organized a voyage to Vella Lavella and brought back two Solomon Island pastors and the Adventist Church to Modo on the northwest cost of Ranongga in the Solomon Islands. The Modo chief organized his voyage as a war raid, thereby transferring pre-established models for gaining power and prestige onto the new Christian institution. On Ambrym it was the manner of purchasing rights that was prominent in the graded society, the *mage*, upon which Magekon modelled his 'purchase of the church' when he set off to West Ambrym with his large pigs. This graded society was initially brought to Ambrym from the neighbouring island of Malekula. The principle of the *mage* was to 'buy' grades with huge numbers of pigs, both through exchange and sacrifice. As a result of their enormous social capacity and relations to ancestral spirits, those with higher grades could hold dangerous power over those with lower grades. When one grade was 'bought', a carved wooden figure would accompany it, and be erected on the ceremonial ground as a representation of the man who bought the grade. This was the way men gained prestige. It was not only in the *mage* society that men bought greatness in this manner, but in rituals predating the *mage* the principles were also quite similar. According to Ambrym kinship principles, a man throughout life had to compensate his mother and her relatives for the blood she gave him. For every such ritual there were different kinds of emblems making the man behind them visible, in the sense that he gained power and prestige (Rio 1997; Patterson 1976).

When the church was introduced, and when the first missionary arrived in Ranon, it seems that the church was also perceived as an emblem. The church became a new *imkon*,[5] the dwelling place of the most sacred men in the *mage*. It did not take the first missionary in the area, Murray, long to translate 'church' into '*imkon*' and thus contribute to the initial association between church and the established male ritual society. When some of the high-ranking men built their own church, other men from other villages wanted to buy rights in this kind of objectification. Just as *mage* was initially 'bought' from a neighbouring island, the church was also a foreign institution they wanted to territorialize in the sense that it was turned into something the people on Ambrym were involved in. The pastor pointed out to me that the church was perceived as being of the same nature as the *mage* and people related to it in this way.

When Magekon went to West Ambrym in search of the SDA church, he wanted to establish himself in this new kind of ritual society. He returned with the promise that SDA missionaries would come to his village, and soon after a German missionary arrived. A church was built, and people in Linbul were part of an SDA congregation. After a while however, the German missionary became too much of an irritation. He became too 'strong'. He introduced rules of conduct, which among other things

---

5   *Im* = house, *kon* = taboo. The *imkon* was usually the house where a man who had high grades in the *mage* lived, separated from the rest of the community. He stayed at a distance, in his *imkon*, because of his potency.

implied the prohibition of eating pork and the rule of attending church every day. Prohibition of pork of course was hard for Magekon, as he based his power on the sacrifice of pigs, and so was the mandate to attend church every day when he would rather be in his garden. The pastor laughed when he told me that Magekon himself grew tired of the church. He finally decided to move to another village where he could lead his life without the influence of the church and where the missionary, which he himself had brought to the island, would leave him alone. So, Magekon moved to the neighbouring village of Fanla. In spite of his final rejection of the church, today Magekon is regarded as the founder of the SDA church in Linbul. He is the 'beginning' of the SDA church, or its *tangbarite*. The origin route of the SDA church on North Ambrym, in other words, traces back to Magekon in Linbul.

How the SDA Church Spread through Marriage

As in all stories of origin told on North Ambrym, the pastor went on in this interview to tell me the story of how the SDA church spread. He pointed out that from the beginning its growth was due to the work of women. When a woman from Linbul married, he explained, there was a strong requirement that the person she married should become a member of the SDA church. This was non-negotiable, and actually, this is still often the case on Ambrym.[6] While I was in Ranon, a Ranon boy agreed to marry a girl from Linbul. She was a member of the SDA church in Linbul. The boy's mother wanted the girl to become a Presbyterian, which had practical advantages. If she were to remain in the SDA church, she could not join the others in their work in the gardens on Saturdays, because this is the day of worship for the SDA members. Saturday is an important gardening day. Youngsters, who normally attend secondary school every day, have weekends off, and everyone works in the gardens on Saturdays. The girl's family in Linbul, however, was determined that not only should she remain in the SDA church, but her future husband as well should gradually become a member. They argued that morals in the Presbyterian Church were getting too low. People were drinking and only occasionally attending church. The boy's family in Ranon agreed that he would become an SDA member, as they realized the matter was beyond negotiation.

The pastor told me how the villages surrounding Linbul became SDA villages gradually as a result of marriage. He outlined how women from Linbul married, and how their brothers demanded that their sisters should remain SDA members and that their future husbands should join the SDA church as well. We clearly see here the similarity between this story and the stories of the origin routes outlined in Chapter 3. In the same manner as women opened the roads into new settlements for their brothers or husbands, 'out marrying' women became the roads for the church as well. Women's movement when marrying and their transformative capacity made them apt as agents for Christianity when the older male-dominated ceremonial institutions such as the *mage* were replaced by the church.

6　　However, there are cases where SDA women convert and become, for instance, Presbyterian, but these are not common. People generally say that an SDA woman seldom converts.

This female agency in conversion is not so often talked about , thus I call it the silent story. I will return to this later in the chapter. First I will outline the experiences of the first missionaries on Ambrym. The voices of the missionaries on the island in the last part of the 1800s reflect the resistance to the church and the men who tried to make the church fit the *mage* manifest; the loud story. However, here we also find small hints of the more hidden story.

The First Missionaries

Through a reading of the diary of the first Ambrym missionary Charles Murray, we catch a glimpse of how difficult it was for him to visit other villages and preach the Christian message. It was seldom welcomed, and people were often hostile. He frequently complained in his diary about sparce attendance at his church sessions, and the few who did come were often old men and children from the neighbourhood. Murray writes in his diary:

4 January 1887:
'A few natives have been around, mainly from Ranon'.

12 January 1887:
'It was hard enough yesterday with only three pupils, but it is much worse today. I have none'.

Then the next day, 13 January 1887:

'At school today had an experience similar to that of yesterday, no pupils, no pupils!'

According to Robert Steel (1880), who visited the island at the end of the 1870s, both the Melanesian Mission and the London Missionary Society, as well as the Presbyterian Mission, had visited the island but experienced great difficulties in getting the people on Ambrym interested in establishing a mission. Markham, who was supervising the labour trade for the Australian authorities, was onboard the *Rosario* which sailed around the islands in the 1860s. He writes:

At noon on the 28th I sent a boat in to communicate with the natives at the north end of Ambrym, some two or three hundred of whom were seen assembled near the beach; but the surf was too heavy, and the natives too numerous and in too threatening an attitude to justify the risk of beaching the boat, and she was therefore recalled ... (Markham 1873, 205)

In spite of this 'attitude' however, in 1883 the Melanesian Mission schooner *Dayspring* anchored on the shores of Ambrym, and the first missionary on Ambrym, William Murray, educated in theology from Scotland, arrived. The Melanesian Mission had agreed with the Presbyterian Mission to let them have the responsibility for establishing a mission on the island (Miller 1989). The Presbyterian Church of New Zealand recruited missionaries from Scotland, and the two brothers William and Charles Murray offered their services. When William Murray had to return home from

Ambrym after only a short period on the island because he contracted tuberculosis, his brother Charles Murray continued the work. He arrived in 1886, along with his wife who died during the first year. The two brothers faced enormous hardships on the island, which are recounted in detail in *Live 6*, by Miller (1989). They lost wives and children, and William Murray died from his illness only shortly after he returned from Ambrym. Although they were both highly optimistic upon their arrival, I believe that they both lost enthusiasm and were truly depressed by the lack of interest they received from the people on Ambrym. Charles Murray's diary gives an impression of hardships in the early period of his work, but also that people eventually started to attend the services, at least those who lived in the vicinity of Ranon, and he had nearly a hundred people in his congregation at the height of attendance.

Malnaim in Ranon, about whom his descendants in Ranon, Rawo and his brothers, have given me insights, had in this period an important position in the village and held the highest grades in the *mage*. He would come to play an important role for Murray, first in the positive sense, but later he destroyed Murray's work. Malnaim had similar motivations as Magekon who founded the SDA Church three decades later: He wanted the church as an emblem of his own power. He therefore, having got to know Murray, helped him recruit members to the church, and it was during this period that the congregation gradually increased in size. Murray always noted in his diary Malnaim's presence or absence at Morning Prayer, and expressed his excitement over the fact that this important man had decided to join him. However, after a while, it became clear to Malnaim that the rules of the game were not something he could accept. Murray wanted to open the church to everyone, including women. Murray called the church *imkon*, as if the church was a house for powerful men in the *mage*, but he wanted the women to be present. This must have been an absurd idea to Malnaim, who wanted Murray to give services for men only. At this point the congregation started to fail Murray. On 17 April Murray writes:

> Bibir came alone. After worship he told me, Malnaim had given orders that no one was to attend school of the female sex …

After a while, Malnaim put a ban on the mission to the entire population, and would not let anyone, not even the men, attend services. People also stopped arriving at the mission-station in order to sell garden crops to Murray. He became completely isolated. He writes in his diary on 24 April 1887:

> Have had some dark days since last entry. The prohibition on school attendance has continued … people proceed to attack my goals … In order to get to work again I said I should be willing to give a goat … My hints at darker purposes and of going away should they not attend, was interpreted to mean that I was timid and frightened. Paying the goat to get an end to the taboo, to get some work done, was understood to mean I wished to appease Malnaim. In one way it was.

Charles Murray had tried to recruit men of high prestige and renown to the church, and Malnaim was one of them. He probably realised that if the these men attended church, it would be easier for others to attend as well, and of course the reverse was even more true; if these men did not want to join the church, no one else saw the point of doing so either. It was probably his mingling with these powerful men, and his ability to speak freely of the changes he regarded as necessary – in particular, his emphasise on the importance of female attendance – which upset the men and led to their ban on both Murray and his mission.

The high-graded men in the *mage* seem to have been important entry points for the church. They can be seen to have established firm grounds for it. Magekon in Linbul and Malnaim in Ranon both took the missionary into their village, although they both ended up breaking with the same missionary. Malnaim's fight against the presence of women was, however, a losing battle. In spite of the fact that Murray's failure in Ranon can be seen as a result of his eagerness to open the church to women, and Malnaim's view on the matter had destructive consequences for Murray, in the long run Malnaim's view of the church did not become formative for the church. In the following years the church congregation grew without the presence of the big men. Mansfield, who visited North Ambrym in 1922, thirty years after Murray had gone, reported:

> I found things at Ranon very bright. The Christian party there have decided to … cut off their connection with the heathen – they will not trade nor intermarry with them. They are now building on the old mission ground at Ranon a large central church, of native material, where they may all meet on Sunday afternoons. This has all come from themselves. The work here is ripe for a man to step in (Miller 1989, 174).

It was not a new missionary which made a difference for the growth of the North Ambrym church however. It was Ambrym women who came to play important roles in the formation of the North Ambrym church, not only as roads for the church into new villages, like we saw for the SDA church in Linbul, but also for the development of practices in the church and the idea of what the church was (which I will go into in more detail in the next chapter). In the early 1920s the missionary Frater toured North Ambrym and describes a baptism scene he witnessed:

> To me the most striking feature of the occasion was the courage shown by the women. An Ambrym woman, in ordinary circumstances, is the shyest and most timid of mortals. They shrink from anything which brings them prominently into public notice. It would have been quite in keeping with island ways if the assistance of the teacher had been found necessary to lead them to the platform. But their faith and love were equal to the great occasion. No sooner were their names called than they immediately responded and in the presence of 600 people signified their faith in Christ by baptism (Frater 1922, 52).

Some decades after Murray's surrender, during a period when no missionary was permanently placed in the area, women had entered the church in great numbers. During this great public display of Christianity described by Frater, women played a prominent part. In the years to come, the mission became more associated with women than with the men of the *mage*. For instance, after Murray returned to New Zealand, an Ambrym teacher, Kalsong, was left in charge of the mission-station in Ranon, and the station then became the refuge for women, runaways and sick people. Dr. Lamb visited the station run by Kalsong about a decade after Murray's departure:

> Kalsong, the teacher, had beat the school drum; and, in response, some twenty to thirty
> ill-looking, limping specimens, of all sizes and both sexes, gathered on the verandah …
> (Lamb 1905, 43).

As a result of the turn away from the church by the high-graded men, the church
seems from early on to have been a movement for the outcasts, and those who did
not succeed in the *mage* society; the men of low esteem and women. It was an
alternative movement for the powerless. Although it was the powerful men of the
mage who approached the church first, they were not the driving force of the church
as it later developed. The church became an arena for women, for peace-making and
for alliance.

Returned Labourers Bringing the Church Back from Queensland

In order to understand how the church was distributed on Ambrym, it is useful to
follow the routes of the first Ambrym Christians. These were often returned labour
migrants who had heard about the gospel overseas and who wanted to build their
own churches on their return. By following their stories, which can be found not
only in the mission literature, but also, more importantly, in oral stories of the North
Ambrym people, the role of the church in the creation of new settlements and the
alliance between them is made evident.

From 1860 on, the number of labour recruits to the plantations in Fiji, Queensland
and New Caledonia increased. Most of those who left ended up in Queensland.
Rebecca was one of the few female migrants. Frater (1922) tells us that she worked
on the sugar cane fields in Queensland with her husband, and that she learnt the
gospel.

> … from some kind soul whose memory they ever afterwards cherished…At the end of
> three years' indenture they returned to Ambrym with the passion burning in their hearts to
> spread among their fellow islanders the knowledge of God's love (1922, 61–2).

Frater writes that they became dedicated workers for the mission at Dip Point, in
West Ambrym, at the time lead by Dr. Bowie. Rebecca worked together with her
husband at the mission. He was also a Christian but 'less forceful', as Miller (1989,
166) points out. The story of Rebecca stands in great contrast to other stories of
women by the first missionaries and settlers. Usually women are talked about as shy,
repressed and voiceless, like Frater's (1922) description of the baptism scene above.
This story serves as a source that adds nuance to the picture of Ambrym women in
this period. Rebecca was one of those women who travelled beyond Ambrym at an
early stage, and who, as she returned, brought along new knowledge. However, after
some time, Dr. Bowie noticed scars developing on her face, which he recognized
as leprosy and Rebecca was told that she could no longer remain at the mission-
station. Rebecca then followed her husband to his village, Wilit, in the northern part
of Ambrym. Frater (1922, 63) writes:

Several months afterwards, on the occasion of one of his visits, Rebecca reported to her missionary that they had gained a small following, and that the place was now ripe for the settlement of a resident teacher, suggesting, at the same time the name of James Kaun …

James Kaun is another of the local heroes from the written historical sources. James Kaun was among the very first converts on Ambrym and was baptized in 1893 before being recruited to Queensland. His brother, however, had been to Queensland and had been his source of information about the gospel. James Kaun is described in the mission literature (Frater 1922; Miller 1989) as an unafraid and brave man who fought the will of the respected chiefs, among them his father. He sought the company of the missionaries in West Ambrym, and during this period was one of the first on the island to learn how to read and write.

There were also other men, who returned from labour journeys with new knowledge and a new kind of vision for their home villages, who are not mentioned in the mission literature. One of these stories, which was told repeatedly by people on North Ambrym when we discussed the first Christians, was the story about Peter Ramel. He was originally from the village of Melkonkon. He was recruited to the plantation in Queensland as one of the first who left from North Ambrym. He must have been away for some time, because when he returned, his natal village had been deserted as a result of a war between the villages of Melkonkon and Hawor.[7] Peter Ramel settled in Hawor, were the remaining people of his *buluim* were now living. He preached about salvation and about the Christian ideals, and he urged people to help him build a church on his abandoned *harl* in Melkonkon. After a while he succeeded, and the first church was built on Peter Ramel's *harl*, without the involvement of any white missionary. According to people's stories, this was the first church on North Ambrym, and it was built before Murray's arrival. There is no mention of this church in Charles Murray's diary, nor in Miller's (1989) account of the church planting on Ambrym. In other words, there is no written historical record of this church, but it figures as an important historical event in the local historical imagination. We often walked passed the site where Peter Ramel built his church, on the uphill path between Ranon and Fanrereo, and my companions, knowing my interest in the history of the church, would always stop and ask whether we had heard the story of Peter Ramel.

Another similar story I heard was about the church in Merongrong.[8] This was also the story of the return of a labour migrant who had built a church in his village. I did not obtain any exact information about the church in Merongrong, or the name of the man who founded it. During my work on the old settlements however, people always referred to Merongrong as a Christian place, and it was pointed out that it was a returned labour migrant who had founded the first church here. Melkonkon and Merongrong can be said to have been the two centres of indigenous Christian activity, and the history of the distribution of the church on North Ambrym is tied to the origin routes from these two places. The Melkonkon church was later moved to Hawor where Peter Ramel lived, and later to Fanrereo, where Peter Ramel's

---

7   See Chapter 3 for a map and details of this conflict.
8   See Chapter 3 for a map and a short history of movements from this place.

descendants moved. Today there is a Presbyterian Church in Fanrereo on the grounds where Peter Ramel's son lived. As I outlined in Chapter 3, it was women married into Hawor from Melkonkon and from the other villages such as Nomto and Randyu who connected their families to the Hawor settlement. It was Peter Ramel's daughter who married into Hawor, and who therefore can be said to have extended the road of the church from Melkonkon and into Hawor.

To conclude this section I will point out that the pattern of the distribution of the first churches follows the origin routes which are always triggered by women's 'out marrying' movement. The SDA church had its *tangbarite*, or its origin, in Linbul, and spread through women to other villages such as Fanla. The church built by Peter Ramel was moved by his daughter's marriage into Hawor, and later to Fanrereo. Women brought along the church as they resettled after marriage. Ambrym women were effective missionaries as the church was established on Ambrym from the 1880s and during the latter half of the last century. Women moved and so did the churches. Sometimes the woman was joined by her father and brothers in her new settlement, as the origin stories in Chapter 3 revealed. The history of the development of the church and people's origin routes are intertwined histories triggered by moving women.

Kastom and Christianity: The Beginning of an Oppositional Construct

The discourse about the transformation from the pre-Christian to the Christian life is dominated by the distance that was created between the men in the *mage* who renounced the church, such as Malnaim and Magekon, and those who openly welcomed the church such as Kalsung, Rebecca, James Kaun and Peter Ramel as this citation from Frater (1922, 46–7) expresses:

> On leaving the church the whole congregation accompanied us to see an old chief who is the last remnant of heathenism in the tribe. On accepting Christianity, the people, in order to make the cleavage with heathenism as distinct as possible left their old homes and founded the Moru village of to-day, which stands in a beautiful situation, with a neat weatherboard church in the centre of the village. But the old chief would have none of it. With his three wives, he remained in the heathen village, surrounded by the painted symbols of pagan worship. We found old Horseham within the sacred enclosure, with his naked breast covered with pigs' tusks and his arms and legs covered with croton leaves …

This very common scene is often described in the missionaries' biographies and memoirs. The pagan chiefs were left behind in the traditional villages in the interior, whilst the newly saved souls joined the missionary on the sunny coast of the island where the mission-station was built. I have already pointed out that those who sought the church at the early stage were those who did not have a strong position in the *mage*. They were the powerless and the outcasts. When they converted, they moved away from the 'heathen' villages and they needed the missionaries' protection because they were in most cases regarded as enemies by those remaining in the interior. Most of those who resisted the mission were of course the highly graded and most respected old men, like the chief described in Frater's (1922) citation above. These were also men with a lot of knowledge about sorcery and the ones who controlled the ancestral spirits. It was often the fear of the effect of this knowledge – namely sorcery – that was the most common reason for people's refuge at the mission-station.

At the turn of the century, the degree of sorcery accusations and threats and war between villages escalated. John Rawo in Ranon, a descendant of the great Malnaim who chased away the missionary Murray, described the situation in the early part of the twentieth century as a crisis. He had heard his father, Worwor, talk about the war between villages, and about the great number of people who died because of sorcery. There were almost no young men left in this period, according to John Rawo. This might indirectly have been a result of the new diseases introduced by the white settlers. A growing number of people became ill and, as always on Ambrym, sorcery was used as the explanation for both illness and death. In this period the conflict level between villages escalated into war in some cases. When the fear of sorcery was too strong people moved down to the coast, that is, to the mission-stations. The missionaries presented the mission-stations as peaceful areas.

Murray also wrote in his diary about conflicts between different villages in the interior as a result of sorcery accusations. He tried to make the connection between belief, church attendance and good health:

> Returning home in the company of a Ranon man, I made the remark that quite a number of Metanmerbul people had died recently. As none of the latter come to school, while the Ranon people do, he at once connected the Ranon people's good health with their school attendance (29 January 1887)

The gospel was portrayed as something in contrast to the ways of the 'heathens', so much in contrast, it is a matter of life or death. This strong opposition between those who left the interior and those who remained 'in the dark areas', might partially account for why the concept of *kastom* developed historically. It developed as a concept in the first part of the twentieth century at the time when the church had been firmly established on most of the islands in Vanuatu.

Kastom as an 'Invented Tradition': The Effect of the Loud Story in Anthropological Theory

Kastom is a pan-Melanesian concept, and its significance has been widely discussed in the regional anthropological literature since the early 1980s (Keesing and Tonkinson, 1982; Keesing, 1992; Jolly, 1992; Lindstrom and White, 1993; Bolton, 1993; and others) when *kastom* had already been a powerful concept for at least a couple of decades during the process leading up to Independence in the colonies. It worked as a self-conscious reification of a 'local way'. Keesing has pointed out that *kastom* is 'discourses about the past situated in the present and oriented towards the future' (1993, 587–97). Lindstrom (1993b) has argued that *kastom* is an oppositional concept, always operating as a resistance toward something else, very often foreign, Western, and Christian ideas. In various accounts of how Melanesian people reacted to the missionization, there has been an emphasis on how people tended to either join the church or become oppositional, to either become Christian or *kastom*. On Ambrym this can be seen as a result of the division between the men in the *mage* who resisted the church and the men without power in the *mage* who were eager to join.

Malnaim in Ranon and Magekon in Linbul realized quite soon that the church threatened the foundations of the *mage*, and therefore also their position. The 'outcasts' who moved to the mission-station had nothing to lose in this world. This conflict between men such as Malnaim and Magekon on the one hand, and those who joined the mission, such as Kalsong and his followers on the other, can be seen as a conflict between *kastom* and church, where the men of the *mage* represented *kastom*. In a similar way other accounts from Vanuatu show how *kastom* came to oppose much of what was brought from the outside during colonialism. Jolly (1995) outlines how on South Pentecost, in the northern region of Vanuatu, there was a strong division between villages that were Christian and usually referred to by the Bislama word *skul villij*, and those villages that were not Christian and usually referred to as *kastom villij*. Keesing (1982) has described a parallel phenomenon among the Kwaio people in the Malaita province in the Solomon Islands. As a result of external pressure on land and resources, there developed a strong opposition between the Kwaio traditionalists and the converts. The traditionalists reacted strongly against the church and the external forces it represented, and were never even seen to enter the Christian villages where the traditional taboos and rituals were no longer followed, and where the ancestors' anger could be harmful. On Tanna, in South Vanuatu, a similar process has taken place. *Kastom* was used as the counterpart to new ideas and in particular Christianity. This opposition created a strong division between new social movements such as the 'John Frum cult' and the church (Lindstrom 1982).

This focus on *kastom* being developed as a reaction to mission and Christianity can be compared to Thomas's (1989, 1992) perspective on the development of a similar concept, *Kerekere,* on Fiji. *Kerekere*, as Sahlins (1962) describes it, is the practice of sharing among relatives. It has often been translated as 'begging', which, according to Sahlins, is a completely inaccurate interpretation of it. He states that *Kerekere* is more a way of requesting something from relatives in which the whole kinship ethic and the values of reciprocity need to be considered. In short, *Kerekere* is, and was historically, a mechanism for transforming material inequality into social inequality on the grounds that givers are always superior to receivers. Thomas (1989), on the other hand, compares the use of the concept in the early period of trading, from about 1800–1860, with the more intensive colonial period from 1860 onward. He concludes that *Kerekere* was created as a symbol of the customary and communal on Fiji in reaction to colonial politics. He points out that there is no evidence for the existence of *Kerekere* before the colonial period. Moreover, he argues that much of the Pan-Pacific idea of sharing in a similar way is constructed as a political reaction, or what Keesing (1989) calls a 'political symbol', by the colonised. Thomas points out that the polarities Gregory (1982) outlined in *Gifts and Commodities*, between gift relations creating social value and transactions based upon profit and use-value, are reproduced as stereotypes in neo-traditional systems. Thomas (1989, 76) argues, 'modern Pacific cultures and practices are organised oppositionally'. This view of *Kerekere* implies a specific concept of 'culture' which in many ways can be summed up by Keesing's view of it as 'a strategically useful abstraction from the distributed knowledge of individuals in communities' (1981, 72). Thus, *Kerekere* was reified as a tradition, or an essentialized Fijian culture, by those in position to do so, mainly the chiefs interacting with the colonial agents.

Thomas's argument must also apply to the Melanesian *kastom* concept that also, in line with Thomas, could be termed a neo-traditional concept, and an oppositional concept, being a result of European contact. Just as *kerekere* was created as an oppositional ideological construct during colonial times, *kastom* can, following this argument, in a similar way be regarded as a reaction to western ideas of Christianity.

I believe that to some extent the oppositional reading of *kastom* is useful. It is, for instance, obvious that, as I have outlined, some of the most dominant big men of the *mage* actively worked against the mission and thus created the foundations of *kastom* as an opposition–discourse. However, Foster has argued that the triggering mechanisms for the development of the *kastom* concept might not be 'a noisy confrontation with colonizers' (1995, 28). *Kastom* does not necessarily distinguish between what is authentic and local and what is foreign. *Kastom* might be an 'internal' concept, referring to 'internal' distinctions. For the Tanga islanders in Papua New Guinea, *kastom* is what connects the matrilineages, whereas the household, which, of course, is as much Tangan as the matrilineage, is concerned with business and not primarily *kastom*. It is thus not always in the 'noisy' confrontation we should look for the distinctions that make *kastom* meaningful. In the same manner I argue that in the case of Ambrym, seeing *kastom* as oppositional is based on the 'loud story'. It thus only tells half the story. The accounts I have given about the development of the church on Ambrym, and how it hooked onto marriage structures and people's movements, indicate that the opposition between *kastom* and church only accounts for part of the history. It is a useful way to describe the conflict between Malnaim and Murray, and later some of the local converts. However, if we let the 'noisy' oppositional construct of *kastom* and Christianity dominate the reading, or 'hearing', of history entirely, then the way the church is seen to be part of a local process of appropriation, is neglected, and *kastom* comes to refer solely to the views and practices of the men in the *mage*. If we remain within a dualistic portrayal of *kastom* and Christianity, the agency of women and those outside the *mage* is forgotten. The *kastom*-opposed–to-Christianity discourse highlights only the local agency in the creation of the *kastom* discourse, as a sort of resistance to colonialism.

Sahlins argues against the view of tradition as 'fabricated with an eye politic to the present situation' and as 'self serving inversions of the colonisers' tradition' (1999, 402). Following this invention of tradition argument (Hobsbawm and Ranger 1983; Carrier 1992) or another variant of it, the inversion of tradition (Thomas 1992), culture is reduced to 'a myth, a fabrication, a mystification – the collective misrepresentation of someone's particular interest' (Sahlins 1999, 403). Sahlins sees such an argument to be fundamentally functionalist in the sense that, for instance, *Kerekere* remains nothing but a reaction to colonial powers, which functions as a concept portraying the Fijians as dramatically different from the Westerners. Following Sahlins's argument, *kerekere* could not be a result of strategic thinking by some chiefs on Fiji, or, the argument transferred to the *kastom* concept on Ambrym, does not only refer to the resistance of Malnaim and Magekon.

An oppositional reading of *kastom* produces an oppositional reading of Christianity. Christianity becomes white man's agency and the resistance to the first missionaries by the high-graded men in the *mage* becomes the most appropriate reaction. The agency of women and men outside of the *mage* is then forgotten. I have shown in the first part of this chapter that only some opposed Christianity on Ambrym, and that the distribution of the church was based on principles of kinship and marriage. The portrayal of the dualism between Christianity and *kastom* serves to glorify those men who resisted Christianity and the converts become the 'losers', or those who did not have the strength to remain among those who resisted. If our analyses of *kastom* are not narrowed down to the resistance of the high-graded men, and Christianity is seen to be part of a local initiative, a wide range of people's historical accounts fit our concepts, and not only the version where the high-graded men in the *mage* play the leading roles.

I want to highlight another agency in the process of Christianization in addition to the resistance. Christianity is tied to female agency not only in the sense that it was the women who married away from the first Christian villages who brought this new knowledge along to other villages, but also in the sense that the church came to stand for an alternative movement in relation to the traditional male graded society. The church became a feminine movement as it developed in Ranon, which I will take up in more depth in the next chapter. The church thus became an alternative to the more masculine *mage*. So, in other words, the relevant distinction for understanding the development of Christianity on Ambrym is not so much the distinction between local *kastom* and Christianity, as it is the distinction between a male established institution and a new alternative female movement. The concept of *kastom,* analysed as an oppositional construct, only serves to highlight the reaction of some of the old and high-graded men in their encounter with the new and alternative movement. To understand the women's roles and the role played by those who did not have an established position in the *mage*, we must look beyond the opposition between Christianity and *kastom*.

Conjunctural Agency and Women

The dualism created in the *kastom*-opposed-to-Christianity analysis eclipses the agency of local men and women who were not prominent in the *mage* society, but who played important roles in the process of establishing firm grounds for the church on Ambrym. One might view the agency of the high-graded men in the *mage*, such as Malnaim and Magekon, and the men outside the *mage*, such as Peter Ramel, along with the women who brought the church to new villages, as representing a contrast between systemic and conjunctural agency. Sahlins (2004) has argued that there is a difference between men like Napoleon or Fijian high ranking chiefs commanding wars on the one hand, and people who more accidentally become the person Sahlins (2004, 178) calls 'unlikely celebrities'. Napoleon and the divine Fijian chiefs based their agency on an institutionalized power. So did Magekon and Malnaim, who, because of their high positions in the well established male institution, the *mage*, had the power to chase away the missionary and prevent women from going to church. Peter Ramel, and his daughter who moved the church into Hawor, had, along with other women and men outside of the *mage*, an agency in the process of Christianization that did not build on an institutionalized power. Rather the effect of their actions, it can be said, was based on the combination of the structure of marriage, on the one hand, which made women move into new villages and connect people and places, and, on the other, on the new ideas of Christianity which women now brought with them when they moved. The combination of the return of some of the labour migrants who had brought along the ideas of Christianity, the failure of Murray, and the already existing marriage practice which made women move, created an agency of conjuncture where women and men such as Peter Ramel and James Kaun came to play key roles. The agency of women in the church after Murray's departure from the island was based on the intertwining of marriage structure and the fact that the new knowledge had been renounced by the great men such as Magekon and Malnaim, which thereby made it open to women and those who did not have great names. It was as if the church, as it steadily grew as a movement in the twentieth century, had given a name to a movement that already existed, namely the practices of women as they married and created alliances laterally instead of competing hierarchically, and at the same time had created something completely new; an organized movement which, after a while, seriously challenged the already existing *mage* institution.

Chapter 6

Women, Churches and Communities[1]

Women and the Church

In 1912 Pastor T. Watt Legatt wrote a letter to *The New Hebridean Magazine*, the journal for the British colonialists in the New Hebrides. In this letter he expressed his utter horror at the position of the Melanesian women:

> The outstanding feature of Woman's position is that of inferiority. In some places she cannot pass in front of a man. She may be bowed to the earth with a heavy load, but if a man comes along she must crush herself into the bush at the wayside to allow him a clear road. When he is seated she must make her way behind him, and if he is of high rank, crawl out of the sight on her hands and knees.

He was not alone in his opinion. Frater, who visited the northern islands of New Hebrides in the early part of the 1900s, wrote:

> Apart from the fact that we are carrying out the Lord's command, I do not think a stronger argument for mission work could be obtained than the great change it makes for the lives of women (Frater 1922, 119).

In spite of the church's influence on the lives of women in this region, it has traditionally, first and foremost, been looked upon as a new arena for male power, and male leadership in the church has been considered a continuation of traditional male leadership (Allen 1981; Rubenstein 1981). However, more recently the connection between church and women's lives has been a matter of more anthropological focus (Jolly and Macintyre 1989; Jolly 2003; Douglas 2002, 2003; McDougall 2003; Paini 2003).

Having argued in the previous chapter that women played an important role in the process of missionization on Ambrym, and that the church from the outset has been tied to women and men outside of the *mage*, in this chapter I look at how women's agency in the mission history of Ambrym has not only transformed the relationship between the *mage* and the church, but also opened new arenas in which women move and operate. The church became a new space for a social form that negated the hierarchy of the *mage*. It was mostly women, but not solely,[2] who came to form this space. In this chapter I thus continue the focus from Chapters 2, 3 and 4 on women's

---

1 This chapter has also appeared, in a different version, as an article in *Oceania*, 2005, 75 (3).

2 Peter Ramel, referred to in the previous chapter, is an example of a man operating within the new alternatively gendered space of the church.

ability to move, make connections into new places, and represent alternative 'roads'. I also continue the argument began in Chapter 5 on the transformative capacity of women in relation to the church and I will show that today, more than making great men, the church creates communities, and the dynamics of this process is tied to 'connecting women' and historical origin routes.

Churches and Communities: The Presbyterian Church in Ranon

Arriving in Ranon, or most places in Vanuatu, on a Sunday just before church time you will witness a whole community – young and old, women and men – dressed in their best clothes. Men wear their newest pair of trousers and cleanest white shirt and women wear long spectacular colourful 'Mother Hubbard' dresses while holding umbrellas against the sun, everyone carrying a Bible or a psalm book under their arms. Inside the church, women are seated on one side and the men on the other, while the children run between the rows and join either side. Long before the service begins there are people in the church, and often someone starts singing, and those present join in while waiting for the service. I never saw or heard of anyone in Ranon doing any other work than cooking on a Sunday. There were no activities in the gardens, and no one cleaned their houses or washed their clothes on a Sunday. Even the cooking was done before church time. The women of a household got up early in the morning and prepared a *laplap* that was placed in the ground-oven before the family set off to church. It was amazing how almost everybody attended church. Although the Ranon church was quite large, with seats for about a hundred, there was always a crowd outside because the church was full. People sat on their mats in the shade of a tree and joined in on the singing of psalms. It was therefore no surprise to me that when I returned for my second visit to Ranon in 1999 they had started building a new and bigger church, which they were still working on during my last visit in 2000.

In 1996 they had only one pastor in the Presbyterian Church in Ranon. He was a man from West Ambrym and during most of our stays he was in the West. However, the community did not suffer without him, as one of the community elders held Sunday ceremonies and regular morning sessions with Bible readings. There were five elders, one of them a woman, and they were all very capable of saying prayers and performing church services. My impression was that the church in Ranon, which was the one I most frequently visited, was locally run. Jolly (1989) as well has pointed out that Protestant organizations in Melanesia with a congregational ideology have made an effort to train indigenous people to be leaders of the church, and the Protestant organizations such as the Presbyterian church are today predominantly run by *ni-Vanuatu*. This is in contrast to the Catholic Church, which is based on a much more hierarchical structure, and is even today run mainly by Europeans. The Catholic Church in West Ambrym, for instance, had a resident French priest.

Fund-raising and 'Heathen' Rituals

The Presbyterian Church in Ranon involves much more than Sunday services. Quite often people organize different kinds of fund-raising events for the church. This is a part of the church activity that is almost exclusively performed by women. Sometimes women in Ranon organize small markets and sell produce among themselves and give the money to the church. This was organized every Tuesday morning on the lawn in front of the secondary school when I was there in 1999. On other occasions larger fund-raising activities are organized that involve a number of people and are something of a happening in the village. The women start to cook early and already at dusk the fires in the kitchen houses show that women are busy preparing food for the occasion. Some make *laplap*, others kill a fowl, and some just bring their garden produce. These larger occasions often take place in front of the church where there is an open space under the shade of two huge breadfruit trees. The women sit around on their mats and sell the food. On these days no one prepares an evening meal as usual. Everyone eats the food made for the fund-raising event together.

During my fieldwork in 1999, people in Ranon organized a fund-raising event which they called 'mate to meet' after an Australian fund-raising concept. The idea was that everyone should bring along a plate with food and then the organizers would read aloud names of people who should eat their meals together. Two families would exchange plates and pay for the food they got from the other family, and then sit down together and eat. The money would then be contributed to the church. This particular fund-raising event was organized on the lawn in front of the secondary school and had been planned and announced during church service the week before. It was one of the village chiefs who organized the event and he showed up early in the school-yard. He had made accurate lists of all the households in Ranon and decided who should eat together. People started arriving with beautifully decorated dishes. They had wrapped *laplap* and meat in green banana leaves, tying the leaves together with red hibiscus flowers. Most of the food brought to the event was traditional style cooking based on crops from the gardens. Every household in Ranon turned up at the event, and sat in groups around an open space where the chief stood and called out the names of those who should eat together.

These fund-raising events do not involve a great deal of money. Actually they 'sell' their products rather cheaply compared to prices of rice and tinned meat in the cooperative store. I suggest that the main reason for organizing these markets is not economic. The time and energy they invest far exceed the money they bring to the church. At the 'mate to meat' event every dish, each large enough to feed a whole family, was sold for a hundred vatu, which is less than a kilo of rice in the store. It seemed that people were eager to arrange different kinds of fund-raising events almost for the fun of it. These events broke up the routine of everyday life. The children played, women laughed together, and men sat around in groups smoking their stick tobacco. However, perhaps the most important reason for holding these events was that they brought people together for a common purpose – sharing food.

It was often pointed out to us that a kitchen house full of garden produce – yams, taro, and bananas – is not a pleasant sight. This produce should not be harvested in order to be just piled in the kitchen house. Rather, this produce should be circulated

Photo 6.1   Communal meal in front of the church, Ranon 1999

among the villagers and even beyond the village. An economy based on frequent sharing easily adapts to fund-raising regimes which make produce from individual's labour circulate in the village. The ceremonial economy on Ambrym, based to a large degree on generalized exchange, such as at marriage, circumcision ceremonies, *yengfah*, or death ceremonies, also provides contexts for the circulation of this garden produce. As I showed in Chapter 4, a large number of people contribute to the payments during these ceremonies, and thus transform garden produce from private into communal produce. In the past there was a greater repertoire of ceremonies that had this effect. Patterson (1981) has described some rites that were common on North Ambrym before the church was established. The *Serebuan* rite for instance was closely connected to the joking relationship that exists between a man and some of the kinsfolk from his mother's place, on North Ambrym called the *wuren*'s place. This ceremony is no longer performed on North Ambrym, because it is no longer regarded proper to do so. The church has banned it because it entails the singing of insulting and 'improper' songs with reference to sexual intercourse. The rite involved payments between a man and his *wuren* for the right to sing these songs in public, by which the singer would gain status and metaphysical power. Another ceremony, which is still performed to a certain degree, but which is becoming less frequent, is the *taoboan* ceremony. This ceremony is directed towards the mother's place as well, and involves payment of pigs and yams. The *taoboan* can also be directed towards the wife's place, as a way of paying respect to the maternal place of the children. On Ambrym in 1999 we observed the *taoboan* ceremony described below.

A Ranon man wanted to pay his respects to the wife's place. His wife was actually from Pentecost, but he killed pigs to his own mother's mother's place [his *mukuen*], which was the preferred place from which he should have received his wife. His wife had up until then been barren, and rumours had it that they were quite unhappy about this. Some people hinted that perhaps they believed that this ceremony would make way for children. By performing a *taoboan* rite the man would open up the road for new blood from his future children's maternal place. Only women can transfer blood through pregnancy. The *wuren*, or the mothers' place, is the source of one's blood and the place to which one owes an eternal debt. This debt is repaid at every life cycle ceremony, and, as in this case, the payment is made to the future children's *wuren*, even before these children are born. In order to make a contribution of some size to the *wuren*, which was especially necessary in this case in order to increase the hope of getting children, the man who performs the ceremony needs contributions from a large number of relatives. Some days before the ceremony Billy and Nelly, who were classified as this man's classificatory *gemalsul* [that is, of his place], went to their gardens and returned with a couple of large yams and bundles of bananas. On the morning of the ceremony, as we were climbing the steep hills to Fanrereo where this man's classificatory *mukuen* (and his future children's *wuren*) lived, I saw people from several of the households in Ranon carrying garden produce on their way to the same event. They were mostly people classified as brothers, fathers, and also sisters of the man who was to perform the ceremony. When they arrived in Fanrereo, people sat in a circle around the ceremonial ground waiting for the man to make his presentation of food to his *mukuen*. The man and some of his brothers organized all the food into one large heap. They had also brought along a medium sized pig that was killed on the ceremonial ground by the man before he gave his speech and presented the food to his *mukuen*. Afterwards the people in Fanrereo who had received the raw food, the *mukuen* of the Ranon man, presented a *laplap* they had prepared and meat from a pig killed that morning. There were five different kinds of *laplap* made from banana, taro and yam. The women from Fanrereo distributed this food to the clusters of people sitting around the ceremonial ground. Most people ate together on the spot, while some took the cooked food away with them in baskets to give to some relatives in Ranon who had not been able to come to Fanrereo, but who had contributed to the *taoboan* payment.

The North Ambrym ceremonial economy was, and still is, to a large degree based on people contributing to each other's ceremonies. In the *taoboan* ceremony just described there were at least ten different households contributing. I view the fund-raising events as part of this economy. In addition to raising money for the church, people share the food in their kitchen houses. Although there were no heaps of food piled up on a ceremonial ground during the 'mate to meat' event as there was during the *taoboan* ceremony, in both cases people shared cooked food. During a market where the money is contributed to the church, the syntax is also the same: people pool and share.

The Aesthetics of the Church: Creating Social Wholes

McDougall (2003) has pointed out in the case of people in Ranongga in the Solomon Islands, that the church offered a new kind of opportunity for collective action, in particular through fund-raising events. In a similar manner I found that the fund-raising events make the products of individual labour circulate and thereby become communal. In the name of the church, individual products are transformed into relational products. The events of history have decreased the repertoire of elaborate kinship ceremonies on Ambrym and given way to the church, but the church has not remained foreign. M. Strathern's hypothesis about social life in Melanesia that 'relations are only recognized if they assume a particular form' (1988, 180–81) is particularly relevant in this context. It is as if the principles governing the old ceremonies are now present in the church activities. In M. Strathern's terms the appropriate 'forms' are a matter of 'aesthetics' (M. Strathern 1988). Relations can either be closed or open. Ceremonies where people share food are a means to open relations, and new relations are generated. The new kind of ceremonies, such as church fund-raising, must be pressed into these 'appearances'. Contributions of foodstuffs and the sharing of other household's contributions make the fund-raising events into events that pull an individual household into the larger community. In this way the fund-raising events open the relations between households. The old ceremonies, as the *taoboan* ceremony described earlier, had the same effect. The individual household contributed and then shared a meal with those who were given the original contribution. Both the older ceremonies and the fund-raising events open relations in this manner and thus merge households into a social whole.

However, these events – both the ceremonies and the fund-raisers – also mark distinctions and close off certain relations. On the one hand relations are opened between those who share, and on the other, those who do not participate are clearly marked as such. Relations with those who did not turn up at the 'mate to meat' were closed off. The distinction between those who participate in the fund-raising of the Presbyterian Church in Ranon and those who do not is an essential distinction. It is a matter of being or not being included in a social whole.

Connecting Origin Routes and Churches

The Presbyterian Church is the dominant church in Ranon, and most of the people in the surrounding villages, such as Ranbwe and Lonbwe, join the services in Ranon's Presbyterian Church. In Fantor, however, the village that seems to be almost an extension of Ranon, there is another church called the Church of Holiness or the Neil Thomas Ministry [NTM], named after its Australian founder. I was told that the NTM in Fantor was established in the early eighties and that during this period there had been much turbulence and also violence between people in Ranon and people in Fantor. The NTM members in Fantor had previously been part of the Presbyterian Church in Ranon, and their break with the Ranon church triggered fights and accusations of sorcery for years afterwards. At its peak, the conflict culminated in a big fight on the beach where men from Ranon fought men from Fantor with clubs and knives. This fight is still talked about as one of the big events in recent history. The police from the capital had to show up and cool matters down. Today most of the people in Fantor are members of the NTM church community, and they have recruited some members from Ranon and other surrounding villages as well.

The different churches, the Presbyterian and the NTM, form two distinct communities, and participation in one automatically excludes participation in the other, and not only in regard to church-services. The church defines the community. The preferred marriage is, for instance, church endogamous. During my 1995–96 fieldwork on Ambrym, three couples got married in Fantor, and all of the marriages were between two people from the same church. The borders between the different church communities are not random and the breakaway from the Presbyterian Church and the establishment of the NTM church in Fantor is significant. In order to analyse the factors relevant to this process of splitting a church and the borders created between them, I include an analysis of the relation between church and origin routes.

Ranon was the site of the first mission station on North Ambrym and it was the site of the only plantation on the island. The plantation owner also ran a store and Ranon became a centre for commerce and trade on Ambrym. I have outlined in Chapter 3 how people moved from the inland settlements to the mission station and plantation in Ranon. Old people remember how their grandparents decided to leave the old settlements because of the fear of *posen* [B: black magic] or as a result of war and conflict with neighbouring villages. Accusations of *posen* led to tensions, and club fights broke out between villages. When the fear of *posen* and tensions escalated, people sought refuge in Ranon close to the mission station. Ranon became a settlement of people from different areas, all with different origin routes.

In Map 6.1 I show some of the routes followed by people who settled in Ranon two and three generations ago. One of the routes goes from Hawor down to Ranon, another one goes from Wilifil and ends up in Ranon, and the third goes from Fante in West Ambrym, through Port Vila, and ends up in Ranon.[3] The last two routes going into Ranon, the Wilifil route and the Fante route, end up in Fantor. This last route is interesting for the Ranon-Fantor division, because it was men of this route who were the main actors in the drama between Ranon and Fantor that culminated in the fight.

The story of Willy and Balkon[4]

I first became aware of the deep roots of the Ranon-Fantor conflict when the founder of the NTM church in Fantor died in 1999, and a man living in Ranon was accused of sorcery. The accusations and tensions were so strong that the accused had to leave the village and live in Port Vila for a time. There were accusations both ways however. People in Ranon said that the men in the NTM congregation had access to knowledge of sorcery and had used it. The Bible they carried was only a camouflage, people in Ranon said during the village court case in 1999; the NTM people were really sorcerers.

---

3   There are other routes into Ranon. I have just drawn the most significant to illustrate my argument.

4   The descendants of Balkon still living in Ranon and Fantor told us this story. The facts of the story seemed to be undisputed. Both the descendents of Willy and Balkon tell the same story.

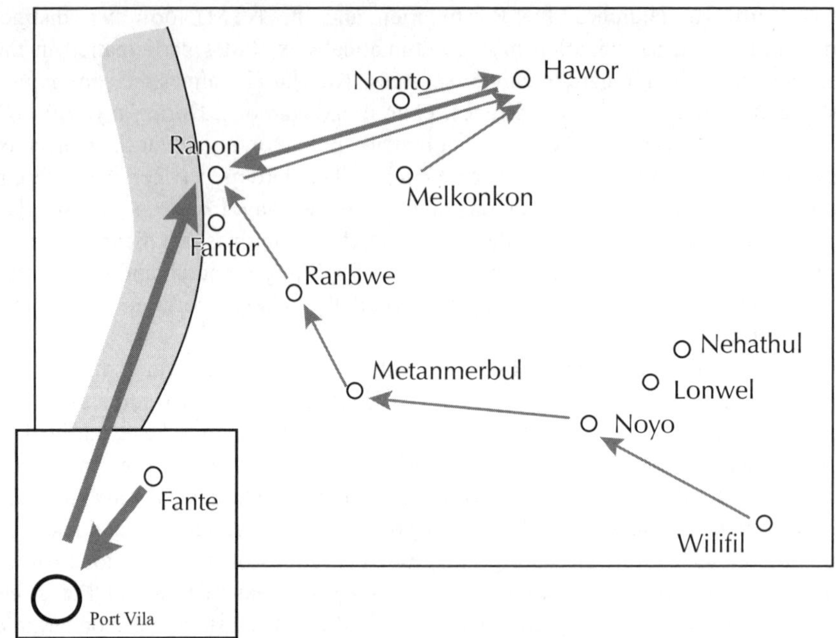

Map 6.1   Origin routes into Ranon

I was told that the diseased founder of the NTM church was the grandson of Balkon, a man who was not from Ranon, and actually not from North Ambrym at all. He was from Fante in West Ambrym, and had been one of survivors of the volcanic eruption in West Ambrym in 1913. The area became uninhabitable and Balkon moved to Port Vila (see Map 6.1). Here he met Willy, a *tarin Ranon* [L: a Ranon man, man of the place]. Balkon accompanied Willy to Ranon, and after a while he married Willy's sister, Mareng. Balkon and Mareng settled just outside of Ranon, where the village of Fantor lies today. They had a son, Tantan. Balkon's wife Mareng died young, and Balkon was without a wife. Willy had several wives, and one of them had an affair with Balkon. People in Ranon today say that Balkon stole Willy's wife. This, of course, was unacceptable to Willy, who in the end shot Balkon with his rifle. Tantan, (Balkon and Mareng's son and Willy's sister son), was adopted by a woman in Hawor village and grew up there. He married a girl from Ranon and moved back down to this village. He and his wife had eleven children, eight of them boys. One of these boys founded the NTM church in Fantor, and all of the remaining brothers still alive today have joined this church. We see here the interconnection between the division and conflict lines between the churches and the historical movements of people.

Origin Routes and Churches 1: Ranon and Fantor

As shown in Chapter 3, people on Ambrym move and change residence, and in particular during the last hundred years, and the degree of population movements has increased as a result of the colonial economy and plantation in Ranon. The level of conflicts concerning land rights increased as well after Independence when land was to be reclaimed by the '*kastom* owners'. Both on the national as well as the local level, efforts have been made to negotiate and find solutions to land disputes. The land department's local representatives have carried out land surveys and genealogical enquiries, but this is not an easy task because there are no agreements on the relevance of the different origin routes: Who came first? Who have stayed longest? and so on.

When Fantor was established as a new village with its own church, it was only people in Ranon who had origin routes from elsewhere who moved to Fantor (see Map 6.1). Moreover, it was people with problematic origin routes who settled here. Balkon's descendants had only access to land though their matrilateral links, because their patrilineal land was located in West Ambrym. Balkon's descendants depended on rights to use land through their mother in Ranon. Establishing themselves in Fantor might have been a way of manifesting themselves more strongly in the area and an effort to root their place on North Ambrym. They had worked the land their mother worked in Ranon for a long time, but because of their disrupted route of origin from Balkon, they needed to emphasize their connection to the place more strongly. Fantor village and the NTM church were ways of doing this: by establishing a new village, their own village, they emphasized their relation to the place.

Another route into Ranon and later into Fantor is the route from Willit. It is not so disrupted, but the length of the route, the long walking-distance to Metanmerbul and Noyo and even Willit in order to work gardens (see Map 6.1), may have contributed to these people's decisions to join the NTM church. By moving they emphasize themselves as different from the others in Ranon and by changing church this is highlighted.

The descendants of Balkon, as well as those with their origin route from Willit, all talk about the establishment of the NTM church as a religious decision. The attitudes and actions of the Presbyterian congregation are not sufficiently Christian according to the NTM adherents. One of Balkon's grandsons argued that the church in Ranon was doomed because of the low morals of the congregation: they drank alcohol and kava, the women smoked and the young people danced. This discourse, making the break with the Presbyterian Church a matter of morals, can also be seen as related to this conflict-line with roots in the past. By emphasizing themselves as even more Christian and acting morally superior to the Presbyterians in Ranon, they have corrected the mistakes Balkon made. The new village of Fantor emerges as more Christian and morally above the *men of the place* in Ranon.

Origin Routes and Churches 2: Fanrereo

In the same way as Ranon is a composite village where people from different areas of North Ambrym live, Fanrereo as well is a relatively recently established village where people from abandoned villages have settled.[5] People who live in Fanrereo

---

5   Fanrereo is an inland village north of Ranon.

are mainly from Hawor, Randyo, Numto and Melkonkon.[6] In the same way as the Fantor-Ranon conflict illustrated how the relationship between the churches incorporates historical movement and different origin routes, the division between the church communities in Fanrereo shows that there is a connection between church and origin route as well.

In Fanrereo the conflict between the churches is tied into a land dispute. The Presbyterian Church lies on Peter Ramel's ground in Fanrereo. As I outlined in the previous chapter, Peter Ramel[7] was a returned labour migrant who found his old settlement, Melkonkon, empty and who moved to Hawor. Later he built a church in Fanrereo, close to where the previous village Melkonkon had been located, where people from Hawor later resettled. Peter Ramel is regarded as the founder of both Fanrereo and the Presbyterian Church. Fanrereo, like Ranon, is a village founded on a church in the sense that first the church was established and then converts gradually settled in its vicinity. In the same way as the conflict between Ranon and Fantor is intertwined in the historical process of movement, this conflict in Fanrereo is also connected to resettlements of the past. Peter Ramel built his church on his abandoned ground. This ground is today disputed. Peter Ramel had only one child, a daughter, and it is the son of this daughter who founded a new Apostolic Church in Fanrereo. Peter Ramel had, however, an adopted son whose descendants have remained Presbyterian. Today, the Apostolic Church wants to own the ground on which the Presbyterian Church in Fanrereo is built, and its members claim that since Peter Ramel had no son, the descendants of his daughter are entitled to this ground. They argue that since they are the true descendants of Pita Ramel, the ground and church that stand there now belong to them, and they want to make the church into an Apostolic Church. The Presbyterians in Fanrereo argue that Peter Ramel gave his ground to the Presbyterian Church and, since the members of the Apostolic Church have turned away from this church, they no longer have any rights to the ground it stands on.

Differences Expressed through Church Adherence

The stories of Ranon and Fantor and of the conflict between the two churches in Fanrereo show that there is a connection between the complex compositions of villages today on Ambrym, and the establishment of new church communities. This complex composition of settlements is characteristic of most villages on North Ambrym, and Patterson (2002, 206) has described this for Fona village north of Fanrereo in the following manner:

> In 1968 the only Fona residents who were also Fona people in the senses of the origin narratives, comprised male and junior or elderly, divorced female members of two out of eleven households. The majority of Fona residents were actually 'other' people, who, while strongly maintaining their domain of affiliation, had been drawn to Fona by

---

6   See Chapter 3 for a detailed map of these villages.

7   For the story about Peter Ramel see Chapters 3 and 5.

preachers, stores and the persuasive powers of the senior man of the village, the yam master Koran, over which eponymous ritual he presided annually.

Fona's scenario also holds true in Fanrereo and in Ranon, as I pointed out earlier. Negotiations between different origin routes take place through the churches in Fanrereo, and the distinction between Ranon and Fantor is made visible through their different church communities. This process of negotiating and signalling origin through the church takes place at different levels. Sometimes a village is divided, and sometimes it is only one man or one woman or one household who breaks away from the church. In the vicinity of Ranon there is an SDA household. This family has to walk for an hour uphill to the village of Fanla where the closest SDA church is situated. All the other households in Ranon are Presbyterian or NTM. This family has an origin route different from those in Ranon and Fantor, and maybe this difference is made visible through their SDA adherence.

To a certain extent it seems as if the church, or rather the specific church one belongs to on Ambrym, works like an idiom for conflicts and difference. As we have seen, these conflicts often centre on political control over land and resources, and people use the church as a way of expressing adherence and rights to specific areas. By remaining Presbyterian in Ranon one shows that one is *of the place*, and consequently has access to the land in the area. The conflicts between Ranon and Fantor, or between the Presbyterian Church and the NTM Church, is a matter of emphasizing origin, but churches can be used as an idiom for conflicts at other, more personal, levels. The story of Balkon and Willy and the conflicts following them in Ranon can be seen as an expression of conflict between men of the place and men from the outside, but it was also a personal conflict which led to a break away from the Presbyterian Church some generations after the dramatic shooting episode. There are other such personal conflicts, which show how the church works as an expression of conflicts at different levels.

For instance, in Ranon an elderly woman had for some time been dissatisfied with her son's wife. The wife had lived with her son for close to two years without yet becoming pregnant. There were rumours in the village that the wife was drinking abortive substances to prevent pregnancy. The two women, the wife and her husband's mother, were often observed having loud arguments, and the young wife often ran home to her mother, only to return quietly before nightfall. The conflict culminated with the mother of the man demanding that the wife of the son should return to her natal place; in other words divorce her son. A village council, a *kot* [B: court] run by the three chiefs gathered, and the whole village attended. Several of the girl's relatives spoke in her favour, arguing that the mother-in-law was too *stronghed* [B: strong head, determined]. The chiefs asked the young man himself whether he was unhappy with his wife, and he replied that he did not want her to leave. The mother, however, argued that the couple were only *merred long bus* [B: married in the bush[8]] and were not properly married in the church. After loud arguments and a lot of crying by the women present, the man's mother's brother spoke to the woman

---

8   *Merred long bus* implies that the couple is married in the sense that the man has given some valuables, probably a pig, to the girl's father and brother as a preliminary payment

(his sister), and said: 'You call yourself a Christian woman. You carry the Bible under your arm. But you kill love!' The village court ended without reaching any agreement. The following Sunday, however, the mother-in-law did not turn up in the Presbyterian Church as she usually did, but was seen on her way to Fantor, to the NTM Church, carrying her bright umbrella and Bible.

Another woman in Ranon broke away from the Presbyterian Church as well and joined the NTM Church after a domestic conflict. Her natal family lived in Fantor, but she had married a Ranon man and lived in Ranon with her mother-in-law and her four children. Her husband was never in the village during any of my fieldwork periods, as he was working on a cargo ship abroad. He sent her money now and then, but this could not compensate for his absence and all the work she had to carry out alone in the garden as well as at home. The mother-in-law was old and sick, and needed care. Gradually the Fantor women started joining the NTM Church instead of the Presbyterian Church, and people saw this as the beginning of a movement back to Fantor.

Both the mother-in-law from the case above and the Fantor woman felt let down and left alone. They made their views visible by changing churches. They used an already established division between the churches, to make their own differences visible. The church manifests social wholes, or social communities based on origin route. Sometimes conflicts that are not related to land and historical movements are expressed in terms of this already established conflict line. This is related to the way the church operates as the most basic and the primary social group to which one relates. I noticed during my stay in Ranon that when work parties were organized, such as those to make copra, it was done within the churches. So that when, for instance, a woman living in Ranon, but a member of the NTM Church in Fantor, recruited people to help her on her copra plot, she only called upon people who were members of the NTM Church in Fantor. This emphasized the way the church defines social communities, and divisions between them.

The Gendered Church

We have seen how the church marks difference and how the distinction between the churches has long historical roots. But how does the internal 'tying together' of the church take place, and how does the church operate as a community?

On the one hand the church has, through different kinds of fund-raising activities, taken on a relational form creating social wholes. In this way the church takes on the same form as the older ceremonies. The church maintains the open relational form that the traditional ceremonial economy required. It is not the case, however, that the church has just replaced the old ceremonies, and thereby merely given the old content a new appearance. I will show how women in the church have transformed certain aspects of the ceremonial economy tied to gender relations.

---

before the real marriage ceremony. It is common on Ambrym for couples to live together for several years before they get married in the church.

The social structure of the Ambrym ceremonial economy has an inherent internal contradiction. On the one hand, the principles of sharing and creating social wholes lie at the bottom of every ceremony, whether it is a marriage, a *malyel,* a *taoboan* or any other ceremony. The prestations in every ceremony are based on generalized exchange, as I argued in Chapter 4. On the other hand, the main persons of the ceremony eclipse this generalized exchange. The man who pays for his *taoboan,* as in the *taoboan* ceremony described in the first part of this chapter, presents the heap of food he has received from a large number of relatives *as if* it was a gift *from him* to the wife's place, and he thus emerges as an industrious man. This illusion is only momentary, because after the presentation of food to the wife's place, the return prestation, which in the case of the *taoboan* ceremony described previously was a number of *laplaps* and pork, is shared among the many relatives who contributed to the *taoboan* payment. This tension between the social whole and the one person who emerges as the big man (Sahlins 1963) is present in all ceremonies, whether it is a marriage, a *malyel,* a *yengfah,* or other such events.

For instance, in Fanrereo in 2000 I observed the payment of one of the largest 'bride prices', to my knowledge, in North Ambrym. It had been rumoured for quite a while before the ceremony that the bride's brothers had signalled that they expected to receive a rather large sum of money and a great number of pigs. The groom's father had, on his side, mentioned figures that made people wonder where he would be able get that kind of money. I was told that one of the bride's brothers,[9] a neighbour of ours in Ranon, expected 200,000 vatu, at least. The average on Ambrym is often lower than the national standard of 80,000 vatu. The groom and his father had been watched as they walked around and visited villages and people from whom they expected contributions. They visited the groom's father's sisters who were married and living other places, and they visited classificatory fathers and brothers of the groom in other villages. Rio (2002a) has followed in detail the collections of contributions to ceremonies of this kind, and has concluded that contributions come from different kinds of relatives, and not only agnates. Relations to other affines, and to the agnates of the mother are also used to collect contributions. As I argued earlier, in a marriage, the total population who participates is divided into two sides – the groom's side and the bride's side – and people choose on which side they contribute based on which kin-relations they emphasize.[10]

In the days before the ceremony, people walked to Fanrereo where the groom lived and put their contributions in the groom's kitchen house. Some just left a yam or two. Others arrived with several bundles of bananas as well as money. On the morning of the ceremony, people were still arriving with contributions to the 'bride price'. From Ranon people carried heavy burdens of garden crops and live pigs. On the ceremonial ground in Fanrereo everything was gathered in ten different heaps. Beside each heap, there was a stick with money fastened on the top, and to each stick

---

9   Her father was dead and her brothers represented her side. She had a number of brothers who had interest in this ceremony because she had been adopted after her father's death, and several families had to be compensated for losing her.

10   Those who contribute to the bride's presents during the *sakkem presen* ceremony are those who receive payment from the 'bride price'.

a pig of variable size, was fastened by a rope. At this point, when all the contributors on the groom's side were present and busy helping the groom make different heaps to go to different parties on the bride's side, the communal effort to gather the 'bride price' was highly visible. As the ceremony officially started and the father's sister led the bride, who was covered by the red mat, to the ceremonial ground, the groom's father played the leading role. The relatives who had contributed food and money left to sit at the outskirts of the ceremonial ground. No one but the groom and his father and a father's brother was allowed to enter the ceremonial ground as the payment of the 'bride price' began. This was emphasized to me strongly several times. It was as if no one should disturb the image created when the groom's father initially gave an envelope to the bride's brother. This was the father's sister's cue to lift the red mat, which until then had covered the bride, and the father of the groom continued to call out the names of the different parties on the bride's side who should receive their share of the 'bride price'. The envelope given had contained the 'bride price', which I later heard had been somewhere near 200,000 vatu in cash. In varying shares, this amount represented contributions from half the population in the area, and the father of the groom gave it as if it was a payment from him to the bride's brother. At this moment the groom and his father represented all those who had contributed; the others were only spectators. It was the groom and his father's show altogether. They were the big men, eclipsing all the others who had contributed during the last few weeks.

This transformation of a number of small items from a number of people into one large contribution given by the groom and his father, was only momentary however, because as the payment was being made, the large heaps disappeared into small pieces given in different directions on the bride's side.[11] The pigs were given to each of the bride's brothers in Ranon.

During this ceremony there was a shift from the communal contribution to the personal achievements of the groom and his father. This tension can be seen as gendered on Ambrym. It is a male capacity to emerge as the one person who eclipses the social whole, and it is thus a female capacity to be backgrounded and 'eclipsed' (M. Strathern 1988) as the ones who contribute without being highlighted.[12] One might say that the total social whole is female gendered and the man who represents this whole, what we might call the male 'personification' (M. Strathern 1988, 177) is, during the payment phase in the ceremony, seeking to eclipse this. I will, in Chapter 7 and 8, go more into the dynamics of the tension between the social whole and the individual and then include a discussion of the men's graded society, the *mage,* in relation to this, but for now it will suffice to point out this gendered contradiction in the ceremonies. It is this tension that has been affected when the church became the

---

11   See also Rio (2002a, 235) on these processes in relation to a comparable *malyel* ceremony.

12   By this I do not mean that only men can become the agents of a ceremony and that only women contribute. A woman can, for instance, perform ceremonial compensations by handing over yam and pigs. She thus takes on male qualities. Likewise, contributing to a ceremony involves taking on female gendered capacities. On Ambrym however, it is often (but not always) men who take the leading role in a ceremony and it is often women, and relations through sisters, that are followed when collecting resources for a ceremony.

new arena for the ceremonial economy. To emerge as a 'personification' or as a big man has become harder. The church does not emphasize singular men the way older ceremonial institutions did.

Christianity and Change

The relation between the church and older ceremonies in northern Vanuatu has been given some attention in the anthropological literature from the area. Allen (1981) has argued that the men's graded society in West Ambae in northern Vanuatu, is somehow reflected in the title-hierarchy of the church. After missionization men sought these titles in order to make the church into a new form of graded society. Allen has pointed out that even the numbers of grades coincide, respectively: *moli, levuhi, vira* with deacon, teachers and elders. Whereas earlier political authority was achieved through titles in the graded society, the *namange* or the *hungwe,* the church is now the road to leadership. Allen has pointed out that the different church communities – the Church of Christ, which was the dominating Church in West Ambae, the Melanesian mission, the French Marists, the SDA, and the Apostolic Church – were 'the modern equivalent of local differences in graded society hierarchies and rituals' (1981, 127).

Rubinstein (1981) argued along the same lines when he regarded how Christianity was first introduced on Malo in northern Vanuatu. The traditional power structures remained. The local graded society, the *sumbuea,* had fifteen ranked eating classes, implying that the holders of each grade had to eat separately, as was common in the graded societies in northern Vanuatu. The higher the rank, the higher are the prestige and the political power. Major pig-killing ceremonies opened for the entry into new eating classes. Big men attracted followers by sponsoring the pig-killing ceremonies of others. The introduction of the church did not alter this conception of 'following': 'lesser men still followed greater men, in this instance the greater men being those who were best versed in Christianity; women still followed men' (1981, 143).

I believe that this process may not have worked exactly like this in North Ambrym. Women run the church markets and the fund-raising events and serve as teachers as well as elders in the church. Women's involvement in the church not only parallels, but far exceeds, men's preoccupation with the church. Both men and women go to church regularly, but in addition, women have their own church organization, the PWMU (Presbyterian Women's Mission Union) and attend church meetings exclusively for women. There is no such church organization exclusively for men. Every Tuesday morning the Presbyterian women in Ranon and the neighbouring villages gather in the church, either in the big concrete church in Ranon or in smaller bamboo-churches in the other villages, for meetings of the PWMU. Once a month or so they have their so-called 'combined meetings', which involve PWMU women from all over North Ambrym. Every year there are General Assemblies in Port Vila. Quite a few of the women in Ranon had been to one or two of these assemblies. In addition to these formal meetings, women often just gather in the church in order to make handicrafts in each other's company. These handicrafts, like flutes and pandanus mats, will be sold and the money given to the church.

The church is not a continuation of the graded society. It presented itself as more open to women than some of the older institutions and ceremonies, and as shown in the previous chapter, it was important for the first Christians on the island to emphasize that the church was open to both genders. It was his repeated emphasis on this that finally drove the first missionary off the island. Women have been present in the church since the very beginning. One might say that the church has been presented as an *alternative* to the already existing social order where men performed the leading parts of the ceremonial economy.

Barker (1992) has argued that we must stop regarding Christianity as a substitution for traditional religion, but rather look for the changes it brought, and how it has become integrated and adapted. Robbins (2004, 2007) has more recently argued that Christianity often brings along radical breaks with the past but that anthropologists have tended to interpret Christianity as a continuation of previous cultural categories, only in a new disguise. In Vanuatu ethnography Philibert (1992), for instance, has outlined the changes that the introduction of Christianity has had on the lives of the ni-Vanuatu in Erakor village on Efate in Vanuatu. He has stressed that the 'traditional institutions' were lost in the villagers' 'new life'. Not only changes of spiritual order but also the political organization of the village was altered. Philibert argues that, 'By adopting Christianity the people of Erakor obtained a new tool, a new model, for thinking about themselves, for defining themselves, and for guiding their actions' (1992, 116). However, in spite of these changes, Philibert concludes that 'Erakor villagers in a sense simply replaced one set of sacred figures by another' (1992, 117).

For the case of Ambrym I stress that the while the church has taken on an open relational form that includes ceremonies where the sharing of food is central, and thus somehow continues the pre-Christian relational form, Christianity has also changed important aspects of the ceremonial economy. I will describe one ceremony, a New Yam ceremony, which illustrates the relational dynamics of the church today. This is a ceremony that had another form before the establishment of the church that was not only about creating social wholes, but also a way for big men to show off. As will become apparent, this latter part of the ceremony is non-existent today.

New Yam 1995

I took part in the New Yam ceremony in Ranon in 1996. It is an event that can be compared to other Melanesian first-fruit ceremonies and is performed before the harvest of the yams in the gardens. The day that was selected for the New Yam ceremony some time in advance by a ritual expert from Fona village, started with a church ceremony blessing the yams. The day before, everyone had been to their gardens to dig up the first yam tubers. This is something of a ritual in itself. Extreme care has to be taken. If one of the yams breaks on the way down to the village, it implies that a man in the village will die. On the morning of the day of New Yam, however, everyone brought some of their fresh and unbroken yams to the church. The church was not as crowded as usual, and nearly all those present were women except for the male elder who was to lead the ceremony. The women placed the yams in front of the altar, and the elder held a brief ceremony and blessed the yams. Shortly afterwards some women gathered in the front and placed the yams in different heaps with price tags on them. Then all the women bought some, and the money was collected for the church.

Immediately after the church service everyone gathered outside the old *Nakamal* [B: communal house] bringing new yams. This time almost the whole community gathered. The men, however, sat in the background except for one of the chiefs who helped the women organize the yams in different heaps. They took quite a long time on this process. Tubers were carried back and forth between heaps in order to make all of the heaps equal in size. When I asked about possible patterns in the yam distribution, I was told that the important thing was that no one left with the same yams they had brought. After the women finished their work, the chief called out the names of various women who were to cook the New Yam meal together. These women were *gemasul* [related through husband]. The different women collected the yams and went off to prepare their meal.

The yam was mixed with taro and 'island cabbage', sprinkled with coconut milk, wrapped in *laplap* leaves, and then baked in a ground-oven. At dusk the women who had cooked together gathered with their children and ate. For a while I wondered where the men were, because they usually eat with the women. I quickly found out that almost all the men were drunk. They had gathered together just after the yams were distributed and shared some bottles of wine and whiskey that were purchased the day before when the skipper of the community-owned speed boat ran an errand in West Ambrym. For many of them the day ended without the New Yam meal.

New Yam is about distributing yams in the village, and thereby making the product of individual labour into something communal, in the same way as the other ceremonies I have described. The church is the framework for this transformation. As we can see from the description above, women are the organizers of the distribution. I was surprised when I learnt about the key roles women have in this ceremony, because as a symbol, the yam is used in various male contexts (cf. Deacon 1934; Layard 1942; Patterson 1976; Rio 1997, 2002a). Jolly (1995, 67) reports that on South Pentecost women do not take part in the planting of yams, because yams are associated with men and connected to male work, whereas taro is associated with women, and appropriate as women's work. It is also the case that women on North Ambrym do not plant yams, and as Jolly explains for South Pentecost, this has to do with the yam being associated with maleness and the male part in procreation, which makes it inappropriate for the women to plant. Furthermore, in descriptions of New Yam ceremonies from the past, women played quite another role in the ceremony.

New Yam in 1887

Murray, in his diary, gives an account of a New Yam ceremony he attended in Metanmerbul. On 10 March 1887 he writes:

> As there is to be a great feast of "First Fruits" tomorrow, and as all the missionaries on their islands set their faces against it as being an unmitigated evil, I asked Bongnaim about it … 'Is there any evil about it then?'
> 'no'

'do you offer the first fruits to spirits or demons?'
'no'
'before you allot the large heap into its several portions, do you say anything?'
'no, we just beat the drum, and each individual comes to take his share'.
Bongnaim's replies were clear and firm, and from my opinion of Bong, I was inclined to believe him.

On 11 March he walked to Metanmerbul, having told himself that perhaps the other missionaries were wrong about these first-fruit ceremonies. Maybe these ceremonies were not a matter of sacrifice to demons, but had another dimension:

On arriving found all busy, sat down … they spoke of the feast "Yes" I said, "I am to watch it, and what is more, I am to return thanks to God for his goodness for supplying us with so much food, for it was he that made it grow".

Leaving my position I went to see the chief (…) I next proceed to the "har" – the public place in the village. As we approached, the drum beat for them to gather the things into one heap. This took some time. During the interval I spoke with the chief Magmagmelun, who sat on my left. I was to return thanks to God for his goodness. He said that there had been a great deal of rain. The yams were small. "Tell him to send no more rain, but plenty of sunshine", which I undertook to do. Seeing one of those in charge of piling up the heaps, I said I was as soon as all was gathered together, to return thanks to God.

Murray went on to thank God, and prayed for more sunshine. He held a long talk about good and evil, and in the end asked for forgiveness for all sins:

The men then proceeded to allot with dignity and gravity, becoming judges. They spoke in whispers so that none might know where their portions lay. This took a long time. Everyone in the village of the male sex, had to get their share. After the allotment, came the counting by a couple of tellers. The moment the counting began, the drum struck up at exactly the same second. No English hand could have been more prompt. The counting took a long time…I had incidentally come to learn there was an allotment for me. So, I said I am a white man and I won't deprive you of your food. "No," they shouted, "you are one of ourselves – a native". I had to submit (…) This part of the program over, the old chief on my left and one of the tellers arose. The chief pronounced the names of the owners of the lots … After the lots were all assigned, the chief gave a speech. He had a very dull commonplace style of talking. Stepping from side to side, from one foot to the other. He got slightly more animated, but only a little … His spoke of what had recently taken place amongst them. He alluded to deaths, and to charges of poison. (…) I enjoyed the whole affair very much, and could for my part see no evil in it.

Murray did not mention women much in his account, and it is uncertain whether his remark that all the men in the village should receive their share of the yams, was something he was told, or whether it was he himself who deduced this. However, he remarks that he, half way during the proceedings, 'went visiting the women', while the men were busy allotting the yams, and from this I surmise that the women were not present on the 'har' and were not taking an active part in the proceedings he was describing.

New Yam in 1943

Paton (1971) described a New Yam ceremony that took place in 1943, and this description reveals interesting innovations with regard to the church as well as to the role of women.

The whole ceremony takes place at a ceremonial ground, which he calls the *hara*, where the Chief of Fanla at the time, Hanlam, had the leading part:

> When all seemed ready, the men took the yams and bananas into the centre of the enclosure, and placed them in a heap, yams resting against the bananas. Hanlam took in his hand a small bundle of sticks called *muju*, which represents yam. With the *muju* in his left hand, he moved to the further side of the *hara*, enclosure, and made passes with the *muju* in various directions. He was said to be thinking about the yam in all the surrounding villages, and, in a sense, to be "praying for a good crop for all". He then turned full on to the gathering of men, and gave the sign for the climax of the ceremony.
>
> One man, squatted in front of the two drums [atingting], heartily began to beat a specific rhythm … Being specific rhythms significant of the New Yam ceremonies, they carried the message to the surrounding villages, where other drums began to beat and spread the message further … The rhythm was said to represent the sound of rainwater …
>
> During all these proceedings the women stood watching from beyond the stone walls of the enclosure.
>
> At the same time as the vigorous beating of the drums, the conch shells were blown, and all the men shouted and cheered, and threw oranges out beyond the enclosure, mainly in the direction beyond the spot where Hanlam stood during his part in the ritual. They were said to be chasing away the old year, or the old yam.
>
> To end the formal proceedings, the food is piled in little heaps, much care being taken to divide it equally or fairly equally; and the piles are then distributed, as free gifts, among all the men (1979, 42).

Comparing the role of women in the three descriptions, it becomes obvious that this has changed dramatically. Murray described a scene where only men are present and in Paton's description the women where outside the enclosure. What has happened?

Today women's roles in the ceremony have become much more prominent. Not only are women now made visible in the ceremony, but their parts are also far more dominant than the parts the men play. Whereas before, men performed the whole ceremony by themselves behind the large stone walls of the enclosure, today men have lost their prominence in this ceremony altogether.

As my account of the ceremony in 1996 reveals, men were not present in the church at all, and although they were present outside the *Nakamal* when the actual redistribution was taking place, they only watched the whole procedure. Only the chief and the women were taking part in the distribution of the yams. The chief did not have the prominent role that Hanlam did in 1943 or Chief Magmagmelun in 1887. The Chief who helped the women allot the yams during New Yam in 1995 had a very quiet role.

One might say that men and women have changed parts in this ceremony. Whereas women some decades ago were the observers of the ceremony, men are the spectators today. Not only have women been able to take part in the ceremony, but they have also replaced the men. Why is this so? I argue that it is because of the female appropriation of the church historically and women's continued presence in the church, particularly through the fund-raising events. Because the ceremonies now are taking place within the framework of the church, they are dominated by women. The church, as the new arena for conducting ceremonies, has changed the structural principles on which the ceremonies are conducted. The role of men who seek to take a leading role in the ceremonial context, by presenting the food and giving speeches, has disappeared as the ceremony has come to be a church-based event. The other aspect of the ceremony, the contributions and distribution of food within the social whole, remains as the main aspect of the ceremony.

Before the establishment of the church women were, of course, also part of this generalized exchange, although their physical presence on the *harl* was tabooed. Women worked in the gardens with their husbands to produce what the husbands brought along to the ceremony and they received the yams their husbands brought back. Women's work was eclipsed (M. Strathern 1988) by men's ceremonial performance during the New Yam ceremony, as well as in other ceremonies where men exchanged food that women had contributed. During church-based ceremonies women's roles have become visualized to a much larger extent than was the case during the older ceremonies. The old ritual place, the *harl,* was tabooed for women, a place for ceremonies that created big men. The church, as an alternative movement, opened the ceremonies to women, replacing the older ceremonial structures privileging men. The change in symbolic systems, the shift from the *harl* to the church, has given women access to a previously forbidden ceremonial domain.

Sexton's (1982) well known analysis of the Wok Meri movement in the New Guinea Highlands from the seventies is also a story about women entering what has until then been male domains. Sexton shows how women took on male roles in what looked like traditional ceremonies but which also were development and business events for women. Ambrym women not only opened the church, and public ceremonies like New Yam, to women. They also inverted the structural principles on which these ceremonies were conducted. Understanding the relation between gender, Christianity and change on Ambrym implies not only an understanding of how women came to enter a previously male domain (the ceremonial domain) through the gender neutral church but also how the female social form came to structure the conception of the church in line with the egalitarian Christian ethos.

Presbyterian Women and *Kastom*

I suggest that women are prominent not only in the New Yam ceremony, but also in the church, because transformations and opening up of new domains have been tied to female agency in many respects. In Chapter 2 I argued that it is the links through women, often mothers, which stand out as alternative roads of relation making, and in Chapter 3 I pointed out that movement and creation of new settlements relied on women opening up the roads. Furthermore, as I argued in Chapter 4, during movement into completely new territories, such as the urban spaces of Port Vila and Luganville, women became key points for their male relatives on their journeys to and from the towns. Christianity represents another such new territory opened up by the female movement. This movement has taken place on different levels. Women have 'transported' the church as they married into new places, as I argued in Chapter 5, but more than this it is women's ability to make connections, or to be 'roads', particularly after marriage, which has facilitated the making of social wholes, the creation of communities, a female capacity. At the same time as the church has made women more visible in the ceremonial domain, women have made the church into a communal movement. The church today has through the visualized female agency become the most important social institution on North Ambrym. The church is thus 'female' in the sense that it connects people and operates as a whole socially in regard to most important community activities. However, why cannot the church become an expression of male capacities?

Practices that are male gendered on Ambrym are more about emphasizing oneself than about emphasizing the social whole. It is a male gendered practice to create objectifications that refer back to oneself as a great person. These objectifications can be regarded as personal representations. In the male graded society, for instance, large three-fern figures were erected after every grade-taking. This three-fern figure represented the man and his grade, as well as the number of pigs he killed and his new name and status. The figures remain as a representation of the person (see Rio 1997). The church has no room for such objectifications. Although it was renowned males of this kind who purchased the church in the early days of colonial history, as shown in my account of Magekon who travelled to West Ambrym to purchase the SDA church in Chapter 5, the church, as it historically developed, became unattractive to these men who sought objectifications and representations of their greatness. During the 1960s for instance the church launched large campaigns against traditional objects, such as magical stones, because they were regarded as strengthening the 'heathen religion' (see Tonkinson 1981).

The churches on Ambrym today are manifestations of social communities, and of social 'wholes'. The church cannot be the manifestation of one man as an isolated person. Within the church there is no room for objectification referring to only one person's achievement, like the men's graded society, the *mage,* did. During those ceremonies, the sacrificed pigs, as well as the three-fern statues that were erected, pointed to one man and his greatness. The church on the other hand, both in contexts such as fund-raising events and markets, as well as in ceremonies such as the New Yam, does the opposite. I have outlined how men in traditional exchange contexts seek to eclipse the social whole in order to emerge as the one person who performs an exchange. Traditional ceremonies facilitated these kinds of performances, and in particular the ceremonies in the *mage* highlighted individual men's performances. Church-based ceremonies, such as fund-raising events and New Yam distributions, do not make room for these male practices. As I argued in the previous chapter, the church cannot serve as an arena for male accomplishment and promote individual men's greatness, because the church is based on a much more communal and egalitarian ideology. One might claim that the old ceremonies in the graded society focused on one particular person and eclipsed the total social whole, whereas the church does the opposite. In the New Yam ceremony, specific work relations are eclipsed and the focus turns toward the total social whole. I will claim that this ceremonial shift has drained the male ceremonial energy. Men today have lost interest in ceremonies as the New Yam, and perhaps the drinking and lack of ceremonial commitment is a result of this. There are few ceremonies left that provide a forum for male objectifications.

The church, as I argued, became an alternative movement in relation to the established male ceremonial practises. Although the repertoire of these ceremonies has decreased, there are still arenas for men to perform their greatness and achieve personal glory. However, this is not achieved in the church, because there are no specific relations within the church that are emphasized. The priest or the elder in the church can never achieve the position of a big man as men in the traditional graded society, the *mage*, did. The priest and the elder fill a rhetorical position. They speak in the church, but their roles do not, for instance, involve any control over amassed food, as did the role of the ceremonial performer in the *mage* or in other ceremonies. The priest and the elders in Ranon are not men of great reputation like men who have climbed the grades in the *mage*.

I will go further into this topic in the next two chapters. Here it suffices to emphasize that through the church one is not able to focus upon particular relations or particular persons. The ceremonial contexts outside of the church are generally talked about as *kastom,* and it is through *kastom* today on Ambrym that one can emphasize particular persons and relations. The conflict I described between an elderly woman and her son's wife illustrates this point well. As the young wife herself expressed, her husband's mother was too strong. In the end the wife did leave the village, and the old woman had to compensate her act of driving the wife away. She said to me that the only way she could do this was through *kastom*. Only through *kastom* could she compensate the young woman. She could not use the church as a framework for this event because the church has no means of objectifying or representing this particular relation. Through a *kastom* ceremony the old woman gave a pig, which she had bought from one of the few remaining *kastom* chiefs who still performs grade-taking ceremonies, to the girl's father.

One might say that *kastom* on Ambrym today provides for social reproduction in situations where 'cuts' in the network (M. Strathern 1996) have been created. The church cannot deal with such cuts in the network of the total social whole. On Ambrym today, men dominate *kastom*, both in talk about *kastom*, as well as in *kastom* ceremonies still being performed. *Kastom* is important to men because *kastom* provides objectifications and individual glory. This does not imply that women are not involved in *kastom*, as my reference to the old women who had to compensate her son's wife through a *kastom* ceremony shows. Rather *kastom* provides for male objectification and the church makes 'female' social wholes visible, but both men and women are participants in the church and performers of *kastom*. However, it is the case that men to a larger extent than women use *kastom*, and women, to a larger extent than men, participate in the church.

Chapter 7

From Churches to Councils and Cults

Alternative Social Movements and Female Agency

In the previous chapter I presented the church as an alternative movement in relation to the graded society. Whereas the graded society produced big men, the church produces communities. I have pointed out that this contrast between the church and the graded society is gendered. In this chapter I will continue this focus on the gendered distinction between the church and other social institutions such as the graded society and organizations from more recent history such as the politico-religious movement 'NaGriamel' and the Local Council.

I argued in the previous chapter that the shift between emphasizing the community, or the social whole, on the one hand, and the achievement of a particular person who eclipses the collective contributions – what we might call personifications (M. Strathern 1988, 177) – on the other, is particularly relevant in an analysis of the ceremonial economy on Ambrym. By the ceremonial economy I only imply here the ceremonies connected to life-cycle rituals, such as birth, puberty, marriage, and death ceremonies. During these ceremonies there is a constant shift in emphasis between the contributions of the whole community and the achievement of the key person of the ceremony. As I argued in relation to the *tauboan* ceremony and the bride-price ceremony in the previous chapter, in the ceremonial economy one might say that both aspects are present, and that the personification/male gendered aspect and the collective/non-personified and female gendered aspect alternate during the ceremony.

Other social institutions, such as the graded society and the church, have a different gender balance than these ceremonies. The church is dominated by the collective/non-personified and female gendered social from, whereas the graded society, as I will show in this chapter, is dominated by the personification/male gendered social from. This tension between the personal/male gendered aspect and the communal/female gendered aspect is central to my analysis of how other social institutions on Ambrym besides the ceremonial economy and the church, work. An understanding of the political development on the island after Independence, such as the development of the chief role, the operations of the Local Council (and later the Development Council), is also premised on the tension between gendered aspects of relationships. I will initially give a historically focused outline of how the Local Council and one of the most significant and interesting social movements to emerge during the period leading up to Independence, the NaGriamel, developed on Ambrym. Then, in the second part of the chapter, I analyse these movements in terms of this gendered distinction I have outlined.

Movements on Ambrym from the 1960s and Onwards

Understanding political developments on North Ambrym during the period leading up to Independence, from 1960 onward, requires analysis of movements other than the church movement. I believe that the NaGriamel movement represents a particularly interesting phenomenon of this period because of its paradoxical mixture of what I will call modernism and traditionalism. It was both a local movement with its own local social dynamic, which I will return to below, but it was from the beginning a large nationwide movement as well, originating on Santo in the northern part of the archipelago.

The NaGriamel movement was started as a reaction to land alienation by cattle farmers who had bought land from local people, and the word 'NaGriamel' was created from the Bislama names for two *kastom* leaves; the *namele* and the *nagria*. In its infancy the movement was based on the relation between two Santo men, Jimmy Stephens and a man called Chief Buluk. Jimmy Stephens grew up in Luganville and from early on lived in close association with the white presence on the island. Chief Buluk was a *kastom* chief from the interior of Santo who also experienced the struggle against land alienation at close hand. Chief Buluk and Jimmy Stephens provoked the expatriate land owners by settling on land that had been alienated. They established their own *kastom*-based community on an uncultivated bush area on Santo, naming it Tanafo.[1] They declared the 'Act of Dark Bush' in 1965, which stated that no colonial landlords could expand their lands further into the uncleared bush.

It was a rapidly growing community, and during the 1970s there were NaGriamel villages on most of the northern islands. Stephens had set up a system that made it possible for NaGriamel members from other islands to own land at Tanafo (see Beasant 1984). In Tanafo they built a huge *nakamal* [B: community house] for meetings, and NaGriamel supporters not only from Santo, but also from Ambrym, Malekula, Amabe, Paama, Maewo and Malo took part. The giant *nakamal* at Tanafo became a community *nakamal* for a movement with wide support in most of the northern islands. The movement also had a ceremonial ground under a great banyan tree. Here Stephens staged annual pig-killing ceremonies in order to climb the grades in the male society. Photographs in newspapers and elsewhere of Jimmy Stephens in front of the *nakamal* and under the Banyan tree became iconic for the movement as a whole. This was an image that reflected what I will call the traditionalism of the movement. I will argue that the NaGriamel movement was different from the general *kastom* movement. The traditionalism of the NaGriamel movement merged with an extreme search for modernism in the form of development. On the one hand, Jimmy Stephens and his people retrieved alienated land back to *kastom* owners, but on the other hand, they wanted to use this land themselves for building industry and developing business interests. They sought to establish a free state and a tax paradise in association with American business capital.

The NaGriamel grew into perhaps the most important, national oppositional movement in the 1970s and Stephens, despite his great disrespect for colonial churches, built his own church, which he called 'NaGriamel Federation Independent

---

1   Sometimes also called Fanafo or Vanafo.

United Royal Church'. Stephens was related to the monarchs from Tonga, being a descendant of a Scottish seaman and a Tongan princess, and the 'royal' of his church signified these connections (see also Beasant 1984). During the 1970s the movement on Santo established its own large Tanafo community, its own church and its own radio station that broadcasted NaGriamel programs. It is difficult to label NaGriamel as a specific kind of movement, since it had religious, political and economic ambitions. It is, however, safe to say that it was not a political party comparable to The National Party of the same time, which had won considerable support in the islands and fiercely advocated Independence. Rather, as Van Trease (1987, 163) puts it:

> NaGriamel was, to Jimmy Stephens, … a system for ordering Melanesian society based on custom which the government of Vanuatu – both the Condominium and a future independent government – had to recognize.

However, as I have pointed out, the *kastom* nostalgia of the NaGriamel movement also merged with a great appetite for modern production schemes and alliance with foreign, mostly American, business interests. This extreme form of traditionalism combined with the search for extreme development made the movement very different from the more moderate National Party led by the Anglican pastor, Father Walter Lini. As Miles (1998, 21) argues: 'Father Lini's organization spoke the modern language of nationalism and had wider appeal than Jimmy Stephens' Santo centred, traditionalism-grounded movement.'

After the late 1960s the NaGriamel movement was firmly established on North Ambrym as a significant movement in the area in addition to the church movement and the *kastom* movement. One might say that the heritage of persons like Malnaim and Magekon (see Chapter 5) represented in the *kastom* movement, and the heritage of Peter Ramel others represented in the church movement and, lastly, the anomaly NaGriamel, made up the dominant movements in the area. The relationship between them, and the different values and political views they advocated, came to influence not only the island of Ambrym, but also the formation of the new nation.

The Movements and the Chiefs

The different chiefs represented different movements. Bolton (1998b) has commented on the irony in the fact that chiefs today in Vanuatu are generally associated with *kastom* and traditional leadership, but they were in fact installed by the Presbyterian missionaries and later reinforced as local government on the islands of Vanuatu in the early colonial period by the Condominium government. The establishment of the position as chief was the first step in setting up a local government that culminated with the establishment of the Local Council in the late 1970s.

Scarr (1967a) has also pointed out how important the Presbyterian missionaries were in establishing a local government in the early colonial period. She argued that the reason why the Presbyterian missionaries were eager to organize such a local government was their belief that this would halt the influence of the French traders and recruiters.

This organization was a local government system, which initially applied to church members. It was based on meetings of the senior men of the community, who formed a court of trial of breaches of the moral code and petty offences (Scarr 1967a, 236).

Scarr further points out, 'whenever Christianity had a foothold, a local government of this sort was set up, with courts of whose decisions the missionaries or native teachers were the inspiration' (Scarr 1967a, 236). On Tanna for instance, the local government had great success and was given Condominium recognition in 1909 (Scarr 1967a, 243). However, in 1912 and subsequently on other islands, the local government on Tanna was altered in the sense that the chiefs were no longer chosen from among converts, but rather were representatives of the Condominium administration and were chosen from 'heathen' as well as Christian communities. Bolton (1998a) writes that the Condominium administration created offices they could use as entry points into the local community. The position as chief was one such office and the assessor was another. The assessor was to function as a consultant to the district agents, one British and one French. These district agents were the Condominium representatives who regularly toured the islands.

As I have outlined earlier, the Presbyterian mission on North Ambrym was not very successful in the late nineteenth and early twentieth centuries. Neither Charles nor William Murray, the first missionaries on the island representing the Presbyterian mission, had enough authority nor enough converts to organize a local government. They did try to ally themselves with locally respected men of high rank, but this was the cause of the mission's final isolation (see Chapter 5). It was the Condominium that, through its district agents, organised the chief system on Ambrym, although this was not very effective before the 1960s. Although these chiefs all got their formalized authority from being Condominium chiefs, the Ambrym chiefs were not so much an entry point into the local community the way the first chiefs elsewhere (as on Tanna) had been. The chiefs on Ambrym had their own agenda.

Firstly, there was the chief who was closely associated with the Presbyterian Church. Then there was the chief who relied on what was becoming increasingly important, namely *kastom* authority, implying that he was taking grades in the traditional male graded society, the *mage*. Then there was the chief who was associated with the NaGriamel movement. The reports written by the British District Agent [BDA] and his assistant [ABDA] after their tours on North Ambrym during this period reflect the difference between these chiefs and the conflicts between them. For instance, during a tour in 1969 (extract from tour notes by BDA Ambrym and Pentecost, 10–15 October 1969 from National Archives, NA):

> NaGriamel-rumours of Jimmy Stephens' visit are widespread and it is proposed that a 'station' be set up well above Olal. Chief Wilfred of Fonah is being criticised by the rest of the village for having joined Jimmy; Wilfred of course likes to keep one foot in each camp.

Chief Wilfred is repeatedly referred to in the BDA reports as a NaGriamel supporter. He was a charismatic leader and promoter of NaGriamel on Ambrym along with Olsen Kai, whom I will return to below. As in the national political arena, the local political arena was coloured by conflicts between NaGriamel and other movements. For instance, BDA Touring notes 15–21 October:

> ... had discussion with all the assessors and chiefs for this region. I pointed out that continued internal division and urging for power was getting the region nowhere ...

These conflicts reflect the tension that developed between the NaGriamel movement, the church movement and the *kastom* movement. The *kastom* movement during the 1960s and 1970s was advocated first and foremost by the famous Chief Tofor, son of the even more famous *kastom* Chief Tainmal. The two chiefs, father and son, were strongly opposed to the church and in particular the Presbyterian Church. In their rhetoric the two of them used *kastom* to oppose the actions and plans of the chiefs associated with the Presbyterian Church. To a certain extent Tainmal and Tofor continued the projects started by the high graded men in the *mage* in the 1880s. In the same way as Malnaim and Magekon, referred to in Chapter 5, renounced the church when they realized that there was no room for the development of their personal glory in this movement, Tainmal and Tofor in the 1960s and 1970s actively worked to counter the church and used the rhetoric of *kastom* in their work. Rio (2002a) has written on how these chiefs managed to appropriate the very concept of *kastom* and make it theirs in the sense that they had the authority, in every situation, to define what was right according to *kastom*. This was particularly so in relation to the carving industry which developed on North Ambrym as part of the tourism economy (see also Geismar 2005). Chief Tainmal, and later his son Chief Tofor, managed to create an image of themselves as the true *kastom* chiefs, and they were keen to stage ceremonies and take grades in the *mage*, often announcing it in advance, giving access to onlookers not only from neighbouring villages but also to visiting tourists. The Presbyterian chiefs, of whom Chief Willie in Ranmuhu was the most prominent, had constant arguments with Tainmal and Tofor. These chiefs played at allying themselves with others against each other, as noted for instance in BDA touring notes Tuesday 29–Sunday 25 January 1976:

> The alliance between the Catholic Olal supporters and Chief Tofor is not an uneasy one as it first seems though clearly Olal is using Tofor to counteract Willie and the N.P.'s influence.

Both Chief Willie and Chief Tofor garnered the support of the different district agents. When the dispute around rights to carving designs and the selling of carved products was at its peak, the British District Agent [BDA] and the French District Agent [FDA] were drawn into the conflict on different sides, the BDA supporting Chief Tofor and his father Tainmal by arguing the importance of preserving traditional culture and protecting it from degradation as a result of commercial abuse. The FDA was then taking the contrary stance, supporting the Christian carvers against the monopolistic claims of Tofor and Tainmal. In his touring notes from Ambrym 16–21 March 1967 the BDA Wilkins writes:

> Despite FDA's effort to oppose the chiefs agreement, the agreement that artefacts be made by those interested in accordance with their grades, is being adhered to ...

This agreement had been established after strong pressure on the BDA from Tofor and Tainmal. Once those with high grades controlled carvings, Tofor and Tainmal had great say in the carving production.

However, the alliances gradually shifted. The reports from the BDA become more and more sceptical in their description and assessment of, in particular, Chief Tofor. It almost seems as if the BDA got tired of Tofor and his campaign to advocate for himself as the only true *kastom* chief. A couple of years after the BDA had supported Tofor in his effort to control the carving production, he refers to Tofor's 'Napoleonic image build up' (BDA report 1969, NA), and portrays him as an obstacle to development and progress on the island.

The Development of the Local Council

In the early 1970s, the BDA initiated the organization of a Local Council on Ambrym. This was part of a policy from the Condominium government to prevent recruitment to the NaGriamel movement. The NaGriamel was seen as much more dangerous than the National Party and its advocates for independence. Bolton (1998b, 186) comments:

> During the 1970s the New Hebrides National Party, afterwards known as the Vanuaku Pati, was founded. This was an Anglophone party, committed to Independence, which was supported by the Protestant church and also, implicitly, the British Residency.

In other words, the National Party advocated for the kind of independence the British accepted. The NaGriamel however, was a movement much more beyond their control, with visions for the government of the country that did not match the British ideas. The NaGriamel and Jimmy Stephens had, on the other hand, the support of the French Residency (see Van Trease 1987). Almost like a natural law, the French Residency supported what the British resisted and vice versa. The formation of the Local Council was an attempt by the British to create a movement that could work as a counterpart to the NaGriamel movement, which, on Ambrym, it did. In the biannual report from 1964, the BDA writes the following:

> There is currently no other council operating but it appears that in North Ambrym there is considerable opinion in favour of the creation of a Local Council amongst the Presbyterian and SDA populations; it is hoped that other religious elements in the area can be persuaded to join in such an organization.

As we have seen, from the start the Condominiums' political recruitment was religiously motivated, in the sense that the BDA recruited among the Presbyterian adherents and the FDA among the Catholics, and both recruited among the non-Christians. When the BDA initiated the Local Council, the Catholics were opposed to it, and the other 'religious elements', which at this time probably included the NaGriamel,[2] opposed it as well. The non-convert community associated with Tainmal

---

2   The NaGriamel was sometime spoken of as a religious movement, mostly because of its association with Church of Christ communities on other islands such as Ambae. See Van Trease 1987.

and Tofor were equally reluctant. Four years later, there had been little progress in the development of the Local Council, and the Presbyterian chiefs became impatient, and wanted to go ahead without support from the other 'religious elements'. From the point of view of the British Residency and its district agents, the goal was to organize a Local Council with broad local support. In 1968 however, it seemed as if they were giving up hope of achieving this on Ambrym:

BDA report, North and West Ambrym, 9–14 September 1968, NA:
I spoke to the elders and the chiefs (in Ranon) ... and they all agreed to form a Local Council. They asked me if it is possible for only the Presbyterian Church from Ranon to Magam to form a Local Council. They said: it is no use waiting for the blind. Let us get started now; the one who is blind will follow the one who can see. But if we try to wait for the blind we shall wait for another 25 years. I told them that I can see their problem, it is quite true, but we shall keep trying. The Bullock and Stephens business is drawing everyone into their net so we have to ask both resident commissioners to persuade the people to form a Local Council.

And then three years later:

Annual report CD2, 1971, NA:
North Ambrym: A council was formed in this region in December 1971 with continued strong opposition from the NaGriamel supporters and less outspoken opposition from some Roman Catholic adherents who preferred to wait and see. Nonetheless, approximately half of the population from the region (1600) supported the council and a tax rate of $4 was proposed for 1972.

The Catholics during this period were also a social movement to be reckoned with, having a strong alliance with the French Residency, just as the Presbyterians had with the British. The Catholics were of course fighting against the Local Council in the same way, and as an ally of the *kastom* chiefs. The NaGriamel was not interested in forming a Local Council, which would work as an extended arm of the Condominium government, and it had already formed its own Local Council and set up a 'station', an area for NaGriamel supporters, in the interior of North Ambrym. The NaGriamel organization was creating a new society, and was not at all interested in cooperation with the Local Council, which had been created by the Condominium to work against them.

The *kastom* chiefs, the Catholics and the NaGriamel supporters had thus at times similar interests and seem to have created alliances, thus making the situation one of a Presbyterian versus a Catholic/*kastom*/NaGriamel position. The latter was not necessary pro-Independence either. The Catholics could not support the Independence scheme built up and controlled (on Ambrym) by Presbyterians in the National Party, and the NaGriamel and the *kastom* chiefs did not see the difference between the colonial and the independent state. Miles (1998, 66) points out:

Stephens and NaGriamel did not strive for independences for all of the New Hebrides – indeed they rejected the very notion of a New Hebridean political entity – but rather preferred to carve out an autonomous space for themselves ...

Their interests lay at another level. They were more concerned about the local situation, and argued that Condominium government or independent government would not matter so much. On Ambrym people told me that Chief Tofor, the *kastom* spokesman, did not work for Independence like the Presbyterian chiefs did either. However, it was important for him to make a firm stance against the Presbyterian chiefs, and in particular against Chief Willie, the Presbyterian chief who dominated the pro-Local Council work. He therefore engaged himself in a campaign against Chief Willie in national politics.

The Chief's Election

The New Hebrides and the Condominium government were planning the Independence that everyone knew would come. During the latter part of the 1970s, it was decided that chiefs should be elected to the Representative Assembly. The chiefs should contribute their knowledge of *kastom*, and on Ambrym this created more stirrings between the different movements. Lindstrom (1997) has argued that the specific qualifications for the chiefs who could commit their candidature was blurred and undefined, which again resulted in a local electoral process where anyone 'willing publicly to assume the status label and willing to confront anyone who might dispute his claim' (Lindstrom 1997, 215) was included among possible candidates.

On Ambrym however, two main alliances were created, mainly for or against the candidature of the Presbyterian Chief Willie from Ranmuhu. Chief Willie had been a central element in the foundation of the Local Council, and had been working closely with the BDA, first as an assessor and later as a chief (see also Bolton 1998b). Chief Willie was not originally from North Ambrym, but from West Ambrym. There are a number of people in North Ambrym who have relatively recent routes of origin going back to West Ambrym. These movements were caused by the volcanic eruptions in West Ambrym in 1913 and in 1951, but also by labour movement to the plantation in the North.

Chief Willie's father settled in North Ambrym as a pastor. He was the son of one of the early converts who had laboured in Queensland and brought the Gospel home. The main argument used against Chief Willie was that he did not know about *kastom*. He had not himself climbed the *mage*, nor had his father. Chief Tofor in Fanla, the main spokesman against Chief Willie's candidature, allied himself with the FDA and the Catholics in Olal, the neighbouring village to Ranmuhu, where Chief Willie was working as a chief. The Catholics were also opposed to Willie, of course, as he was a Presbyterian. The FDA and the Catholics however, used the same arguments as Tofor in their campaign against him. The NaGriamel seems to have been less visible in this dispute, but is mentioned in the reports as the 'Linbul faction' that boycotts the meetings. NaGriamel supporters were probably against the election on the same grounds as they opposed the Local Council.

In 1975 an election was held and Chief Willie won the majority of the votes. Tofor and the Catholics would not recognize the results, and started a new campaign.

The BDA report 1975:
The UCNH leaders [the francophone party dominated by Catholics, my comment] led by Tessa Fowler and Tofor visited the area and held public meetings to discuss the (…) chief's election. It is apparently being assumed by UCNH that another election will take place, and Tofor is already campaigning.

The BDA in his report in 1976 refers to both argumentative and conciliatory meetings. These meetings were always boycotted by one of the factions. At its peak, the Olal faction (the Catholics) and Tofor and his supporters wanted to evict Chief Willie and the other Presbyterians originally from West Ambrym who were living in Ranmuhu, and asked them to return to their place in the West. In an undated report, probably from 1976, the BDA reports:

There is still tension between the Magam, Olal and the NaGriamel at Linbul; a conciliatory meeting arranged for Monday the 12th December was not attended by the Olal and Linbul chiefs. There is a strong feeling of insecurity in the Magam community, and Willie Bongmatur is supervising the construction of a house and the planting of gardens at Dip Point (the Magam people's traditional land), which suggests that he is seriously afraid that his people will be expelled from the north.

Chief Willie, at one point, did actually agree to withdraw his candidature in return for being allowed to remain in North Ambrym (BDA report January 1976), but eventually took the chance of going to the Assembly meeting on Malekula where his candidature for the Representative Assembly was suggested. At this meeting, described by Bolton (1998b) based on interviews with Chief Willie, the different factions, mainly fronted by Chief Tofor and Chief Willie, argued once more. Tofor again claimed that Chief Willie could not be elected because he was not a *kastom* chief. He had not entered the *mage* society that was the traditional way of earning power and respect. Chief Willie argued back that it was his forefathers who had returned from Malekula with the rights to the *mage* grades, and that Chief Tofor's forefathers had bought these rights from Chief Willie's line.

Chief Willie was eventually elected, but on his return to Ambrym he was met with great opposition and new threats of eviction. In the forthcoming development, as the nation was becoming independent, Chief Willie became a major person on the national level, contributing to the drafting of the constitution as well as being elected as the Chief of the Malvatumauri, the national council of chiefs. This, according to Lindstrom (1997a, 214), was an expression of 'local attempts to reproduce at the national level the sorts of joint conclaves and assemblies of elders and leaders that people regularly convene within their villages and regions'. The Malvatumauri subsequently developed as an advisory body on matters of *kastom* to the National Assembly. Chief Willie moved to Port Vila and lived there with his family until the late 1990s when he retired as the Chief of the Malvatumauri and returned to Ambrym. He was still faced with opposition here, however, and when we last visited him in 2000, he had moved back to Port Vila and was not planning on a return to Ambrym.

NaGriamel on Ambrym

Although the NaGriamel movement on Ambrym was initially part of the wider NaGriamel movement with its headquarter on Santo, the local faction on Ambrym gradually developed into a movement based on local people and local ideas, and in the end as a separate organization which broke off its ties to the mother organization on Santo.

When the NaGriamel movement was in its infancy and was building its headquarters in Tanfao, Santo, Olsen Kai, an Ambrym man with strong beliefs and ideas for the future, was elected as Secretary, and was responsible for all the paperwork for the organization. I met with Olsen Kai in Port Vila in June 2000, and he gave me the story of how the NaGriamel on Ambrym developed:

> The NaGriamel started in 1960, and it was started in order to give a voice to the ground the white man had stolen. They started talking about ground. There were six men. I was at the time a member of the Sabbath mission, the SDA. They held a meeting in Santo, and I was called for. They asked me if I wanted to come and have the job as a secretary. I went to Santo. I worked there for a long time.

From early on, Olsen Kai had ambitions for the NaGriamel movement to manage its own production and to form alliances with international organizations, which could in due time support their own independence claim. Olsen Kai worked for an independence that was not based on a nation-state, but on the NaGriamel organization. The idea of the nation-state never appealed to him because in his view it would only be a continuation of the same social order as under the Condominium. The social system he worked to implement, first in Tanafo and later on Ambrym, was based on self-sustained local communities such as the Tanafo community on Santo. When asked if he wanted a return to a sort of pre-colonial social formation on the islands, he argued that what he wanted was for local people to take control of social development. He argued that he was not a *kastom* man, but more a promoter of new ideas on how to organize local production. When he sought international alliances it was to achieve recognition of his ideas for the future of the islands. He was not seeking capital for international investment, which was what the association between Stephens and American business interests, primarily represented by Michael Oliver of the so-called Phoenix Foundation, sought to achieve. Olsen Kai argued strongly against involving foreigners in local production. His goal was to create a production apparatus that the local people themselves controlled. On this point however, his ideological partnership with Stephens started to crack. Olsen Kai himself recounts what happened when he broke away from the NaGriamel in Tanafo:

> Then there were trouble in the NaGriamel. The leader of the NaGriamel was a rebel in the New Hebrides. They said [the leader, Jimmy Stephens and his group, my comment] that I was breaking down the work of the NaGriamel. I held the office in six years and then, after six years, they kicked me out in 24 hours. I lost everything. I lost big money; I lost the tractor, and all the work tools, all the peanuts which belonged to my people. We had big harvest. So, I lost everything.

> When I returned to Ambrym I had realized that the work of the NaGriamel was no good.
> I built my own office. It had broken away from the NaGriamel now. I worked here. I
> was not a big leader in the NaGriamel, but I built my own office. I did not want to get
> involved with the business of Jimmy Stephens, because I knew that Jimmy Stephens
> would bring the office into trouble. I wanted that my office should be clean. And when I
> left for Ambrym I brought with me every book, every register. I have two big books with
> all the 23,000 members in the New Hebrides, the constitution, everything. I took it and
> went to Ambrym.

Although Olsen Kai broke away from the NaGriamel and Stephens, he retained its
ideological platform. As Van Trease (1987) has argued, Stephens' NaGriamel was
not a political party, but a system for ordering society. Van Trease visited Stephens'
Tanafo-based society and argued:

> From discussion with Jimmy Stephens and observations made during a visit to Tanafo, it
> was clear that NaGriamel was more than a figment of his imagination. It was physically
> well organized and included an office complex and meeting hall and several well-developed
> agricultural projects including forestry, oil palm and peanut production. (1987, 163)

In addition, Olsen Kai's movement on Ambrym was not only visionary, but also
realized many of NaGriamel's ambitions, ideas and agricultural projects. In essence,
Olsen Kai simply transferred or copied the whole movement as it existed on Santo
to Ambrym. He organized headquarters, wanted to buy and clear a special area of
land where he could organize agricultural production, and he organized different
committees responsible for different parts of the operation.

In my interview with Olsen Kai, he proceeded to talk about his ideas and what
his vision had been for the Ambrym NaGriamel. He argues for the importance of
local production, instead of imports. The country keeps importing rice instead of
producing its own food, he kept repeating. On Ambrym he raised funds for tools
and tractors and cleared areas for local production. However, he pointed out that he
never got any help from the Condominium government, nor from the Independent
government.

> The government is not working for the people in the country. We never got any help from
> any of the governments. I was a leader but I never received any help. They looked upon
> me as dirt. If I wanted money for any of the projects, I never received anything.

Olsen Kai had big ambitions, and he talked of how communal production would
create new societies, external to the state. Many had somehow given up the idea of
having the power to influence the national proceedings, at least Olsen Kai and his
movement on Ambrym had given it up. Although the Ambrym NaGriamel movement
was described as a political party in many of the district agent's reports, Olsen Kai's
ambitions were not linked to the new independent state and national politics. The
NaGriamel movement on Santo, however, was still a part of national politics and
Jimmy Stephens was elected to the Representative Assembly (Van Trease 1987), but
Olsen Kai concentrated on Ambrym, and his vision of an ideal community there.

There has not been much written on the NaGriamel movement (but see Miles
1998; Van Trease 1987; Beasant 1984), and very little on the internal dispute and

the rivalry between Olsen Kai and Jimmy Stephens. Van Trease (1987), however, mentions that there had been questions regarding Jimmy Stephens's use of funds, and that money intended for development projects was used in order to promote Stephens himself, and then also notes 'Olsen Kai – a rival from Ambrym – … used finance and other issues to strengthen his position vis-à-vis Jimmy Stephens's (Van Trease 1987, 165). Olsen Kai did not approve of Stephens's use of funds from abroad and he did not approve of Stephens's way of spending money. It was most likely these issues that led to Olsen Kai's eviction. He became too much of a threat to Jimmy Stephens, both with his financial inquiries as well as his charismatic leadership qualities. Olsen Kai is a great agitator and speaker and must have been a useful man for recruiting supporters to the movement, but not very useful when his speeches turned against Jimmy Stephens himself.

Olsen Kai then returned to Ambrym and realized his visions for a better community by creating his own movement. In the interview Olsen Kai talked proudly about what he called the 'peanut factory' he had established on Ambrym. He had a grand production scheme that would make the NaGriamel movement on Ambrym able to export peanuts and make a lot of money. It was working perfectly, he said, and great prospects lay ahead. In the BDA report from a tour in August 1976, the District Agent writes:

> Olsen talked to me of various things. He has now re-named Ambrym, NA Griamel, NH Native Custom United Council Opposition Party, and has organized committees on West and North to supervise social, financial, and political activities. He has cash problems at the moment, especially his payment of the tractor loan from Santo, but has started ambitious agricultural projects up in the bush behind Linbul, including potatoes and peanuts. He is very anti-Stephens, anti-UCNH and professes to be pro-Local Council, only he is thinking in very loose alliance, without financial assistance.

Olsen Kai's Ambrym-based NaGriamel movement was well organized into different committees all over the island. He told me that during this time NaGriamel on Ambrym had over a thousand members, most of them recruited from his own place Linbul and from the SDA communities of which he himself had been a part. Chief Wilfred from Fonah, a neighbouring village, was considered Olsen Kai's second in command at this time. Another report from 1975 gives an impression of their very visible presence on Ambrym:

> **Report from North Ambrym tour 1975:**
> Na-Griamel activity: While I was sitting at the council headquarters at Magam, a group of about six people, led I think by one Wilfred, came ostentatiously and loudly past carrying their NaGriamel leaves and wearing their party t-shirts. They were reluctant to tell where they were going and for what purpose, and it seemed likely that this was a mere show of strength. It was reported that NaGriamel were planning to set up a rival council on North Ambrym, with an annual tax of ten dollars a person (they may have no difficulty in extracting this amount from rabid supporters, but I fear others might be understandably reluctant to contribute) In any case they could not receive any condominium support…

The leaves referred to in this report are *kastom* leaves, probably the croton *liha* or *lira* used in ritual performances connected to the *mage*, and used by the NaGriamel on Ambrym to mark their ideals of *kastom* as the fundamental moral code which could govern society without the interference of outside forces.

Olsen Kai's idea was a radical one. He wanted to build an Ambrym community on its own terms, without the interference of the colonial or the independent government, and as the BDA reports above, the government never supported the NaGriamel movement, neither on Santo nor on Ambrym. It seems as if Olsen Kai and his NaGriamel movement on Ambrym managed without Condominium support. However, after Independence when the Lini government was in power, this movement was becoming a threat. In his interview Olsen Kai outlines:

> I worked for six years in Ambrym. I came in 1975 and worked until 1982. In October 1980 the Lini government sent 400 people to beat me and my people. They killed 13 men. I got my limp leg.

I have heard other stories on Ambrym about this event. The police from the capital arrived and people fled into the bush. Beasant (1984) describes how the Vanuatu Mobile Force visited several of the northern islands in 1980 after a rebellion among the NaGriamel members on Santo. When the Independent government was elected, it was in many respects a defeat for the NaGriamel movement that had opposed the National Party and its leader Father Walter Lini. During the Santo rebellion the night of 28 May 1980 NaGriamel supporters had marched against the government, clapping hands and shouting threats. This had escalated when the police threw tear gas grenades and fights broke out. People fled from their homes, and gardens and empty houses were smashed and destroyed. As part of the 'mopping up' operation after the Santo rebellion in August 1980, the military visited islands other than Santo as well. According to Beasant (1984, 141):

> Arriving on the island of Ambrym on October 20th, they spent three days interviewing people in the western and northern part of the island and arresting the total number of 507 suspects, all of whom were shipped to the prison at Lakatoro on Malekula.

After this the NaGriamel movement on Ambrym was no longer so loud and visible, and Olsen Kai moved to Port Vila, which was where I met him in July 2000.

The NaGriamel on Ambrym as a (Cargo) Cult

Van Tease (1987) has shown links between NaGriamel and earlier cargo cults on Santo. These movements, from the early part of the 1900s, were established in the context of European land alienation. Stories of large ships arriving to deport the white men were circulating, and one cult leader on Santo urged people to destroy their gardens and houses, live communally and share women in the advent of the ships.

To some extent one might argue that the NaGriamel movement had cargo cultic characteristics in its emphasis on the new wealth and the new system. There are, however, ambivalences in applying this concept. Lindstrom (1993a), in his outline of the genealogy of this concept, has argued that anthropologists adopted the tem cargo cult from the missionaries and colonial administrators in the 1940s, and transformed the practises described from being 'madness' to something specifically Melanesian. In the anthropological discourse on cargo cults, cargo has come to represent not so much Melanesian cravings for Western commodities, as Melanesian desire for equality and independence, according to Lindstrom. In the 1980s and 1990s the term cargo cult was deconstructed altogether, because of its derogatory connotations and because it was argued that the term classified different phenomena altogether. Cultic practices were seen to be something not only related to desire for cargo, but as part of a Melanesian religiosity. Lindstrom (1993, 60) argues that the anthropological conclusion was:

> Melanesians ordinarily expect and strive to change their lives in a total and disjunctive manner. The cult is a normal institution of social innovation,

and,

> Melanesians ordinarily conduct politics along cultic lines. Big men and prophets, as leaders, share similar political interests, characteristics, and strategies.

Lindstrom sees the danger in equating what has been described as cargo cults with general Melanesian sociality. Jebens (2005) as well has pointed out that the term 'cargo cult' has become such a problematic analytic category that different writers have suggested the concept be abandoned altogether (see, for instance, Hermann, 1992, 69).

Although I appreciate this reflexive awareness of the use of the concept, the imposing of a self-other dichotomy, and the concept's problematic heritage, I think that the concept might still have a mission. In my analysis of Ambrym social organization I have repeatedly pointed to the alternation between different, gendered social formations. As a category that, on a very general level, refers to movements that break away from ordinary sociality and create, for a period, an alternative and often contrasting social organization, the term 'cargo cult' might be useful. There are of course other movements that also break away from ordinary sociality, periodically or on a more established basis, that are not cargo cults. The establishment of the church, as I described in Chapters 5 and 6, can be seen as one such alternative movement without, of course, being about cargo. I do think however that by recognizing the 'alternativeness' of the cargo cult, the problem of associating it with 'ordinary' Melanesian sociality is to some extent solved. It is obvious, but perhaps useful, to point out that cargo movements, like other alternative movements, are developed not as something 'ordinary', but rather 'extraordinary'. Extraordinary movements seek to carve out a new, autonomous space for sociality which is external to everyday social life. There is a power in such movements to confront the values on which the everyday life is governed, either by purifying these values, highlighting them and elaborating on them in new contexts, which one might say is the case with the graded society as I will show below, or inverting them, turning them upside down, and thus challenge them, as I have argued for the church. Cargo movements achieve this.

An understanding of the NaGriamel movement and the development of the Local Council might also be developed along these lines.

Social Movements Compared

The graded society, the NaGriamel and the local council

In previous chapters I described how the church played on a different gender logic than the *mage* society. Along the same lines I will argue that in order to understand the social form of the NaGriamel and the Local Council, this notion of alternative movements playing on contrasting gender logics, must be part of the analysis. I want to show how the different movements on Ambrym since the 1960s can be understood as different gendered principles of sociality working against each other. I have already shown how this works in the case of the church and I now, in the rest of this chapter, want to include both the NaGriamel movement and the Local Council in this analysis. Before entering into a discussion of these movements however, I will outline my understanding of the workings of the graded society and the way the ceremonies connected to the *mage* society were gendered. This analysis of the graded society will then work as a comparative background for an analysis of the newer movements.

I have briefly pointed out before that the male graded society was the most important social institution for creating a person with a great reputation and respect. Through climbing the hierarchy of the *mage,* one achieved personal glory. I will argue that the male graded society existed in a certain sense outside the wider community, and the principles that governed it did not govern the general ceremonial economy on Ambrym. My view of the graded society is of course coloured by the fact that very few are still active in the *mage,* and that these, mostly elderly men, seem perhaps even more isolated and part of a social reality that did not concern the majority of people in the villages. However, I believe that the grades in the *mage* and the goods that circulated within this male society were in fundamental contrast to the egalitarian ethos of everyday life. Whereas the general ceremonial economy, in for instance marriage ceremonies, is based on emphasis placed upon both the person who performs the ceremony as well as the collective who contributes, the ceremonies in the graded society to a greater extent glorified the person who climbed the grades. The male gendered practices of objectification and personification dominated the ceremonies of the *mage.* The ceremonies were conducted for the sole purpose of achieving a new grade, a new name and new objectification of this. The *mage* consisted of thirteen (Rio 2002a) to fifteen (Patterson 1981) individually named grades. Each grade involved payment in the form of pigs, live and dead (see Rio 2002a for detailed account of each grade). For the highest grade, of which there existed three variants all called *mal,* 40 pigs were required. Tree fern images were carved for each grade, and roofs were erected above the statues. When the candidate climbed up on the roof, he literally climbed the *mage.*

It was generally known on Ambrym that *mage* was a relatively recently introduced ritual concept, and Patterson (2002) estimates the arrival of the *mage* between the seventeenth and eighteenth century, and even in the early twentieth century men from Ambrym still travelled to Malekula in order to be initiated into grades in the *mage*. However, according to Patterson (1981, 2002), before the introduction of the *mage*, another variant of the graded society existed on Ambrym, which was to a greater extent part of the kinship structure, building on the principles of making tributes to the mother's place, and the idea of the three places[3]. These ceremonial institutions were called *berang yanyan* and *fenbi*. These ceremonies involved ritual 'shooting' of the father and the father's father, who were mourned by the spectators, and payments were made to the 'deceased's' mother's place. This was a way of securing regeneration of life and the continuity of kinship structures. When the 'killers' compensated for the blood that was lost by killing boars to the mother's place, focus was placed on women as carriers of blood and the importance of attributing offerings of food and pigs to her natal group. By doing this, the 'path' was opened for the next generation, and intermarriage between the two places could continue. Because the shooting was only pretended, and the father turned back to life, one might claim that the rite made the 'candidates' realize that the relation to the mother's place was life-giving. According to Patterson, these ceremonies also involved grade-taking, killing of pigs and erection of tree fern statues. This last aspect of this ceremonial complex caused Patterson to argue that, 'Far from secular, these rites in North Ambrym were the creative basis of ontological and cosmological ideas as well as the means of status differentiation between individuals and group' (2002, 128). The competitive aspect of the *berang yanyan* and the *fenbi* ceremonies were then replaced by the *mage*.

There seems to be little left of the *berangyanyan* and *fenbi* parts of the ritual, because *mage* today is not tied to the structure of the kinship system, and is not centred on repaying maternal relatives. The powers that were achieved in the *mage* seem to have been beyond any everyday matter. The ceremonies of the *mage* were not, as with the older rituals Patterson has studied, part of the kinship payments, but existed as a separate sphere of ceremonial exchange. The vital matters in the *mage* were not related to the vital matters of kinship, namely, repaying maternal blood. Rather, the vital matter of the *mage* was to glorify the performer who reached a new level of fame. The special character of the *mage* ceremonies, in contrast to the general ceremonial economy on Ambrym, was emphasized by its secrecy, and the way the ceremonies were conducted in places secluded from the female gaze. It was almost as if the participants had to hide to perform these ceremonies because of the shamelessness of fixating on one person's glory.

The graded society as an extra-ordinary movement

There is a lot of regional literature on the relationship between participants in the graded society of northern Vanuatu and their political ambitions outside of it (Allen 1981; Blackwell 1981; Patterson 1981, 2002). Blackwell has argued that:

---

3   The three places: the place of the *wuren*, the *mukuen* and the *gemalsul*. See Chapter 2 for an outline and discussion of this.

the graded society is a competitive domain in which participation, both on one's own account and in supporting others, offers advantages to the political ambitious which are not otherwise available (1981, 40).

This is in line with the general view of the relationship between the graded society and the wider society (Allen 1981; Patterson 1981). The graded society is seen as an institution creating community leaders, and legitimacy is achieved by climbing the graded society. Blackwood, for instance, argues, '…participation in the hierarchy, and especially in its higher echelons, gives a leader access to and potential control over the principal resources of the society: pigs and rank' (1981, 40). He thus implies that control of pigs in the graded society gave access to control of ceremonies outside of the graded society. This might not necessarily have been the case on Ambrym. The other ceremonies which were not part of the *mage* complex were not of the same kind as those of the *mage*. I will argue that there is a great difference between the ceremonial economy of the *mage* and the ceremonial economy outside of it. Ceremonies connected to circumcision, 'bride price' payments, or death payments for instance, are of another social order. Whereas the ceremonies of the *mage* were centred on creating one big name and celebrating this, the ceremonies outside the *mage* expose the successful creation of group alliance. In order to highlight the difference between the ceremonies in the *mage* and other ceremonies and what I perceive to be a lack of continuity between them, I will briefly outline the patterns of contributions to ceremonies outside the *mage*.

Payments from the groom's side to the bride's side in a marriage, for instance, involve dividing people into sides. The premises on which groups are divided, such as into bride's side and groom's side, is not a process persons with high grades in the *mage* can control. There are a number of *buluim* in any particular area, and during a marriage these *buluims* are grouped into two distinct sides, and this division is based on a number of factors. During the marriage in Ramvetlam described in Chapter 4, the division of people into sides seemed to be a matter of practical circumstances. I argued in Chapter 2 that the North Ambrym kinship system works in such a way that people always have a number of potential links, or roads, to follow to other persons. One often has to choose to follow the mother's line or the father's line, and sometimes one follows neither because of one's own marriage, which has changed relationships to certain people. When a couple get married and people have to decide which side they will take part in – the bride's side and give presents or the groom's side and contribute to the 'bride price' – it is a matter of what relationship one emphasizes. In the Ramvetlam marriage I noticed that a woman, Serah, whom I considered to be a classificatory sister of the groom, decided to contribute to the bride's presents instead of contributing to the 'bride price' as people on the groom's side usually do. She told me that usually she followed her husband's line when she related to other people in Ranon and the neighbouring villages (such as Ramvetlam) because she had married into his place. The bride who was to marry the Ramvetlam man was, however, a classificatory sister of hers following her line through her father. Moreover the bride was from the same place as Serah. Serah therefore decided to follow another line than the one through her husband, and she ended up contributing to the bride's presents. Origin route is therefore one relevant factor in decision-making about group divisions.

Contributions to payments are received from a great number of people. When the groom's father, who is normally in charge of presenting the payment, signals that he is about to stage a payment ceremony, contributions come from where he himself has previously contributed to the same sort of ceremonies. Furthermore, people who are classificatory brothers or sisters of both the bride and the groom through crossing kinship ties (following the mother's 'line', the groom is classificatory brother, but following father's 'line', the bride is classificatory sister) can choose which party to join.

Thus, payments of these kinds, whether 'bride price' payments or payments to a boy's maternal uncles in a circumcision ceremony, are always a matter of collective work, exposing the side of the groom as one group and the side of the bride as another. These alliances are shifting, and on another occasion other alliances are created. In ceremonies like this, focus is only momentarily on the achievement of the person who stages the ceremony, and the collective contributions are just as visible.

There is no transference of authority from the *mage* ceremony to a ceremony outside of the *mage*, such as in a marriage ceremony. Those who had a high grade in the *mage* could not use their fame in any way that would influence their position in other ceremonies. As I have shown, other factors are important when ceremonies outside the *mage* are conducted.

The difference between the *mage* ceremonies and other ceremonies on North Ambrym then is tied to the way they are gendered. The *mage* ceremonies, I will claim, were dominated by a male social form; the personification. The relations to those who had contributed were fully eclipsed. Other ceremonies, connected to the kinship ethos, are both male and female gendered by the way the emphasis on personifications and collectivity alternates. On the one hand, the kinship-based ceremonial economy is centred on the creation of sides and distributions between them. On the other hand there is always one person who seems to be able to manage this distribution. This person, however, is not the sole focus of the ceremony. During a *mage* ceremony the person who achieves a new grade is the main actor and this image is not disturbed by the presence of women and other villagers who receive shares of the prestation. The *mage* ceremony is about creating one big and famous name.

We can see the graded society as a purification of the value of personification. Through ceremonies in the *mage*, a key value in everyday social life, namely the ability to stand out as a representation of many and make one's name famous and glorified, is singled out and emphasized. Whereas in everyday life there is a constant shift in focus, the image of the *mage* big man remains almost frozen.

The graded society compared to other ritual cults

Harrison (1985) has discussed how the male hierarchical cult among the Avatip on the East Sepik of New Guinea, operated on a different cultural logic than the secular society. He argued for the existence of two different socio-cultural domains, one ritual and the other non-ritual, or everyday and secular. In a non-ritual context, in matters of kinship for instance, the fundamental ideology is one of equality. The male ritual works as its antithesis. Instead of talking about different domains, such as the political domain of the male cult and the domestic domain of gender relations for instance, Harrison argued that these are different forms of social action. The social action that dominates production, for instance, is one of equality. On Ambrym as well, gardening for example involves cooperation between the spouses. Husband and wife work together with the clearing, planting and harvesting, with the exception of the planting of yams, which is an exclusively male activity. The hierarchy of the male cult does not affect the egalitarian principles that govern the productive work. High-ranking men have no coercive power or any other ways of influencing younger men or women in relation to production. Production of garden crops is also to a very limited degree convertible into pigs that are used to pay for grades in the *mage*. Pigs are usually contributed by affinal relatives in an intricate network of debt relations.

Nor does the hierarchy of the *mage* affect the marriage alliance. Daughters and sons of high-ranking men can marry daughters or sons of low-ranking men, without rank even being a subject of discussion. Rank in the men's graded society is as irrelevant for marriage as it is for production. Other kinship-based activities also seem to be totally unaffected by the hierarchy of the *mage*. The continuing obligation to repay maternal relatives, for instance, is a moral code that does not discriminate on the bases of high or low grades in the *mage*. Every man, whether he is *mal*[4] or not, is obliged to make payments to his mother's brother (see also Patterson 1981). The hierarchical value present in the social action of the *mage* does not create any political power. Power within the hierarchy, which gives persons of high rank the ability to influence who this grade should be transferred to and for how many pigs, etc., is only to a very limited degree transferable to the form of social action that takes place outside the male hierarchy.

Harrison argued, concerning the Avatip, that the only power achieved by men in these hierarchical cults is the 'power to constitute, occasionally and for limited periods, an altered social reality in which women and junior males, are subordinate to them' (1985, 419). I will argue that this was also the power of the high-ranking men on Ambrym. During the rituals of the *mage* on Ambrym, women were subordinate in the sense that they were excluded altogether, whereas junior men were subordinate either because they had not yet entered the society or had lower grades. The power of the high men in the hierarchy then was the power to create an external social reality, or what I have called above, a social order with another gender balance. It is the power to constitute this external social order that is the real power of the men in the hierarchy. However, this external social reality never altered the social reality of everyday life. It existed as a purified version of it, outside of it.

The NaGriamel compared to the graded society

I understand Olsen Kai's NaGriamel movement on Ambrym as an effort to create an external sociality. Building on *kastom* while doing this – for instance wearing the leaves referred to in the BDA report above and, as they did on Santo, building a huge

---

4   *Mal*; L: highest grade in the *mage*. The name is used as a suffix or prefix to a person's name, as in Tainmal.

Nakamal as an icon of the organization – makes a symbolic connection between this new social reality and the social reality of the *mage* society of the past. Moreover, the way NaGriamel was organized on Ambrym has certain hierarchical dimensions that, as I explained above, are not what dominate the normal productive life on Ambrym. The NaGriamel was organized into collective productive units, with leaders and committees with different responsibilities, instead of the conjugal productive partnership. Of course, this comparison between the *mage* and the NaGriamel movement is limited. The NaGriamel did not intend to become the graded society, but perhaps aimed at replacing it. As far as I am aware, the NaGriamel movement was mainly a movement for men without any significant participation of women. As I outlined in Chapter 6, the chances for men today to engage in practices which give them the opportunity to emphasize their own person, and to create objectifications pointing back to their own greatness, creating manhood in other words, are decreasing. The church has become the new ceremonial arena.

One might see the church in the early phase I described in Chapter 5, as an external movement as well. This movement was not purifying the value of personification, however, but radically challenging it. The church thus not only became an extraordinary movement as it developed a hundred years ago, but also an alternative movement. This movement enforced a major historical shift by challenging the dominant male gendered value. Today the church is no longer creating an external reality. The church has become the baseline reality, making the *mage* society peripheral. Men, then, are not as active in the church as women are, and if they are active, it is often as a priest or elder, the only roles giving a certain degree of personal greatness. The NaGriamel movement on Ambrym can be understood within this framework, as an attempt to reclaim the dominating value of the personification at a time when the male hierarchy was vanishing and the church became dominant. Within the NaGriamel movement, male leaders rose and shone in the glory of the movement, like Olsen Kai or Wilfred of Fona, referred to in the BDA reports cited above. These men had established themselves in positions of authority comparable to Tainmal. Theirs was a position of authority within the movement, just as Tainmal's was in the *mage*. In the same way as Tainmal controlled the grades in the *mage*; Olsen Kai controlled the implementation of his grand scheme of local production. The Presbyterian chiefs however, like Chief Willie, had problems in getting that kind of authority, because they operated within the social reality of the church and the Local Council, where there was no room for any *one* person to fill such a position of authority.

The council compared to the graded society and the NaGriamel

What about the Local Council? Can the Local Council be seen as an effort to constitute an extraordinary social movement, the way I have argued that both cultic practices, such as the *mage* hierarchy or the NaGriamel movement, have achieved?

I will argue that in the beginning, in the 1970s, the Local Council operated within the structures of the church, and was not about constituting an arena for the display of great personalities, like the *mage* and the NaGriamel. The Local Council operated on the social form and values established by the Presbyterian Church, as my outline of the process leading up to the establishment of the Local Council above reveals. Therefore, on the one hand, the Local Council was not creating an extraordinary social reality on the local level, because it built on the social relations of the church and the church was by then, in the 1970s, well established. It was the chiefs representing the Presbyterian Church who were the driving force of the council. These chiefs had only limited ability to operate as the main person of the council. The social structure on which the council operated was more gender-balanced, emphasizing the communal aspect. The Local Council even had female representation. Although the chiefs, who were elected members of the council, represented the people of the church, this was only a one-way relationship. The Presbyterian chiefs did not have the kind of power that men in the male hierarchy achieved, controlling others' access to the grades within the society. The Presbyterian chiefs could only represent, but never control, anyone's access to such things as participating in the church, which was the social basis for the council. The Local Council then, operating on the structures of the church and the Presbyterian chiefs, did not constitute an external social reality like the *mage* or the NaGriamel, because the social relations within the council operated on the already-established relations of the church, which, as I have outlined earlier, gave access to both women and younger men and can be regarded as an egalitarian institution creating social communities and signifying historical place identities.

On the other hand, however, the Local Council represented the state apparatus within the local community, in a new and direct way. The Local Council was at the outset part of the state apparatus. It was created as the Condominium government's local alibi, and as an extension of what the chief's role had been in past decades; an entry point into the local community (Bolton 1998b). Although the British were also preparing the islanders for Independence and trying to create administrative structures that would work when they withdrew, they were structures that were invested with the idea of a state. One might perhaps say that internally the Local Council worked on the pre-established structures of the church, and did not create an extraordinary movement representing a reality outside of everyday life. Externally however, when the Local Council operated as part of the wider national administrative apparatus, it created new roads and new opportunities for the chiefs of the island to become part of a wider social reality. Chief Willie Bongmatur, referred to above as the Presbyterian chief who worked for the Local Council and who always opposed the *kastom* Chiefs Tofor and Tainmal, used this opportunity that was created by the Local Council and entered into the national political reality.

Inscribing Movements: Alternative Social Realities

I have in Chapter 5 described the church and the graded society as opposing social forms, the first female and the latter male, and in this chapter I have described other social movements which have inscribed themselves on the social reality on Ambrym by taking different forms. These movements, the NaGriamel and the Local Council, have with varying degrees of success constituted what I have called extraordinary social movements. The Local Council only succeeded at this at the national level, making way for members of the council into national politics, and the NaGriamel had success only for a limited period, before it was violently finished. The mission movement in the previous century was first an extraordinary movement, allied with the men of the *mage*. Building on the structures of the *mage* society, the church was seen as another context in which the value of personification could be expressed and purified. Later it became an alternative movement seriously challenging this dominant value. Today the values of the church are the dominating values of everyday life. Other movements have thus challenged these values, as the NaGriamel movement did.

Historically and today, movements break out of everyday life to either challenge or to purify the values on which routine life is governed. As I showed in this chapter, the *mage* movement can be seen as an example of a purifying movement emphasising the gendered value of personification. The NaGriamel was perhaps a late attempt at regaining the domination of this value in a period when the church had become the main institution of society. One might thus see these movements as competing social realties. Sometimes, when these movements turn into alternative movements challenging the values of society, they become a threat to the wider community. The mission movement headed by Murray in the previous century was one such movement, and Murray was therefore sanctioned and driven off the island. The NaGriamel was another such movement, and was therefore violently crushed in the early 1980s.

Chapter 8

On Council, Development and Leadership

From Local Council to Lolihor Development Council

In this chapter I continue my analysis of how different social movements and organizations on North Ambrym operate, now focusing on the Lolihor Development Council. In the analysis of this council I give particular attention to how leadership in this council has developed and compare it to other organizations, past and present, in terms of the gendered distinction I have outlined in the previous chapters.

When I arrived in Ranon in 1995, the Local Council that operated in the Ranon district in the 1970s had become the LDC [Lolihor Development Council] and was directed not only towards the national government and administration, but also was involved in the global world of NGOs and donor organizations. The state administration works as a facilitator in the process of writing project proposals and strategic plans or mediating between donor agencies and the local development council. In particular the National Planning Office and the Department of Local Government are involved. The British BDA, in his effort to give the local council broad support in the 1970s predicted this development and wrote in his report:

> **Touring notes 8–13 December 1974, NA box 19**
> During the North Ambrym local council meeting which was attended by the NaGriamel committee and the custom villages led by Chief Tofor, I suggested ... that all groups opposed to the local council should in fact join the local council in raising funds for an over-all water supply scheme for North Ambrym ... I emphasized that if all sections of the community participated there would be every chance of third country aid ...

The establishment of the Local Council and the Lolihor Development Council [LDC] had important social consequences regarding leadership recruitment, especially since this happened at the same time as the graded society was in decline. The replacement of ceremonial exchange contexts, as the graded society, by local councils has been described from other parts of Melanesia (White 1991; A. Strathern and P.J. Stewart 2000). Among the Hagen people of New Guinea highlands, A. Strathern and P.J. Stewart (2000, 84) argue that:

> The finance committee of the council became a new centre of power, as well as a new forum of bringing together leaders of disparate groups within the council area as a whole. From the council there emanated a doctrine on development which gradually began to contradict the processes instituted earlier of expanding the sphere of ceremonial exchange.

The LDC also covered villages that before, and still, had conflicting concerns, where people argued with each other in regard to land and church interests. One might to a certain extent argue that the LDC replaced the sphere of ceremonial exchange, as among the Hagen people, in particular the graded society – in the very least, that the LDC increased its activities and importance at the same time as the graded society was in decline. However the LDC operated on quite different social principles than the graded society. This chapter is an effort to single out the dynamics on which leadership works on Ambrym today, in particular with reference to the LDC. In doing this I build on the analyses from the previous chapters where I have outlined what I regard as the most fundamental principle of social organization on Ambrym, namely the distinction and alternation between male/hierarchical and female/egalitarian social structures.

Structures of Leadership

Since Sahlins' reflections on political types in Melanesia and Polynesia, the big man concept has been the topic of discussion in the analyses of different forms of leadership in Melanesia. Godelier (1986, 164) argues that the Melanesian big man 'represents a specific institutional response to a particular type of society' and that 'the big man thus serves as the means through which the wealth and efforts of several local groups are united in the furtherance of common ends'. This might have developed as the result of war, or the organization of ceremonies or as a result of trade. The development of a big man entails the development of a political figure with authority over others. Kelly (1993, 503) has argued '(t)he development of authority over other persons goes hand in hand with the development of a prestige system in which the labour of others can be harnessed to an individual's attainment of prestige'. In systems without these kinds of authority structures, where prestige is not dependent on the control of the labour of others, but rather on individual effort, the power to influence through leadership is weakly developed, according to Kelly. Sahlins' big man then is a person who needs the labour of others in order to further not only common ends but also his own prestige, following Kelly. He compares the Mae Enga of the New Guinea Highlands as described by Meggitt (1977) with the Etoro of the Strickland-Bosavi region of Papa New Guinea where he himself has carried out fieldwork. He argues that the reasons for the development of male domination among the Mae Enga are related to the need of men to control the labour of younger men (their sons) and women (their wives) in the production of the means of exchange. Meggitt has described the punishments that the father may exert over his sons and wives; flogging, cutting of earlobes in the case of the sons, and inserting hot stones in the woman's vagina in cases where wives are guilty of adultery. These kinds of punishments are not developed among the Etoro, because male dominance does not exist in the same manner as it does among the Mae Enga. Authority in secular matters in general is not present to any large degree among the Etoro, Kelly argues. However, in matters of spiritual authority, power, as the means to influence the course of events, is unevenly distributed, and the spirit mediums and the older men are clearly more powerful and in a position of more authority than women and younger men.

Godelier (1986) has developed the concept 'great man' as a comparison and contrast to the big man concept. The great man does not, like the big man, organize the labour and efforts of others; rather he is a specialist in for instance hunting, war, or religious matters. The Etoro spirit medium then is more aptly classified as a great man than a big man. The big man emerges, according to Godelier (1986, 168), under certain structural conditions; 'it is necessary for the reproduction of relations of kinship to be intimately and directly bound up with the production of wealth...(and)...the direct exchange of women must have ceased ...' The substitution of women for wealth, in other words the payment of bride wealth, is a structural condition for the development of big men. Wealth is directly connected to relations of kinship. In great man societies, in contrast, women are only exchanged for women, and cannot be substituted.

The Ambrym case seems at first glance to be an 'in between case'. On the one hand, the existence of the 'bride price' institution should make it structurally possible to develop the big man type, and the ceremonial exchange which takes place in the *mage*, is another element that should make it necessary for men to have the authority to organize others' labour and thus gain the products needed for the ceremonies. On the other hand, I will argue that 'bride price' co-exists with the principle that only a woman can replace another woman. Women are always said to marry back to the place their mother's mother left, and thus replace her. The payment is only intermediary. The real substitution is the return marriage. Furthermore, the kind of male dominance described by Meggitt in the case of Mae Enga, which Kelly argues is a result of the kind of authority needed when leadership depends on others' efforts, is not developed on Ambrym. Men are not able to punish their wives in cases of adultery for instance. Women are often seen to be innocent victims of adultery, as having been seduced by different kinds of love magic. Neither can men exert any particular force on their sons. They cannot for instance force their sons to remain in their household and be part of their productive unit. Rather, sons might change residence, and live in another household periodically or permanently.

What about the men in the *mage*? Does a position in this graded society which involves a kind of spiritual power giving access to 'expert knowledge' on matters of sorcery, for instance, make these men comparable to the great man type (Godelier 1986), or does the position in the graded society also entail secular power and political authority of the big man kind? I argued in the previous chapter that the graded society existed to some extent outside of the wider community, as an extra-ordinary movement purifying an essential value of society. However, if the *mage* society existed outside of the wider community and without the ability to influence the labour of others in the community, where did men in the *mage* get their pigs? The performance of a ceremony involved not only large numbers of pigs as payment for the specific grade one wanted to obtain, but also payments to people who performed different kinds of labour in preparation for the ceremony such as the carver of the three fern figure erected during the ceremony.

To some extent the obtainment of pigs followed the same kind of debt relationships and generalised exchange that other ceremonies outside of the *mage* involved. People contributed to each other's ceremony and expected the same return when they needed it. People have also told me that during the prime time of the *mage* society, candidates for grades in the *mage* and the sponsors would have special pigs bred for these kinds of ceremonies. These pigs were not fed by women, as 'ordinary' pigs were. Rather, they were fed and bred by the *mage* men themselves, in yards behind their men's houses. The costs involved in a grade-taking ceremony therefore did not involve the extraction of pigs from the domestic labour sphere. The position achieved by climbing the grades in the *mage* was not of the big man kind. It did not involve the kind of authority necessary to control other people's labour. Rather, the position in the *mage* gave prestige because of its spiritual dimensions. Layard (1942) described the Malekula *maki,* from which the Ambrym *mage* stems (see Chapter 7) as a spiritual journey, where the different grades in the secret society represented different stages on the journey to the afterlife. The highest grade involved access to the last 'station' of the ancestor spirits; the volcano. The highest graded men of the *mage* on Ambrym, the *Vanten ne hanglam,*[1] are said to be 'like a spirit' – which meant having the ability to perform fantastic magic, having the power to transcend material reality and on the whole, to represent the same kind of spirituality that the ancestors represented. The men of the *mage* thus were outside the materiality of secular society.

In this sense the highly ranked man of the graded society resembles Dumont's 'out-worldly individual' (Dumont 1986, 26). In the same way as Dumont describes the Indian renouncer as self- sufficient and concerned only with himself, the Ambrym high ranking men of the graded society became too powerful for ordinary sociality and had to renounce it, for instance eating by himself in *tambufae* (Deacon 1934; Layard 1942). On Ambrym the 'out-worldly' highly graded man of the *mage* society became dangerous if he re-entered society, becoming an 'in-worldly individual', and was thus denied this, in particular through the practices of eating separately and the building of the sacred house called the *imkon* [L: taboo house]. Built for the man who achieved the highest grades in the ritual society, this house was erected inside the graveyard, where he eventually would be buried, and the high ranking man no longer only ate alone, but lived the rest of his life in complete isolation (see Deacon 1934; Layard 1942; Allen 1981; Patterson 1976; Rio 2002a). This mechanism prevented the highly graded man from becoming a powerful man *in* the world, or in the social reality of everyday life. However, the highly graded man did not just disappear from society. Rather, by living in an *imkon* and eating *tabufae*, he was very visible.

Tofor, for example (see Chapter 7), a *mal* in the *mage* with his own *imkon* house, experienced the peak of his prestige in the period around independence, but during our fieldwork in 1999 he was still a very visible outsider on North Ambrym. On the one hand he was like a superhuman who could do as he liked and a man people would only dare whisper about, but on the other hand, it was almost as if no one took him seriously. He was both a superman and an outcast at the same time. This paradoxical situation is hard to grasp. I think the closest we get to understanding the position of the high-ranking man, is by asserting that he had spiritual and cosmological power, but by being outside of society he did not control this power inside society.

---

1   The highest of men were referred to as *Vanten hanglam.*

The power of the high-ranking men was a total power within the *mage*, but also an ineffective power outside it. This is clearly seen in the cases of sorcery. Rio (2002b) has shown how men with high grades in the *mage* had difficulties in controlling their power in relation to sorcery. A well known *kastom* man on Ambrym, for instance, having climbed grades in the *mage*, was accused of killing his mother with sorcery. He at first denied this, but gradually, during the village court case, he came to realise that it was his powers from the *mage* that had made him involuntarily kill his mother. So, the powers of the men of the *mage*, when transferred from the 'out-worldly', became powerful but uncontrollable and thus ineffective for them.

In conclusion, traditionally on Ambrym there has not existed positions of the big man kind where leadership, as the obtainment of a position wherein authority can be exerted over 'secular matters' (production, distribution), was possible. However, the men in the *mage* were extremely powerful in spiritual matters and enjoyed respect and admiration from the wider community. There were also other kinds of position not connected to the graded society that could give access to a sort of great man position, such as people with magical abilities (the ability to 'see the road', or tell the future), or people who were good gardeners or good organizers of ceremonial events, like the payment of 'bride price', or maternal payments in the circumcision ceremony, or death ceremonies. Being in control of these situations provided grounds for exerting some influence in the organization of these ceremonies, but this position does not entail any access to coercive means, such as among the Mae Enga (Meggitt 1977).

As Ambrym became entangled in the colonial state and later the independent nation-state structures, the social organization based on great man structures was challenged. In this chapter I describe how expectations of another kind of 'leadership' position encountered Ambrym sociality. A new set of leadership positions and very different social structures were put on top of the existing social structure. The position of the LDC chief can be seen as the prime locus of the encounter between these diverging structures. I will therefore compare the LDC position with both the 'traditional' *mage* position as well as the newer *kastom* chief position, in order to reveal different dynamics of this encounter and how different kinds of authority and leadership positions reflect both the gendered based social organization on Ambrym and the effects of external state structures.

LDC Chiefs: Leadership in Projects

The LDC has its headquarters in Ranon but covers the neighbouring region from Fanla and Fanrereo in the north to Ranvetlam in the south. The council is made up of representatives from churches, women's clubs and chiefs, and is led by a community appointed chief. In 1994 the LDC, in cooperation with the National Planning Office and the Department of Local Government, prepared a booklet on project profiles for the community as part of the UNDP program for regional sustainable development. Getting funding for and implementing some of these projects have since been the main business of the LDC. By analyzing these projects it is possible to single out the mechanism on which leadership within the LDC works.

During our 1999 fieldwork in Ranon we observed two American Peace Corps [PC] volunteers in their effort to facilitate the work of the LDC. The PC volunteers not only contributed many of the documents on which I build this account, but also talked to us about their difficulties and problems in dealing with the LDC. Much of the internal accusations and economic disputes within the LDC would probably have remained unknown to me were it not for my conversations with the PC volunteers. We also lived in the households of one of the LDC chiefs who, during our evening meals, sometimes lectured us on development and the prospects of projects in Ranon. Having access to both perspectives; the PC volunteers 'outsider' view of the events, and the LDC chief giving an 'internal' view, has made it possible to conceptualize the differences between these perspectives and see the difficulties the LDC chiefs have not only in satisfying the people in Ranon and neighbouring villages, but also in relating to outside demands, in particular the demands of the donor agencies. The conflict that developed between the LDC chiefs and the PC volunteers was based on their very different views on how leadership was conducted. I will outline of some of the LDC projects, with particular attention given to to role of the appointed chiefs of the projects and the problems they faced with regard to leadership abilities.

The water pipes

The Water Pipe Project, already mentioned as a desired project by the BDA in the late 1970s (see the introduction to this chapter), was officially described in the 1994 profile guide mentioned above. The project, however, was not started properly until 1998–99. The chief of the Water Pipe Project, Rawo from Ranon, had worked on it for a long time. I first heard about the project during my first trip to Ambrym in 1995. Rawo was then leading a water project committee within the LDC. He has long affinal roots in Ranon. Malnaim, the old chief in Murray's time in about 1880 (see Chapters 3 and 5), and his son Malkon belonged to the same *buluim* as Rawo. Malnaim and Malkon were big men in the *mage*, and enjoyed the kind of almost superhuman respect and admiration that men of the *mage* were subject to. Rawo's father, Chief Worwor, was also a man well known for his achievements. He did not climb the graded society however (we never heard any such accounts of him). Rather he was a man of the church and cooperated closely with the plantation owner during the last decades of the colonial period. He was associated with the National Party faction and had worked for independence. He was also a spokesman for alienated land retrieval (see Rio 2002a).

Rawo himself followed his father's example and worked for the church and for development within the LDC. He never entered the *mage*, nor did any of his bothers. Patterson (2002) has argued that being kindred of a *mal* combined with a 'patrilineally traceable origin place in North Ambrym' (Patterson 2002, 135) create a position wherein a powerful leader can develop on North Ambrym. Rawo then has what Patterson would call leadership qualifications; he descended from a long line of men of fame, and men who had climbed the *mage,* and he was also an undisputed *tarin* Ranon [L; man of the place, from Ranon].

Another factor, which is also relevant to Rawo's appointment, is the distribution of the other LDC chief positions. There are said to be different *buluims* in Ranon, or rather, different 'places'. Although the different hamlets are composed of both people originally from this place, as well as descendants of settlers from other villages, three places remain distinct and important as different categories, not least in relation to the ceremonial economy and marriage structure. I noticed that there was one chief from each of these places working on different LDC projects. I never heard anyone talk about 'equal representation' as a principle, but I nevertheless noticed that this was the case.

The Water Committee, led by Rawo, had received funds through the national water supply scheme, which again depended on outside aid. Pipes from sources in the hills led the water into large tanks which again supplied water to connected outlets in the villages Ranon, Fantor, Ranvetlam, as well as smaller villages in the interior such as Ranbwe and Lonbwe. Every household paid a monthly fee for the water, an amount that was bearable to the average household having some access to money from cash cropping copra once in a while.

Initially this project seemed to be a success. People were enthusiastic about finally being able to have piped water in the village. Rawo had appointed a special team responsible for maintenance of the pipes, which would periodically be blocked by leaves and dirt, especially after heavy rainfalls. This team was equipped and trained and was recruited among young men from all the villages connected to the pipes. They managed to clear the pipes and make the system operational after blockages within a day or two. People paid their water fees and seemed to be satisfied with finally having unlimited access to clean water, which before had been a major problem, in particular for the coastal villages in the dry season.

After a while however, the unit faced increasing problems when tending the pipes, because dirt and leaves were no longer the only problems. There seemed to be cases of direct sabotage. The pipes were cut and the costs of fixing them high. People had to wait for weeks before the maintenance unit had equipment to repair them, and by then people were annoyed and did not pay their water fees. I was told that when the argument between the communities of Ranon and Fantor described in Chapter 6 was surfacing, some youths in Fantor had deliberately cut the pipes going down to Ranon, so that everyone in Ranon was without a water supply, except for the old water tanks still installed. The story was also told in reverse; the people in Fantor accused youths in Ranon of having cut the pipes going down to Fantor. The staff of the secondary school, accused people in Fantor as well as people in Ranon of sabotaging each other's pipes, and as a result no one had water. Rawo was unable to do anything else but run between Ranon and the telephone in Ramvetlam contacting the project leaders in the capital and explaining how the project was being sabotaged. The PC volunteers were not so actively involved in this project, because it had already been implemented when they arrived in the village.

The Health Station

The sabotage of the water project was linked to competition over another important project, the Rural Health Station. The LDC consists of representatives from all the main villages in Lolihor, but is dominated by the Presbyterians in Ranon. The chief of the Health Station Project was Billy, who was not originally from Ranon, but from West Ambrym. As I have outlined earlier, his father had settled in Ranon as a plantation worker and had married into Ranon. Billy was also a member of the Presbyterian Church. All the LDC projects were headed by chiefs from the Presbyterian Church, but the Health Station Project became particularly connected to the church.

After church service one Sunday in April 1999, Billy announced that the LDC would organize a 'mate to meat' fundraising ceremony the next week, and that the money would be contributed to the Health Station Project. I was told that the NTM people would also be invited, because, the LDC covers the Lolihor area, and is supposed to work for the benefit of the whole population, not only the Presbyterians. However, on the evening of the ceremony, only the Presbyterian adherents arrived. People in Fantor had decided to work for their own health station project, and not do it through the LDC, but through their own church, the NTM.

The Peace Corps volunteers complained about how hard it was to get people to cooperate on projects crossing church affiliations. In June 1999 however, a new effort to gather the community and work for a health station across church denominations was made, and Billy was again appointed chairman. The last committee had collected a considerable amount of money during the 'mate to meat' arrangement, about 68,000 vatu. Billy, on behalf of the Health Station Committee, negotiated with the *kastom* owner of the agreed-upon site for the Health Station. The PC volunteers drafted a contract and the *kastom* owner signed it, offering the site without rent to the communal health station. The *kastom* owner was an Elder in the Presbyterian Church in Ranon.

In January the next year, in preparing for a meeting with the provincial health officer regarding this project, problems again arose. The money had disappeared, and the *kastom* owner was having second thoughts about giving up his ground. He had also recently changed church affiliation, and joined the NTM after a quarrel with his mother regarding his drinking habits. According to the Peace Corps officers who were at the time members of the Health Station Committee, one of the village chiefs had used the money belonging to the Health Station Project on a trip to Port Vila. I never directly confronted this chief with this story, but I later learnt that he had spent a considerable amount of money on a funeral arrangement in Port Vila, and it was most likely the money from the Health Station Project he had spent. However, he had not spent it on any personal expenditure.

The PC volunteers announced that they would no longer be part of the LDC because of its mismanagement of funds, and declared that they would support the people of the NTM church in their attempt to build a health station. The NTM congregation planned to use the same ground as the LDC had proposed, and had permission from the *kastom* owner who now belonged to their church. The PC volunteers used connections to churches back in the US and were able to raise money for the project. However, the LDC Board, dominated by Presbyterians, stopped the project, arguing that this was not a community-based project. The PC volunteers, at this point so frustrated that they seriously considered giving up their work, decided to use their donated funds for something else, which would benefit the whole community, and not split it.

The Rural Training Centre

The PC volunteers wanted to put the project money for the above project into a Rural Training Centre, also an LDC project. A Rural Training Centre Committee was appointed with Chief Tokon as the headman. Chief Tokon was also a Ranon man, but originally from Hawor. The Rural Training Centre Project also had tight connections to the Presbyterian Church at the outset. Chief Tokon was a Presbyterian and his father was one of the elders in this church.

The PC volunteers helped the LDC apply to the UNDP for additional funds, and received money for a garden-tool and a carving-tool project. The aims of the garden-tool project were to give people, and in particular women and youngsters, access to equipment which would facilitate garden work and make it possible for them to produce more and sell the surplus to the secondary school in the area where the students ate only rice and tinned fish. The aim of the carving-tool project was to establish a workshop where young carvers would learn the skill of carving from their elders, so that they could carve artefacts that were desirable tourist commodities.

These projects were only partly a success. The LDC received the funding, bought the gardening and carving tools, and then, after the first and only workshop had been held, the LDC members, according to the PC volunteers, kept the tools for themselves, both the carving tools as well as the gardening tools, and distributed them among relatives. The PC volunteers told me that they noticed the tools being used by relatives of the board members without any embarrassment or attempted explanation or excuses.

After this last failure by the LDC to implement the project according to the aims in the proposals, the PC volunteers resigned as development workers and concentrated on teaching at the secondary school. The UNDP representatives, who arrived in the village to assess the work of the LDC, decided, according the PC volunteers, that the LDC should receive no further funding for any project because of its continuing mismanagement.

Patterson (2002) has commented that Ambrym is regarded as a 'backward area' within the progressive nation state, and that disputes which breakdown projects are 'symptoms of a much deeper malaise ...' (2002, 127). Patterson argues that the reasons for the failure of projects are linked to the competitive ethos of male leadership, which, as I understand her argument, goes against communal values. There were certainly competitive elements present in the Health Station Project. Chief Billy, as the personification of the Health Station Project in the village, had difficulties in getting cooperation from the NTM faction. They could not look upon him as the personification of any communal project, because of his association with the Presbyterian Church. They clearly expressed this when they decided to form their own health station committee. Membership of a church signals in a very powerful way not only to which community you belong, but also the history of movement. No *tarin* Ranon [L; man from Ranon] is, ordinarily, a member of the NTM church, for instance (see Chapters 3 and 5).

Within the church there is a sense of community and work spirit that the LDC lacks. People will often organize work parties to help each other in the gardens. For instance, when an elderly woman needs help to *serem aut copra* [B: making copra] for cash cropping, people organize within the church to help her. Every Sunday after the ceremony, an Elder in the church gets people to organize themselves into different work groups for different purposes. In particular, work teams for cash cropping are organized through the church, even though the money is not being raised for the church, but for school fees or trips to town, etc. The Health Station Project, when it was turned into a NTM church project, generated a great deal of enthusiasm and work spirit among the congregation. When projects are linked to the church, people have a greater belief in the prospects of the project.

The LDC, as a continuation of the Local Council that developed in the 1970s, has, and to a large extent still is, predominantly associated with people in the Presbyterian Church. The LDC then has become almost an extension of the Presbyterian Church, at least the way it has developed in Ranon. Both the Water Pipe Project and the Health Station Project clearly reveal this, since the NTM people felt the need to define their own project within their own church organization. The LDC does not represent the whole community across church denominations. The LDC is based on the Presbyterian Church on the one hand, but focused on the state and the world of NGOs on the other. This makes the LDC chief something more than a church representative. Internally he has a position within the church, but externally he is expected to have a position exceeding the church. Moreover, the external expectations, clearly shown when the UNDP representatives visited Ranon, imply that the LDC chiefs should be able to control the funds. This seems to be difficult for the LDC chiefs. The local authority of the LDC chief then is limited not only by his church denomination, but also by the extent to which his leadership makes room for controlling resources on behalf of the community. The chief of the LDC is thus unable to exert the kind of leadership the state and the NGOs expect when they fund projects.

Let us look at the position of the LDC chief in terms of the local social structure and its relation to other positions in the village, as that of men in the *mage*.

The *Mals* of the *Mage* Against the State

I have described the men of the *mage* as spiritually powerful but 'outsiders' in relation to the wider community. The *mage* society represented traditionally an external movement where the value central for society at large, the value of 'personification', became distilled and a frozen image. The *mals*, the highest graded men, had to remain 'frozen' and not re-enter ordinary social life. The power they had would become dangerous if it were to become effective on everyday matters.

Clastre's (1989) analysis of the Amazonian Indians who possessed recognized leaders without any actual power is a relevant comparison. Clastre (1989, 29) argues, 'For what needs to be understood is the bizarre persistence of a 'power' that is practically powerless, of a chieftainship without authority, of a function operating in a void'. Clastre argues against the prevailing evolutionary view of societies held by western social science. He argues that classifying societies according to the development of political systems based on coercive power is based on the idea that centralised political power systems is the only possible development. Clastre argues that stateless societies regulate power by preventing the development of a strong chief. The chief's position among the Amazonian Indians is somewhat ritualised. As a 'peacemaker' he gives speeches which no one listens to because he speaks on behalf of all, and not as a commander.[2] 'The discourse of the chief is empty precisely because it is no discourse of power' (1989, 154). Coercive power then is denied the chief, as is the ability to accumulate wealth. The chief is denied reciprocity and is isolated.

Clastre's analyses show how stateless societies prevent the development of centralised powers and the formation of state apparatuses. 'The chief who tries to act the chief is abandoned' (1989, 154). He argues that power, seen as the command–obedience relationship, is regulated in such a way that it does not develop into strong centralised leadership structures. It is an incorrect assumption, according to Clastre, that social systems like the Amazonian, are without relations of power. Rather, they have developed mechanisms that prevent power as a command-obedience structure from becoming dominant. He argues that 'Primitive society is the place where separate power is refused, because society itself, and not the chief, is the real locus of power' (1989, 154).

The same kind of mechanism seems to have operated within the *mage* on Ambrym, preventing the highly ranked men from developing into commanders. The structural workings of the kinship system beyond the *mage*, and the rules of conduct attached to the highly graded men, prevented one man from achieving a position of command. There are, of course, great differences between the South American forest societies described by Clastre and the Ambrym society, in terms of kinship structure, subsistence, and geographical and demographical structures. There are great differences between island societies and forest societies, nomads and gardeners, etc. However, the idea that small-scale societies should not be understood in terms of western political system, and that power relations might have dynamics other than the necessary development of strong leaders, is useful. The *mal* of North Ambrym of course differs from the Amazonian chiefs by the fact that it requires some effort to enter the graded society, not least in amassing the number of pigs demanded, and this reflects some personal qualifications, whereas the Amazonian chief seems to be picked more randomly. However, if renown and spiritual power was what the men in the *mage* achieved more than power in production and circulation of wealth outside the *mage*, it would seem as if Clastre's model is apt in this case.

Jolly (1994) has analysed the different premises on which rank in northern Vanuatu works, and has argued that rank is 'a combination of the ascribed principles of age and seniority and that created by the ritual of the graded society' (1994, 144). She points out that 'the powers associated with the titles [of the graded society, my comment] were those of sacralized potency rather than actual command' (1994, 144). I will argue that the making of a ranked hierarchy which privileges the central and highest positions does not necessarily entail that these are the positions of power in a society. The fact that women and young men are denied access gives *mage* an exclusive character. Exclusiveness however is not the same as power. The ritual domain of men might not even be interesting to women: 'The naïve might ask: since the men are doing this all for themselves and since women are excluded, in what

---

2   'The word of the chief is not spoken in order to be listened to'. Clastre 1989, 153.

sense are men's activities relevant for women?' (M. Strathern 1988, 102). Or why should the young care when the old men do this all for themselves?

Patterson (1981) has described the power of the men in the *mage* as transgressive power. A great man on Ambrym, she argues, is a man who can act outside the system, *and* get away with it. This again points to how the high-ranked man was outside the social system. He could perform outrageous acts, which was in stark contrast to the sanctioned behaviour within the social system.

When understanding the present-day position of men in the *mage*, we should keep in mind the way the graded society has lost ground as an 'extra ordinary' movement and how the dominant values on which the graded society has operated, namely the value of personifications, have lost ground due to the church. The church has brought communal values to the foreground. This implies that the men who still take grades in the *mage* and seek the value of personifications appear even more external and even more arbitrary today. Tofor, one of the last high ranking *mage* men referred to earlier in this chapter, was a product of his time. He climbed the *mage* in a period when the *mage* society was seriously challenged by the values of the church. He was also caught in the struggle between different factions in the period leading up to Independence. On the one hand he was fighting against the new independent state and clinging onto *kastom*, on the other he was closely allied with the colonial officers and had been an important part of the colonial administration on Ambrym. I know very little of the *mals* before Tofor. I know however, that people say that there is no one like Tofor anymore, and that the community chiefs today are not like Tofor. They do not have the kind of transgressive but 'outwordly' power that these *mage* men had. But what are they? Do the state structures give them another kind of power?

Chiefs Today

The bureaucratic chief

Lindstrom and White (1997) define three types of chiefs today. The first type is a national chief, 'the chiefly statesman', representing the nation as a whole, perhaps most prominent in Polynesia, for instance Tonga. The second type of chief is the local chief who mediates between the state and the local context, and, according to Lindstrom and White, advances state operations at a local level. This is what they call 'the bureaucratic chief'. The last type of chief is the contrary to this, working against the state, 'the chiefly opposition'. I want to discuss the second and third type of chief here. Lindstrom and White point out that the chief bureaucrats:

> ... advance a state's political authority and programs, developmental and other wise, into the nation's hinterlands ... at the same time as they improve citizens' access to state bureaus and programs (1997, 13).

The position of the LDC chief might be described as a sort of Janus-headed chief, being both a vehicle of the state, as the chiefly bureaucrat, and a resister of the state.

The 'bureaucratic chief' on Ambrym worked first through the church and then through the local council and then the LDC. Today the chief bureaucrat might also achieve positions in the national administration. These chiefs however, are not out-worldly individuals, like the men in the *mage*, in the local context. Although they are sometimes sons of men who operated in the *mage*, they have seldom climbed the *mage* themselves. Chief Tokon, Billy and Rawo of the LDC, are not regarded as having the kind of transgressive power the men of the *mage* had, which made them out-worldly in the Dumontian sense. However, when the context is widened, and includes the national level of politics and state administration as well as an international network of NGOs, these chiefs become out-worldly in another sense. They hold their positions as chiefs not as a result of entering the graded society, but because they take part in social processes originating outside the local context. They thus become part of another kind of external movement, namely the state structures.

The LDC chief as part of this external structure is very different from the out-worldly *mal* of the graded society, or the NaGriamel described in the previous chapter. Whereas the high graded man of the *mage* stood outside, but nevertheless encapsulated the whole of the society because of his embodiment of the social value of circulation, the chief of the local council who is focused on relations elsewhere is outside society in another way. Although they receive their position as a result of externally originated processes, they are endlessly trying to convert this outside power into an in-worldly power, often without succeeding. Whereas the high graded man of the *mage*, or the leaders of the NaGriamel, were satisfied with the alternative social reality outside everyday life, the local council chief wants to convert the 'outside' powers into 'inside' powers. In the alternative social order of national politics and administration, the chief seeks to create a name for himself, like Chief Willie, described in the previous chapter, who became the president of the national council of chiefs, or local council chiefs who relate to outside agencies, whether governmental or nongovernmental organizations.

In this external context they seem to be able to control the circulation of money and resources into local projects, which Lindstrom and White argue is the role of the 'bureaucratic chief'. The problem they face, however, is that their local platform of power fails them, because they cannot operate as the personifications of circulating money in the everyday social order. These circulations are always presented as collective work. As the *mage* society has declined, the value of the person who is able to represent, the personification, has also lost ground. Everyday village life is dominated by the value of collective effort. The bureaucratic chief thus faces problems not only with the donor agencies, who want them to control the money and to be a representation of the collective, but also with their local relatives who expect them to contribute and who do not recognize the LDC chiefs any privileges. Whereas the donor agencies expect the local council chiefs to be able to exert the power of controlling the money they have received in the village, the people around them deny them this possibility. The chiefs are not able to transfer the power from the external social order (the state structures) on to the local social order. They thus operate as a facilitator for the state, while they are sabotaging the state. They have one face outward and another inward.

Lindstrom (1997, 220) also points out that the chiefs, in particular those who are represented in the Malvatumauri[3] are more focused toward the state, than on the 'unruly villages'. Although the chiefs have tried to codify their powers, in for instance the *kastom polisi* [B: kastom policy] document written by the Malvatumauri (Lindstrom 1997), this has not been too successful, at least on Ambrym. The local power of the chiefs remains limited. When the chiefs of the LDC were accused by the PC volunteers and by the UNDP representatives of mismanagement and failing to control the funds, I believe this must be explained by both the value of circulation and the value of the collective within the everyday social order. When the chiefs are unable to become a personification of the circulating resources, and thus control these resources, they have no other option than to play on the structural premises given to them locally, which make them distribute the money into kin-based relations. I believe this was what happened to the health station money that probably ended up sponsoring a funeral in Port Vila instead of being deposited into a saving account in the chief's name. Sponsoring the funeral and buying food for the participants circulated the money once again. When people ask for contributions to funeral arrangements the chief cannot answer that he is unable to give the money because it belongs to him on behalf of the community. He has to give the money when demanded of him. He is unable to create any 'stops in the network' (M. Strathern 1996), which, as I argued in Chapter 6, the practices connected to *kastom* provide. The same can be said in the case of the tools bought for the Rural Training Centre Project. The tools were immediately distributed, because the chiefs had no authority to control them.

The kastom chief

There is however another position that seems to be a rather new creation, the position of the *kastom* chief. The *kastom* chief is a contradiction in terms of course, since traditionally there were no chiefs. The *kastom* chiefs today, as well as in the colonial period, work in an intermediate position between the external social reality of the *mage* (they are often still taking grades in the *mage* since actually being a *kastom* chief requires some effort to climb the *mage*), and the new structural possibilities provided by the colonial and later the independent state apparatus. A chief is able to be a chief, because the position is instituted by the state, and is thus a position outside the graded society. The *kastom* chief thus combines *mage* with connections to and knowledge of the state. The *kastom* chief is able to personify relations to a larger extent than the LDC chiefs. One might perhaps even argue that the *kastom* chief personifies *kastom*. This is most clearly demonstrated by a case from Ranvetlam village during a marriage ceremony in 1999:

A girl from Lonbwe was to marry a man from Ramvetlam, and after the church ceremony, and as the present ceremony was coming to an end, the groom's fathers and brothers started preparing the handing over of the 'bride price'. First they made piles of *green kakae* [B: garden produce]. Then the groom's brothers and father erected poles next to the piles of produce and tied the pigs to the poles. When this was

---

3   The National Council of Chiefs.

done, the groom and his brothers and father gathered in the centre of the ceremonial ground, and people gathered around them. After having some discussions among themselves they started calling out names of those who were to receive shares of the 'bride price'. Some of the bride's aunts were the first to be called upon. They entered the ceremonial ground one by one, and received small amounts of money, 300, 500, or 1,000 vt. When they seemed to be finished distributing small amounts, the bride's old father stood up at one of the corners of the ceremonial ground, signalled to one of the groom's brothers, and whispered something in his ear. My Ranon companions told me that he was probably asking for more money. The groom's brother returned to the others and they talked among themselves for a while before they announced that the bride's father should be given 60,000 vt. The old man got up once more, entered the ceremonial ground, received the money, and returned. Then one of the groom's brothers declared that all together they had paid 120,000 vt for the bride. Upon hearing this, the bride's father got up again, once more entered the ceremonial ground, and started talking. He complained that the 'bride price' was too low, especially because the bride's mother's brothers were demanding so much. Then one of the mother's brothers of the bride got up, entered the ceremonial ground without having been called upon and thus got the attention of everybody who wondered why he, the mother's brother, would break the taboo of entering the ceremonial ground. He said that all the green food, and the pigs tied to the poles, belonged to him and his brothers and not to the bride's father, because the bride's old father had not yet paid for the bride's mother. He was visibly very angry, and as he talked a couple of his bothers got up next to him.

My companions from Ranon whispered to me that the mother's brothers were 'making shame'. While the bride's mother's brother was talking, the bride's brother got up, looking agitated, and untied the largest pig and started to run away. The crowd of people around looked at him in astonishment, and then started to talk among themselves. Some of them were obviously provoked by the bride's brother's behaviour. People were arguing and waving their arms and I was expecting a huge fight to break loose.

However, suddenly the crowd was mysteriously silenced, and I noticed that the *kastom* Chief Magekon from Fanla (Chief Tofor's brother) had risen. Everybody stared at him in expectation. He talked with a loud and clear voice. He said that he had expected this to happen. The bride's mother's brother had been complaining for a long time that they were not satisfied with the payment they had received from the bride's father when he had married the bride's mother some twenty years ago. The father of the bride, who was now receiving payment, had never himself paid for his own wife. 'We are no longer respecting *kastom*' the chief said, 'and we are getting into trouble because of this'. He then said than everyone should go home to their place and that there would be no further celebrations until the bride's father and the bride's mother's brothers had solved their differences. After his talk, the bride's brother and father seemed to control themselves, and people were just whispering among themselves, saying that the chief had rescued the groom's kin from embarrassment.

This case illustrates the kind of authority the *kastom* chief can elicit in a situation where the code of circulation is disputed. He has this kind of authority not because of his position in the graded society. As I have pointed out earlier this is a position that does not give access to secular power. However, being involved in the graded society today provides access to a new kind of position, namely the *kastom* chief. Magekon was the brother of Tofor and the son of Tainmal, and this association enhances his *kastom* qualifications. He has a long memory of ceremonial events and knows the proceedings. He also speaks with such eloquence that this in itself makes people listen. He intervened because the situation was escalating and might have led to a giant fight. Usually these ceremonies are formal matters, and payments are agreed upon beforehand, but in this case disputes from the past surfaced which made it necessary for someone with authority on the subject to intervene. This kind of authority based on an external social order, namely the state structures instituting the chief role, is made relevant in new contexts because of the new structural possibilities opened by the new chief role.

This kind of authority is not available to the LDC chiefs. Rawo, chief of the water project, was also a man of chiefly descent and with the gift of eloquent speech. However, he was not a *kastom* man. The difference between Magekon as a *kastom* chief and Rawo as a LDC chief was that Magekon built on the kind of position men in the *mage* had. He could do this however, only in matters of *kastom*. He had not this kind of authority outside issues relating to *kastom*. The ceremonial economy is of course part of *kastom*, whereas matters of development are not. Rawo, when trying to reach the kind of position Magekon had within *kastom* matters, built on the authority received from relations to funding agencies. This kind of knowledge about outside agencies has not yet made it possible to achieve the kind of position *kastom* and relations to the *mage* provide.

There is today no position of leadership on Ambrym that gives undisputed authority and power. There are, however, different kinds of chiefs operating on different structural principals and in different arenas. The LDC chief, or the bureaucratic chief, has a position in relation to development matters and local government, but his position is limited with regard to authority. Outside the local context, however, his position might be different and on the national arena leadership of another quality might develop. The *kastom* chief is a development of the *mage* big man and, as the *mal* of the *mage* in the past had no strong influence in matters beyond the *mage*, the *kastom* chief today has no say in matters beyond *kastom*.

Chapter 9

The Social Dynamics of Ambrym in a Comparative Perspective[1]

Gender-based Social Formations

I have repeatedly pointed to female agency as a creator of alternative roads, whether they are matrilateral links making it easier to code potential marriage partners as suitable, paths to new places, or alternative social movements such as the church. I have outlined a gendered social structure that alternates between a male personalised form and a female communal form. I have argued that understanding the dynamics of different aspects of social life on Ambrym – everyday interaction on the one hand, the hierarchical male society on the other, or the local council or the church on the one hand, and NaGriamel on the other – is premised on seeing how these different aspects of social life are gendered. I will claim that gender is a difference on which other differences are ordered. However, on Ambrym the social structure not only builds on gender as a fundamental difference, but it *transforms* itself on a gendered principle. As I have pointed out in the previous chapters, there is a constant alternation between a male personified form of the social structure and a female communal form of the social structure. This alternation is clearly visible in the context of the ceremonial economy, described in detail in previous chapters, where the switch from a focus on the female and communal to the male and the personified takes place as the man who stages a ceremony enters the ceremonial ground and the other participants disappear into the background.

There is a constant tension between the two poles of the social structure. These gendered poles can also be conceptualised as the hierarchical and the egalitarian, or the personalised and the communal. These rarely exist in their pure form, but one or the other of them seems to dominate in different situations. The church for instance, as I have outlined in Chapters 5 and 6, builds on a communal form in its social structure. Through fund-raising and other communal activities, alliances between households are created and the church comes to stand for social wholes. The church on North Ambrym[2] works horizontally more than vertically. The vertical organization

---

1 Parts of this chapter will also appear as a chapter in Rio, Knut and Olaf H. Smedal (eds) (2007). *Hierarchy, Persistence and Transformation in Social Formations* (Oxford: Berghahn Books).

2 I refer here to the Presbyterian Church in Ranon mainly, but also to the Church of Holiness in Fantor and to a lesser degree to the SDA church in Fanla, which I did not visit so frequently. The Catholic Church in Olal I have not visited at all, and I do not include this church in my analysis. I would assume that the hierarchical social structure would be more present in the Catholic Church than in the Presbyterian Church.

of the church with deacons, elders, and the role of the priest are of course present, but the female form of the social structure with its emphasis on communality and inclusion is the basic social mechanism of the church. Furthermore, as I have outlined in previous chapters, the church does not create any opportunities for expressions of grand personalities, like the competitive graded society and the NaGriamel did. The positions of deacons and elders are available to a much larger degree than were positions in previous ritual institutions, such as the graded society.

When I talk about the social structure on Ambrym as gendered, I base this on the social practices I have outlined in the previous chapters. I have shown that it is a female quality to move, to make connections, to create paths and alliances, and that it is a male quality to be rooted, to stand for places, to seek manifestations of places and persons and compete for these manifestations. I could also have discussed these differences as being between alliance and patrilinity, and egalitarianism and hierarchy. However, gender lies at the bottom of all of these concepts. The distinction between an egalitarian and cooperative social form compared to a competitive and hierarchical social form on Ambrym is best described as a difference been male and female social forms because these aspects are both in practice and metaphorically tied to gender (see Chapters 2 and 3). By acknowledging this, one is also able to see how these forms are linked to kinship organization, to ideas of place and immobility and to movement and flexibility. There is thus an underlying social mechanism that ties together the different aspects I have discussed, from kinship and marriage to migration and the working of different social institutions on Ambrym, namely gender.

Gender has been a central feature of theoretically important literature from the region, as in Marilyn Strathern's *The Gender of the Gift* (M. Strathern 1988). Here Strathern has argued that an understanding of the dynamics of social life in Melanesia is premised not so much on an understanding of the relationship between an individual and society, as western social thought has dwelled upon, but is rather a matter of how relations are gendered and changed. Looking at my analysis from the perspective of *The Gender of the Gift*, one could argue that the two forms of the social structure, which I call the female and the male social forms, can be conceptualized as a difference between what she calls 'mediated' and 'unmediated' exchanges.

M. Strathern's model is based on different prototypic exchanges: 'same-sex' and 'cross-sex' exchanges and 'mediated' and 'unmediated' exchanges. The prime example of this is the Hagen couple of the New Guinea Highlands (see for instance M. Strathern 1988, 199–200) who raise pigs that the husband uses in a Moka exchange. The Moka exchange is a grand ceremonial exchange where big men show off their ability to assemble pigs (see also A. Strathern 1971). This exchange is only between men: in other words, a same-sex exchange. The cross-sex relationship in this case is the relationship between the wife and the husband. This cross-sex relationship is prior to the Moka exchange. It is the cross-sex union that produces the pigs needed for the ceremonial exchange (the same-sex event). The cross-sex relation is of an unmediated kind because it does not involve an external object. The same-sex relation is of the mediated kind because it involves the gift, in the form of the pigs, going from the one part of the relation to the other. The husband and wife relationship does not involve any such mediation. It is contained within itself as a unit.

M. Strathern argues that the product of this union (food, pigs, and children) is a substitution for this relationship (M. Strathern 1988, 183). This substitution is itself in a cross-sex state, or, in an alternative phrase, it has an androgynous composition. The unmediated cross-sex relationship between husband and wife results in a substitution and this substitution is the androgynous child or the androgynous pig. In the same-sex relation, where the husband exchanges the pig with a person of the same sex, the pig comes to stand for the previous cross-sex union which caused it. In other words, the grown pig when extracted from the cross-sex relationship is a substitution, or a manifestation, of the unmediated relation between the husband and the wife.

The difference between mediated and unmediated exchange, as outlined by M. Strathern (1988), can be compared to the difference between sharing and exchange, which Gell (1992) has discussed. Sharing is distinguished from exchange on the grounds that only exchange involves status competition. In an exchange, or a mediated relationship in M. Strathern's terms, the process of personification and objectification takes place simultaneously. Firstly, the pig, which in the cross-sex relationship worked as a substitution, becomes in the same-sex transaction an objectification of this relationship. The pig signifies the (politically important) relationship between two big men, where the giver is always superior to the receiver. In other words, the pig not only objectifies the same-sex relationship, but it also points back to an unequal relationship. Furthermore, the process of personification implies that the man who gives the pig represents the previous relationship in which the pig was produced. He contains this relationship within him. The man who gives the pig in a ceremonial same-sex pig exchange gives face to the previous relationship in which the pig figured. Hence, the mediated exchange involves personification and status competition, whereas the unmediated exchange can be said to be like sharing, without the process of personification and competition, involving instead the process of substitution.

We see here how the difference between the competitive and personified social form in relation to the non-personified and egalitarian social form on Ambrym can also be conceptualised as the difference between unmediated and mediated exchanges. Unmediated exchanges are exchanges without 'objectifications'.

On Ambrym personified, mediated relationships are of the male-male kind, and take place during ceremonial exchanges, in the men's graded society, but also, as I have shown, in political movements like the NaGriamel. What I have called the female social form on Ambrym is of the unmediated kind. As I pointed out above, unmediated relationships do not involve personifications, but rather substitutions. On Ambrym the church is a substitution for unmediated relationships; it stands for the total social whole. When people for instance give yams to the church during church service on the morning of the New Yam ceremony (described in Chapter 6) every household, represented (usually) by a woman, contributes a yam to the church, and places it in front of the alter. The yams that have been pooled by various households are then sold and the money is given to the church. This event involves no exchanges, but is a matter of sharing. There are no personifications created in this event. Rather the result of this sharing ceremony is the church itself as a community.

The Hierarchical Nature of the Two Social Forms

The personified social form and the communal social form (or the unmediated versus the mediated social forms) are not only different structures played out in different contexts. These contexts, and these different social structures, also stand in a certain relationship to each other. Through the last chapters of this book I have outlined a historical transformation where the church has come to replace the graded society as the most important ceremonial institution. In this process the female social form (the communal and unmediated) has gained in prominence, and the male social form (the personified and mediated) has become marginalised. Thus, we see how these contexts always are related to each others in terms of foreground and background, or in terms of superior and inferior. The male social form has disappeared into the background, or it has become an inferior social form, whereas a hundred years ago the situation was the reverse. The conceptualization of social forms on Ambrym thus must involve the conceptualization of a hierarchical relationship.

Dumont (1980) has argued that in every cultural system there is one value more sacred than other values: an ultimate value. This ultimate value is the organisational locus of society and the value that makes the world meaningful. This ultimate value is absolute and thus encompasses its counterparts. This is the nature of the hierarchy, according to Dumont. A hierarchical system works by continually submitting opposite values to encompassment. In modern western society for instance, as Dumont outlines in his *Essays on Individualism* (1986), the individual is the primary value. It is a value without compromise. Other values can be accommodated, such as the value of collectivity, of solidarity etc. as long as they do not seriously challenge the value and integrity of individuals.

All differences are related to each other hierarchically in such a way that the one part is the whole and the other its counterpart. There are no neutral differences, according to the Dumontian model. Whenever a distinction is made, a hierarchical ordering of the elements follows. Howell (1985) has argued that there is, however, a difference between inherently value-laden concepts, such as good and evil, and concept pairs that are not inherently value laden, such as left and right. The latter distinction needs to be coupled with a whole in order to emerge as differently positioned in relation to this whole. The 'good-evil' distinction is already value laden, because 'good' is an absolute value. It stands for the whole, and 'evil' is automatically inferior, or encapsulated within the 'good' as a necessary but inferior counterpart. The 'left–right' distinction is related to the whole of the body before it is turned into a hierarchical relationship. The left and the right are differently positioned within the body, and thereby also differently positioned in the hierarchy.

The male-female distinction I have analysed for the Ambrym case is of the latter kind. It is a distinction that is only ordered hierarchically in relation to a whole. It is not in itself ordered hierarchically. Dumont has argued the case for India that the idea of the pure is an encompassing value that contains impure practises such as politics, economics and the juridical within it. Purity is an absolute value. Building on M. Strathern's (1988) model it is possible to argue that 'the relation' is an absolute value in the Ambrym case. The female and the male variants are unequally positioned in relation to this, because, as I have shown, the gendered 'codes' for creating relationships are different. Whereas the male version involves mediated, and often same-sex, relations to achieve manifestation of relations as persons, the female version involves unmediated relations to create manifestations of relations. In unmediated exchanges between women in the church for instance, women seek to create the church as a representation of social relations, whereas men in mediated exchanges during ceremonies seek to create themselves as renowned persons and eclipse the relations that they rely on. The gender difference on Ambrym is a difference between emphasis on persons and emphasis on relations. As M. Strathern (1988) has shown, both person and relation is a variation of each other, and necessary counterparts (just as pure and impure, or good and evil, although these are more self-evidently related as superior and inferior).

The value hierarchy on Ambrym can thus be seen as organised on the value of relationships. The male version of this in contrast to the female version is differently positioned in this hierarchy. The male social form has traditionally been the most valuable form, and thus the encompassing form. Today, as I have shown, the reverse is the case.

Alternations Between Levels or Contexts

Dumont has argued that for comparative social science to be successful, the model that is applied as a conceptual grid must have comparative qualities. He argues (Dumont 1982, 237):

> There is thus in each concrete society the imprint of this universal model, which becomes perceptible to some degree as soon as comparison begins. It is a negative imprint, which authenticates, so to speak, the society as human, and whose precision increases when comparison begins.

In an effort to lift the study of the dynamics of the social structure on Ambrym to a comparative level, and in an effort to use hierarchy as a comparative axis, the value of 'the relationship' can thus be singled out as one 'negative imprint', i.e. something that makes this society distinct. Howell (1985) has made a distinction between what she calls expressive and implicit evidence of hierarchy. She argues that expressive evidence is visible in cosmological conceptions and in ritual performances, whereas implicit evidence of hierarchy can be found in structural analyses. When I ague that there is a hierarchical relationship between 'relation' and 'person', this is based on my analyses of kinship, marriage, migration, church movements and political movements. The personified version of achieving this, which is a male-gendered practice on Ambrym, is today only a partial way of achieving it, and as I have shown, limited to certain contexts which have become rarer and rarer (as the graded society).

Dumont is reluctant to use the concept 'context', and is more comfortable with 'level'. The latter concept implies a 'depth view' (Dumont 1980), because it does not position the different situations as if they were interchangeable, but positions them hierarchically, where the one is superior to the other. In the Ambrym case, the church movement is succeeding as a superior movement, because it explicitly manifests the unmediated relational form more than the mediated and personified. Standing out from the social whole is no longer valorised when the graded society has lost ground. The church became, as I have shown, a countermovement to the graded society, emphasising the previously encompassed value of unmediated relationships. In the graded society the highest value was that of mediated exchanges and personifications. It was as if the greater social whole was eclipsed and forgotten for the sake of letting men create great names. In these contexts the value of the unmediated relations was pushed aside as an inferior value, while the value of the personified relationship rose as the dominating value. In the church, the opposite happens, the contributions from individual households and individual persons merge into a collective whole and the focus is on unmediated sharing.

Phrased within a Dumontian language, what has happened on Ambrym is a reversal of the hierarchy. As the church replaced the graded society, the value of unmediated exchanges, or the female social form, replaced the personified form as a superior value. This reversal is, however, not final. Whenever a ceremony in the graded society is held, although this is very rare today, this ceremonial form is momentarily revived, and the transformation is reversed. The personified form once more gains prestige. However, when the ceremony is over, and everyone knows that there will not be a new one for a long time, the everyday social form is once more dominant. In other words, one might say that the Ambrym value hierarchy has transformed itself historically, from the graded society to the church, and it still transforms itself according to context, or level (following Dumont concepts).

In comparison, in Dumont's own ethnographic material (1980) from India, the priests were normally superior to the Kings because they were purer. The priests had the ability to ceremonially cleanse the kings, and the kings could not achieve this by themselves. However, as Dumont points out, 'the priest would obey the Kings in matters of public order, in *subordinate matters*' (Dumont 1982, 225, emphasis added). When the hierarchy is reversed, this takes place at a subordinate level. The graded society then, which I have argued has been marginalised as a result of the church, is, in Dumontian language, subordinate to the church today. The church has become the new superior form, and this form is purifying the form of everyday life, and not inverting it (like the graded society did). Standing out from the social whole is normally not accepted in everyday matters. Practices that make distinctions and make certain people stand out are sanctioned through *posen* [B: sorcery]. For instance, when the cook at the Ranon Secondary School became ill and had to stop working, a job was suddenly available in the village. A paying job was certainly a scarce resource, because there were not many of them in Ranon. Besides teachers in the primary school and the secondary school and the priest, no one else was paid. A number of people in the village wanted the job, since it would ease the burden of having to cash crop in order to pay for school fees, water fees, etc. The surprising thing was, however, that the woman who got the job remained in the position only a week, and then she moved to Port Vila. She told me that there had been too much *toktok* [B: gossip] in the village, and too many people had pointed to the fact that her father was on the board of the secondary school and also a member of the LDC, and that he had tried to control the process. The woman felt threatened by this, because, as she explained, *toktok* like this always leads to *posen* [B: sorcery]. She was afraid that jealousy would inflict sorcery.

We see here how the communal form, wherein separation and personification is sanctioned, is the primary value in everyday interaction. Getting the job through privilege implied an emphasis on the relationship between her and her father. This way of singling out specific relations were in this context unacceptable and annoyed the people in the village. The values of everyday life in other words completely negate of any sort of 'stops' or 'separations' in the network of relations. The historical transformation and value-reversal following the advent of the church and its development on Ambrym, has resulted in a sacralisation of this everyday social form. Whereas in the past there would be a great difference between the level of the ceremonial and sacred (the graded society) and everyday life, in terms of the value that was emphasized, there is no such great difference today. The ceremonial form in the church resembles the everyday social form.

In everyday life, as well as in the church, the female social form, the unmediated relation, is succeeding as a superior value. However, this does not imply that only women are successful in the church or in everyday life. As I have repeatedly underlined, men can of course also take on a female social form, and they do to a large extent. Men are active in the church and they of course take part in household production. It is interesting however, that men do not seem to be as interested as women in creating their own communal organizations for community development. As the graded society has lost ground, men seem perhaps to have lost a male expression. Women are much more active in their 'all female' organizations. The local women's club and the PWMU [Presbyterian Women's Mission Union] are to date the most successful organizations with regard to communal work. I was even told that some years ago, the PWMU raised money to buy a communal truck in order to ease the burden of walking the distance between the churches on the island when they organized combined meetings for women from different villages. Men, however, seem to have no institutional base for expressing the male social form any longer.

Dumont in Melanesia

Much of the Melanesian-based critique against Dumont has circled around his notion of levels (Mosko 1994; Jolly 1994; see also for other contexts Fox 1989, 1994, etc.). The notion that a reversal only takes place at an inferior level implies that there is always only one encompassing value, and that this never alternates equally with the opposite value, only unequally. Mosko (1994) has, through an analysis of Dumont's early writings in comparison with his later post *Homo Hiearchicus* [HH] writings, argued that it was Dumont's replacement of the pure-impure distinction for the sacred–profane distinction that coloured his model of hierarchy in general. His early writings (Dumont and Pocock 1957; Dumont 1959, etc.) were based on the sacred-profane distinction as the primary distinction and in this sense within the Durkheimian tradition. Durkheim's argument, in *Elementary Forms of Religious Life* (1915), was that the sacred-profane distinction was a universal and absolute distinction. But, the way Mosko reads him, it was in its nature alterable and reversible. The profane could, for instance in initiation rites, become the sacred. As Dumont's works develop, however, he alters the original Durkheimian notion of the sacred-profane distinction, as well as his own sense of it in his early writings, according to Mosko (1994). As the pure-impure distinction was emphasized at the expense of the sacred-profane distinction, the irreversibility of the hierarchy emerged, because pure-impure, in Dumont's analysis of the Indian material, had this character to a greater extent than the sacred-profane distinction. Mosko, in considering Dumont's much discussed Postface to the second complete English edition of HH, finds a different characterization of hierarchy than the one which is uttered in the Preface, 'Hierarchy consists in the combination of these two propositions concerning different levels. In hierarchy thus defined, complementariness and contradiction is contained in a unity of a superior order' (1980, 24). This, according to Mosko, implies that there is no reversal, where the inferior can become the superior without change of level, and 'there is just a single axis of categorical opposition' (1994, 45). In the Postface Dumont expressed it differently, according to Mosko:

> Hierarchy assumes the distinction of (two) levels. In a sense it is this distinction itself ... As soon as we posit a relation of superior to inferior, we must become accustomed to specifying at what level this hierarchical relation itself is sustained ... Hierarchy thus offers the possibility of reversal: that which at a superior level was superior may become inferior at an inferior level. The left can become the right in what might be called a "left situation" (1980, 244; in Mosko 1994, 46).

Mosko points out that this notion of 'levels' is different from the first sense of hierarchy. The inferior level is a different axis, or a second dimension. Mosko argues:

> I suggest therefore, that reversals, rather than indicating changes of level or presupposing relations of encompassment, point to inversions or transpositions of the relations between complementarily or asymmetrically opposed terms in accordance with changes of context (1994, 48).

Then Mosko arrives at the following definition of hierarchy:

> ... hierarchy consists simply in the complementary or asymmetrical relation between two contrary and mutually opposed terms or categories ... each opposition may serve as the axis upon which the asymmetry of the other may be reversed or inverted so as to produce differentiations among contexts (1994, 49).

This definition, he argues, is more apt to find use in Melanesian worlds where, 'In all such hierarchical systems there are ways in which hierarchy is constrained and contested, by co-existing egalitarian values, by alternative sources of power ...' (1994, 10).

It is interesting that Iteanu (1990) has comparable analyses of Durkheim and Dumont, where he, as does Mosko, takes the difference between the impure-pure and the sacred-profane distinction as his point of departure. Contrary to Mosko, Iteanu argues that it is the sacred-profane distinction, the way it has been analyzed by Durkheim, which is problematic rather than the pure-impure distinction the way Dumont has analyzed it. Whereas Mosko sees the pure-impure distinction as changing the initial dynamic character of the sacred-profane distinction, Iteanu sees the pure–

impure distinction as solving the internal contradiction inhered in the sacred-profane distinction. Iteanu argues that Durkheim in *Elementary Forms of Religion*, where he compares two Australian totemic religions, faced a problem because he on the one hand argues that the sacred and the profane are absolutely distinct and comprise two distinct parts of the social order. On the other hand, in rituals of initiation, for example, the profane becomes sacralized as the candidates become more sacred, and this, according to Iteanu, shows that the distinction between the sacred and the profane is not absolute, but rather a matter of degree. Iteanu compares Durkheim's model to Dumont's and argues that by a realization of the hierarchical nature of the concept pair, the paradox is solved. Through a comparison of the pure-impure distinction as outlined by Dumont, Iteanu argues that just as the pure-impure concept pairs create two hierarchies, this is the case for the sacred and profane as well. It is the bi-dimensional character of the hierarchy that makes the profane become the sacred, at another level. At the level of the profane, the profane may become the sacred, because this is at an inferior level.

These different readings of Durkheim and evaluations of Dumont can be attributed to the different evaluation of seeing variation in a society as limited by one axis of differentiation. Jolly (1994) has, through an analysis of historical transformations of hierarchy in Vanuatu, argued that there is not *one* value more prominent than any other that can be credited as structuring a local value hierarchy. She focuses on three hierarchical oppositions in northern Vanuatu, implied in rank, gender and place, and compares these to historical hierarchical principles on Fiji as analyzed by Sahlins. She criticises Sahlins (1985) for privileging the distinction between chief and commoner as a gendered distinction, and applies Toren's (1990) model of how hierarchy on Fiji works. Toren points out that there is no generalized hierarchy between man and woman, but that there is one between wife and husband, between older and younger, etc. Jolly argues that Toren (1990) 'sees the intersection of these oppositions not as contained within an overarching totality but as constantly generating ambiguities and contestations' (Jolly 1994, 157).

In other words, there is no dominant difference to which other differences are related as parts to wholes, in the Dumontian sense. Jolly criticizes Sahlins for taking a position where he puts himself in a privileged place, as a transcendental subject, where he is able to see this totality. There is no such place, according to Jolly, or rather, as she puts it (1994, 161), 'I am rather nervous in the face of this monstrous specter of an overarching intellectual sovereignty and would prefer a location which is more partial ...' No opposition is primary according to Jolly, neither in the Fijian case nor in the case for Vanuatu. She points to the colonial process where chiefs were suddenly selected by untraditional criteria. Appointed chiefs and assessors were often not 'men of significant indigenous rank or influence' (1994, 158).

Jolly argues that there is a range of different axes on which hierarchy is developed, and not only according to one difference. I agree that there is a difference between the relationship between seniors and juniors, and between husbands and wives, and parents and children, etc, but cannot all these be said to be structured by a distinction on a more general level? In the Ambrym case I have argued that it is the difference between the personification and the unmediated relation which orders other relationships, so that 'male' stands for the personified version of the relationship whereas 'female' stands for the non personified version of the relation and that their equally important but contrasting parts constitute a hierarchy. There is thus a locally manifest principle on which historical transformation must be understood, or else there would be nothing but random social activity on which historical circumstance had total power. Arguing for the presence of significant local structures can only be empowering for the way such small-scale societies as villages on North Ambrym are presented and understood. I have argued, in Chapters 5 and 6 for instance , that women in church groupings create communality and manage community fundraising successfully because the church materializes a social form that women enacted even before the church was established.

In his analyses of Urapmin conversion to Christianity, Robbins (2004) also underlines the usefulness of seeing cultures as structured on the importance of one dominant value. This does not imply that variation and change is not recognized. However, both variation and change is structured. In their encounter with Christianity, the Urapmin people realised that their traditional dominant value, 'the relation', lost ground in giving explanatory value to the new colonial and post-colonial reality. This did not imply that the Urapmin, when going to church and when encountering colonial officials, changed their perceptions of what is meaningful and valuable only in these contexts. Rather, the new value of the individual, which is central for the kind of Pentecostal Christianity the Urapmin people converted to, gained a privileged position in the cultural system as a new dominant value. Even radical change is structured according to an encounter between opposing values.

Variation and contextual difference on Ambrym as well is structured according to the hierarchy of gendered social forms. This book has been a demonstration of how these gendered social forms have operated in different constellations in the last century. On Ambrym, the alternation between church and *mage*, and everyday life and ceremonial life, is an alternation in gendered value regimes where the first emphasizes unmediated relations and the second emphasizes personified relations. This transformation from emphasis on personifications to emphasis on the unmediated relation, is perhaps in my material best documented in the description of the development of the church in the last century (Chapters 5 and 6). As I have argued, the church was initially controlled by the high-ranking men in the *mage* who bought rights to the churches and seemed to use the logic of the *mage* within the church, for instance by buying rights and preventing female access to the church. As the high-ranking men turned away from the church after endless battles and quarrels with missionaries over how the church was to be organized, the church was left to women and low-ranking men. The high-ranking men were no longer interested in the church when the missionaries prevented them from creating manifestations of greatness, and prevented them from making the church into an exclusive and partial movement for men only. The church was transformed from a movement that initially worked on the logic of the *mage* where high-ranking men bought 'rights' in the church, so that the church could represent their great names, to a movement which was inclusive and communal. Malnaim who chased away the first missionary in Ranon, described in Chapter 5, would never himself become a Christian as the church was turned into a movement where personal glory was no longer achievable.

As the church developed in the last century into a communal movement, it became a silent and steadily growing movement, without any big names. From the 1920s and onwards the churches on North Ambrym grew from small minority congregations to the most important communal institutions. As the movement transformed from an exclusive relation between competing big men to an open and inclusive movement, people from villages around the mission station were recruited and built their own churches. I have shown how this rapid growth of the church can be tightly connected to women from the mission villages who married into 'heathen' villages and brought the church along.

Besides Peter Ramel, the first returned labour migrant who built the first church, there are few names connected to the growth of the church movement. This is in direct contrast to discussions of *kastom*. The discourse on *kastom* is tied to particular high-graded men, such as Tainmal and Tofor and later, when Tofor died, his brothers Hanghang and Magekon. The church movement and the *kastom* movement then can be contrasted: the first silent and with no names connected to it, the second loud and tightly connected to particular names. One might even argue that men like Willie Bongmatur Maldo from Ranmuhu north of Ranon, discussed in Chapter 7, who became the first President of the National Council of Chiefs and who was a church man opposed to the men of *kastom* like Tofor and his father Tainmal, first became well known after he had raised his voice on *kastom* issues. During the 1970s, when he worked hard for the development of the local council and in cooperation with the Presbyterian Church, he was only involved in issues on a local level. As soon as he faced Tofor on issues of *kastom*, as at the electoral meeting on Malekula described in Chapter 7, he created a name for himself, and he rose as a big man in national politics.

However, we might ask, how do these dynamics of local value hierarchy materialised in gendered social forms relate to developments outside of Ambrym?

No Names: Reflections on Movements Without Big Men

This development on Ambrym where a flat, silent movement grew and became the most important communal institution making it harder for the high-graded men to make manifestations of themselves is paralleled by a similar development on the national level. I will in the final part of this chapter briefly throw light on the development on the national political scene during recent decades in order to compare the local level to the national.

In the period leading up to Independence, in the latter half of the 1970s, the *kastom* movement was at its peak. The NaGriamel movement, which was, as I described in Chapter 7, both part of the *kastom* movement as well as having its own agenda, was also experiencing new heights in its development. American business interests had fuelled money into the movement, and Jimmy Stephens travelled to Australia, America, and France. He had great plans for his movement on Santo. He wanted to establish his own independent 'free-state' on Santo, and used American land speculators in his scheme. Beasant (1984) writes that the plan was to give 100,000 Vietnamese refuge on Santo. This had been planned in cooperation with an American businessman named Oliver who had meetings with the UN Refugee Agency and sponsored Jimmy Stephens's travels to broadcast and get support for his plan. The Vietnamese would secure Jimmy Stephens a majority of votes in the forthcoming elections, and, as they were fleeing from a communist regime, they would 'constitute a natural "bulwark against communism"' (Beasant 1984, 66), which was important for the American business interests. The Vietnamese would also supply skilled manpower that would be needed in the new development on Santo, as envisioned by Jimmy Stephens and the American business interests that operated under the name 'the Phoenix Foundation'.

Jimmy Stephens was in other words experiencing support and getting resources from new sources. In the 1960s and early 1970s, the French administration had been his main supporter (see Chapter 7), but he now built new alliances. Jimmy Stephens had in the early 1960s established the NaGriamel village Tanafo, initiated local production schemes, and built a huge *Nakamal* [B: communal house] for his movement, and was now carried forward by American dollars. His name travelled worldwide. However, just at its peak, he and his movement of which he was the primary personification, was completely smashed. The new Independence government broke down the Santo-based organization with violent intervention (see Chapter 7). In the same way as the famous *kastom* man Tofor on Ambrym experienced a peak of fame in the years leading up to Independence, but was afterwards relegated to a place in the shadow of the new independent government, Jimmy Stephens on Santo fell suddenly from his prestigious pedestal. I believe that this development, where great personifications of the NaGriamel and the *kastom* movement suddenly disappeared and the democratic government was elected, is comparable to the development of the church on Ambrym in the late nineteenth and twentieth centuries. Just as great village men during a few decades lost territory because another movement, founded on other structural principles grew and became more important for village politics, the great men of *kastom* and the NaGriamel movement were suddenly no longer necessary as the nation-state became independent. The elected government was in many respects founded on the principles of the church, as the national slogan 'long God yumi stanap' [with God we raise] indicates. The movement that finally succeeded in controlling the process of Independence, the National Party, was not only a political party but can also be seen as a Christian movement, based on the Anglican and Presbyterian Christian ideals headed by a churchman, Father Walter Lini. The new structural principles of the nation-state followed those of the church, and I believe that, in this period, also at the national level, the church represented an alternative movement to the *kastom* movement and the NaGriamel, in the sense that it was more a communal, democratic and 'flat' movement.

This analysis, in which the development of the national democratic movement is compared to the growth of the church on the local level over the last hundred years, is of course oversimplified here. In order to understand the dynamics of national politics in its own right, other factors need to be included in the analysis, such as issues of class, of island identity and of relations to the wider world. I believe however that there is a significant link between the way the church has developed in the villages and the way the National Party and Father Walter Lini came to government. The

National Party sprung from the people of the Presbyterian Church on Ambrym,[3] and the Presbyterian Church remained, as I showed in Chapter 7, the framework on which persons such as Chief Willie from Ambrym operated as they entered national politics. When the Presbyterian Church celebrated its anniversary in Port Vila in 1998 it was also a celebration of the nation based on the values of the church. I was not in Port Vila at the time, but when I arrived in Ranon in 1999, I was told that I had missed the most important event of the last few decades, and that all the meetings and fundraising events I ever attended afterwards would never become as huge and as important as the celebrations of the anniversary of the Presbyterian Church in Port Vila. Several of the village women from North Ambrym had travelled to the capital for the sole purpose of taking part in this national community of the church. The form of the church extended from the local level to the national level, creating a community that exceeded the village and the island. I found it particularly interesting that when I asked people about the anniversary, it seemed to me that women had been in great majority among the people who had travelled from Ambrym to Port Vila to take part in the celebrations. The idea of a national community as well in many respects seems to be connected to the church and to women. The church is, in other words, also a very successful, although silent, women's movement.

Feminists in National Politics

The success of the Presbyterian Church in mobilizing village women stands in great contrast to the lack of success the urban feminist movement has experienced in the villages. The Vanuatu National Council of Women /Nasonal kaonsel blong ol Woman [VNCW/VNKW] is an NGO with economic support from foreign NGOs, founded officially after the first national conference of native women in Port Vila in 1980, just after Independence. Grace Mera Molisa and Hilda Lini were at this conference and later important to the beginning and the development of the organization. The two women had been part of the Independence movement and had advocated women's rights in the National Party (Bolton, 1993).

The VNCW is today mainly a Port Vila-based organization with its own radio program and its own newsletter. It has been a movement influenced by Western feminists, with a call for equal rights and equal representation and the organization is linked to other international women's rights forums. It has been an important movement for the formation of the egalitarian state project, where women's rights to representation and participation have been recognized. Furthermore, it has been a movement of great significance for many urban women who have lacked social security and family, being single mothers or in violent relationships.

Except for a brief period in the 1980s however, on Ambrym this movement has not been very visible. It was the PWMU [Presbyterian Women's Mission Union] that played the main role for women in the villages. When I visited the headquarters of the VNCW in Port Vila in 1995 and then again in 1999, to discuss their work and

---

3　　On other islands they came from other churches as well; for instance the Anglican Church was important for the National Party.

the reason why they seemed to be mainly an urban movement and lacked success in the villages, it was argued by several women in the organization that *kastom* had too strong a grip on village life and *kastom* remained an obstacle for women wishing to participate in politics. I will however argue that it was almost the other way around. It was the feminist movement's similarity to the *kastom* movement, in terms of social form, that made it foreign for local women to engage in the movement.

The PWMU was based on the structures of the church, which, as I have argued throughout this book, is communal and unmediated. The inclusive and non-personified social form of the church made it attractive to women. The feminist movement had another character. It was a movement for women only, and it thereby had a single-sex character. In this respect the feminist movement is more comparable to the exclusive movements for men, like the graded society and, to a certain extent, the *kastom* movement. Whereas the urban feminists argued that *kastom* was an obstacle to rural women's involvement in the feminist movement, from the point of view of North Ambrym women, it was the structural similarity of the feminist movement to the *kastom* movement which made it foreign. The feminist movements seemed to create personifications in the same way as the exclusive male social movements had done. The VNCW had entered national politics with key persons in the front, and in 1995 several of the centrally positioned women in the VNCW campaigned for their seats in the national assembly. While constantly arguing against men of *kastom*, in particular by protesting decisions made by the Malvatumauri, the VNCW operated on the same social form as did the *kastom* movement.

Although changes in gender relations were taking place during these decades, it was in another arena perhaps than the one the urban feminists were watching. Women became important within the 'silent' movement of the church. Because the church was opposed by the *kastom* men, it became a female movement and as such it grew and became a more important social institution than the *mage*. The combination of the structural position of women in relation to marriage and movement and the transfer of the church from high men to low men and women, made way for a new social movement on the local level on Ambrym, which has been more successful with regard to changes in gender relations than the urban-based feminist movement. Gender relations were changed in the sense that when the church replaced the *mage* as the most important social institution, the capacity of women to work collectively became more visualized and gained a new importance. Moreover, as the Presbyterian Church became a national movement, the church provided women with a network exceeding the local community, and urban events such as anniversary celebrations of the church in Port Vila gathered women from all over the archipelago.

Concluding Perspectives on Christianity and Change

What kind of change is this, however, when a cultural system transforms itself, or inverts its value hierarchy, in the encounter with Christianity? The message the Christian movements of various kinds brought along as the mission spread to various parts of the world often echoed the values of individualism and egalitarianism (see also Robbins 2004). These values, often expressed through terms like 'liberation', have been a radical force for change. Perhaps the most famous anthropological description and analysis of a Christian transformation is the work by Comaroff and Comaroff (1991) on the Tswana in South Africa. They describe how: '… parts of the evangelical message insinuated themselves into the warp and weft of an evangelical hegemony, while others gave rise to a novel form of consciousness and action' (1991, 12). It was the novel form of consciousness that gave the Tswana new concepts and a language for resisting the colonial government and its inequalities. However, the Comaroffs do not emphasize the new values of the new religion, but rather argue that these new signifiers of the colonizers became unfixed. The Africans refashioned them and turned them into vehicles for their own signifying needs. The language of the mission became, not solely but nevertheless significantly, the language of liberation from the colonial hegemony by referring not to new value regimes but to old ones.

Robbins (2007) has recently argued that anthropologists often fail to recognize the change involved in conversion to Christianity, and takes the Comaroffs' analyses of the Tswana conversion as a specific example. He argues that instead of focusing on what Christianity itself implied for the Tswana, they concentrated on how the pre-Christian cultural system is played out in a new language. The Comaroffs describe how the cultural change involved in Christianity was resisted. The Tswana people of South Africa turned the significance of the evangelical message from a 'civilising' project to a liberating project based mostly on their pre-existing cultural scheme. They applied what they found useful in the Christian message, but did not accept Christianity as a new 'total' system, structured on a new dominant value. Rather, the Comaroffs describe the process of evangelization in South Africa as conversion and conversation. The Tswana tried to draw out of the conversation the power of the mission to protect an endangered world. The missionaries tried to get other things out of the conversation, such as fixing the image of the Tswana as the 'savage other' 'into the currency of the Christian Commonwealth' (1991, 198).

To some extent the Tswana are described as if they were 'in-between' the Tswana cultural system and the Christian. The change that comes about is a result of a manipulation of the Christian signifiers merging with their own cultural schemata. This situation is quite different from the kind of change Robbins (2004) has described among the Urapmin, a group of less than 400 people in the Mountain Ok region of the western highlands of Papua New Guinea. By embracing the new Christian worldview and the value of individualism, their cultural system was radically changed. The Urapmin faced a situation where their previous position vis-à-vis their neighbours was weakened. As a result of their peripheral position in relation to the colonial centres of powers, both religious and political, they lost a certain sense of pride in their own cultural system. They could not make sense of how they had lost their position and this humiliating experience made them seek alternative explanations. In a Christian cosmology they found answers. They resorted to an ideology where their 'sinfulness' could explain lack of success.

Comparing the Urapmin to the Tswana, one might say that whereas the Urapmin radically changed their cultural system in a 'total' way, the Tswana only partially did. The Ambrym case is different from both of these in the sense that it was on the one hand totally changed; turning the value hierarchy upside down, but on the other the cultural system was maintained as a whole based on the value of the relation.

The Ambrym situation must be understood as a result of a particular colonial situation, which was quite different both from the Tswana and from the Urapmin. In South Africa colonial settlers, both Dutch and British, built large and powerful settlements on the coast, and adventurers and missionaries, mostly from non-conformist churches (the Methodists, Calvinists, etc) travelled into the 'unknown interiors'. The Tswana felt that their world was being threatened and the chiefs, as the Comaroffs illustrate by citing missionary reports, warned their people of contact with missionaries whom they regarded as only 'precursors of the government, who would soon follow in their train and make soldiers of every one of them' (1991, 192). The Comaroffs describe political battles between the Tswana and the missionaries 'to control the dominant material and symbolic values' (1991, 199). It was a battle between the values of the expanding Western hegemony and the values and life world of the Tswana chiefdoms. The Comaroffs outline how, 'The curricula of church and school together set out to reorganize the flow of seasons and events that configured space and time for Tswana' (1991, 234). Among the Urapmin, the situation was perhaps even more dramatic. The Urapmin live in a remote area of Papua New Guinea and had not until the late colonial period, at the end of the 1950s, any contact with the colonial state apparatus. The encounter was thus not of the gradual kind such as the Tswana experienced. It was a rather more dramatic and shocking experience where the world around them, their neighbours and regional partners had become part of a new system they themselves were excluded from because of their marginal situation. Whereas the Tswana had to fight a long battle, in the form of a fight over signifiers, the Urapmin lost the ground for their signifiers long before the fight had begun. When the Urapmin were drawn into the colonial apparatus, the law system and the new religion, they were faced with an established system that they, a group of not even 400, had extreme difficulty rejecting.

On Ambrym there was no battle. The colonial situation was not of the South African kind, nor of the Urapmin kind. As I have outlined in previous chapters, the condominium government never had any efficient state apparatuses, and the District Agents were to a large degree more puppets for the different chiefs in the area than an authoritarian force of any kind. Ambrym ideas of place and movement were not threatened. The initial power struggle between the missionary and the high-graded men was so uneven in strength that the missionary never had any real chance of success. On Ambrym it was not a battle between the Western hegemonic values and the values of the traditional community, but rather a battle over how the church was to be gendered. This fight, as I have shown, did not last long, as the high-graded men withdrew and used their energy to protect the existing male institution, the *mage*.

In South Africa however, in spite of how the mission was at first resisted, the churches also came to represent collective identities the way the churches did on Ambrym. In South Africa, the Comaroffs argue, this was a novel form of collective identity. The Tswana in pre-colonial times had not engaged in this kind of collective self-representation. Rather, the self-representation of the Tswana in pre-mission times had been one that stressed undifferentiated humanity. The mission church came to represent a new form of collective identity:

And so the Christians, by turning the visage of shared identity back on "their" people, became a medium for its construction and representation – the human equivalent, almost, of the mirrors they had given the Tswana fifty years before, except that now the reflected image was not individual but collective. Sometime the fabrication of ethnic consciousness involved such flamboyant gestures as founding a state, a "united Nation". But most of all, it lay the way in which the missionaries tried to remake the everyday world of these Africans and, as they insinuated themselves into it, to redefine its significant coordinates and constituencies. For instance both the LMS and the WMMS established a "Bechuana District"… (1991, 288)

The mission church in South Africa reorganized ideas of what tied people together. On Ambrym it was the other way around. It was the idea of what tied people together which organized the church. The church came to represent place identities in a time of mobility. In South Africa a significant difference developed between the nonconformist mission church on the one hand and the state-oriented church of the whites. The 'proper' church was for the whites and the mission church was for the blacks, and according to the Comaroffs, a novel form of black consciousness developed. On Ambrym collective identities that the church was based on were not formed by such a distinction between mission church and proper church. The colonial representation was not so forcefully present on Ambrym. Rather, as I have outlined, the church on Ambrym hooked onto collective identities tied to historical village relocations and 'connecting women'. Whereas this new expression of collective identity on Ambrym foregrounded women's work, it was the black consciousness movement which was being institutionalized through the mission church in South Africa.

The Comaroffs talk about the colonization of consciousness in South Africa. It is obvious that this was less the case on Ambrym. Although the church did bring along changes, these changes were more a matter of foregrounding something which had been in the background all along. This form of social change however is talked about as a form of liberation by women on the islands of Vanuatu, as in this poem by Avin which was published after the National Women's Festival in 1990 in the booklet *Who Will Carry the Bag*:

Woman	**Woman**[4]
Sista	Sister
Wanem ia bigfala krae	What is this big cry
Long medel naet	In the middle of the night
Yu we	You who
Yu gat wok ful dei	You have work all day
Yu we	You who
Yu no save luk taet o sik	You cannot be tired or sick
Yu we	You who
Yu no gat raet blong tok	You have not got the right to talk
Yu we	You who
Oli save kilim i tet	They might kill you

---

4   My translation

Yu we	You who
Man I pem blong plisim hem	Man pays for you in order for you to please him
Yu we	You who
Yu stampa blong laef blong wol	You are the source of life in the world today
Sista	Sister
Stanap	Raise
Yu no blong wan man	You do not belong to one man
Yu blong God.	You belong to God.

My claim is that the church movement has been the most important social movement on Ambrym in the colonial and post-colonial era. As I have described above, the church developed not only as a new expression of the origin identities and connections between people, but made roads for new connections on other parts of the island and in the urban centers. I read the poem above as an expression of how the church has changed gender relations. The church has become an expression of the role of women in the local social organization.

Women's efforts in communal work have become visualized and gained in importacen through the church, and this visualization has contributed to a new kind of consciousness among women. The poem above expresses this, showing how a woman is not primarily a wife and a mother in a conjugal household. In spite of how she carries the burden of daily care for children and husband, her role is not confined to this arena. 'You have not got the right to talk' the poem says, and by this I believe the poet directs attention to the ways in which women have been denied access to the traditionally exclusive male organizations. However, in spite of work burdens and in spite of limited access to traditional political institutions, it is through the church that women on Ambrym and in the islands of Vanuatu generally, have built powerful frameworks for their concerns, ambitions and activities.

References

Allen, M. (ed.) (1981), *Vanuatu: Politics, Economics and Ritual in Island Melanesia* (Sydney: Academic Press Australia).

– (1981), 'Innovation, Inversion and Revolution as Political Tactics in West Aoba', in Allen (ed.).

– (1984), 'Elders, Chiefs and Big Men: Authority, Legitimation and Political Evolution in Melanesia', *American Ethnologist* 11:1, 20–41.

Asad, T. (1993), *Genealogies of Religion: Discipline and Reasons of Powering Christianity and Isla* (Baltimore: The John Hopkins University Press).

Avin (1990), 'Woman', in *Who Will Carry the Bag.* (Booklet from the National Women's Festival, Port Vila).

Barker, J. (1992), 'Christianity in Western Melanesian Ethnography' in J. Carrier (ed.).

– (1996), 'Village Inventions: Historical Variations upon a Regional Theme in Uiaku, Papua New Guinea', *Oceania*, vol. 66:3, 211–30.

Beasant, J. (1984), *The Santo Rebellion: An Imperial Reckoning* (Honolulu: University of Hawaii Press).

Barnard, T.T. (1986), 'The Regulation of Marriage in Ambrym and Paama', in Gisele De Meur (ed.), *New Trends in Mathematical Anthropology* (London: Routledge and Kegan Paul).

BDA (British District Agent Report) Bi annual report from 1964, National Archives, Port Vila, Vanuatu.

– Annual report CD2, 1971, National Archives, Port Vila, Vanuatu.

– report 1975, National Archives, Port Vila, Vanuatu.

– report from a tour in August 1976, National Archives, Port Vila, Vanuatu.

– Touring notes, 16–21 March 1967, National Archives, Port Vila, Vanuatu.

– Touring notes, 9–14 September 1968, National Archives, Port Vila, Vanuatu.

– Touring notes 10–15 October 1969, National Archives, Port Vila, Vanuatu.

– Touring notes 8–13 December 1974, National Archives, Port Vila, Vanuatu.

– Touring notes 29–25 January 1976, National Archives, Port Vila, Vanuatu.

– Touring notes 15–21 October, year undated, National Archives, Port Vila, Vanuatu.

– undated report, probably from 1976, National Archives, Port Vila, Vanuatu.

Blackwell, P. (1981), 'Rank, Exchange and Leadership in Four Vanuatu Societies', in Allen (ed.).

Bolton, L. (1993), *Dancing in Mats: Extending Kastom to Women in Vanuatu*, PhD thesis, University of Manchester.

– (1998a), 'Praying for the Revival of Kastom: Women and Christianity in the Vanuatu Cultural Centre', Paper given in the Workshop, State, Society, and Governance in Melanesia Project. ANU.

– (1998b), 'Chief Willie Bongmatur Maldo and the Role of Chiefs in Vanuatu', *Journal of Pacific History*, 33:2, 179–95.

– (1999a), 'Radio and the Redefinition of Kastom in Vanuatu', *The Contemporary Pacific*, 11:2, 335–60.

– (1999b), 'Women, Place and Practice in Vanuatu: A View from Ambae', *Oceania* 70:1, 43–55.

– (2003), *Unfolding the Moon: Enacting Women's Kastom in Vanuatu,* (Honolulu: University of Hawaii Press).

Bonnemaison, J. (1985), *The Tree and the Canoe: Roots and Mobility in Vanuatu Societies,* in M. Chapman (ed.).

– (1994), The Tree and the Canoe: History and Ethnography of Vanuatu, transl. and adapted by Josee-Demetry, South Sea Books, (Honolulu: University of Hawaii Press).

Butler, J. (1990), *Gender Trouble: Feminism and the Subversion of Identity* (London: Routledge).

Carrier, J.G. (ed.) (1992), *History and Tradition in Melanesian Anthropology* (Berkeley: University of California Press).

– (1992), 'Introduction', in Carrier, J. (ed.).

Carrier J. and Carrier, A. (1991), *Structure and Process in a Melanesian Society: Ponam's Progress in the Twentieth Century*, (Philadelphia: Harwood Academic Publishers).

Chapman, M. (ed.) (1985), 'Mobility and Identity in Island Pacific' *Pacific Viewpoint,* Special Issue 26:1.

Clastres, P. (1989), *Society Against the State*, transl. by Robert Huxley in collaboration with Abe Stein (New York: Zone Books).

Collier, Jane F. and Rosaldo, M. (1981), 'Gender and Politics in Simple Societies', in *Sexual Meaning*, S.B. Ortner and H. Whitehead (eds) (New York: Cambridge University Press).

Collier, J.F. (1988), *Marriage and Inequality in Classless Societies* (Stanford: Stanford University Press).

Comaroff, J. and J. (1991), *Of Revelation and Revolution: Christianity, Colonialism and Consciousness in South Africa, Vol. 1* (Chicago: The University of Chicago Press).

Corris, P. (1970), 'Pacific Island Migration in Queensland', *Journal of Pacific History,* 5, 43–64.

Crowly, T. (1995), *A New Bislama Dictionary* (Institute of Pacific Studies, Suva, Fiji and Pacific Languages Unit, Vila, Vanuatu).

Curtis, T. (1999), 'Tom's Tambu House: Spacing, Status, and Sacredness in South Malekula, Vanuatu', *Oceania,* 70:1, 56–71.

Deacon, B. (1927), 'The Regulation of Marriage on Ambrym', *Journal of the Royal Anthropological Society* 57, 325–42.

– (1934), *Malekula: A Vanishing People in the New Hebrides (*London: Routledge and Keegan).

De Certeau, M. (1984), *The Practice of Everyday Life* (Berkeley and Los Angeles: University of California Press).

De Coppet, D. (1992), 'Comparison, a Universal for Anthropology', in Adam Kuper (ed.), *Conceptualizing Society,* pp. 59–75. (London : Routledge).

Douglas, B. (2002), Christian Citizens: Women and Negotiations of Modernity in Vanuatu', *The Contemporary Pacific* 14:1, 1–38.

– (2003) 'Christianity, Tradition, and Everyday Modernity: Towards an Anatomy of Women's Groupings in Melanesia', *Oceania,* vol. 74:1/2, 6–23.

Deleuze G. and Guattari, F. (1983/1972), *Anti-Oedipus: Capitalism and Schizophrenia* (Minneapolis: University of Minnesota Press).

– (1988), *A Thousand Plateaus: Capitalism and Schizophrenia* (London: The Athlone Press).

Dumont, L. (1959), 'Purity and Impurity', *Contributions to Indian Sociology,* **3**, 9–39.

– (1979), 'The Anthropological Community and Ideology', *Social Science Information*, 18, 785–817.

– (1980), *Homo Hirarchicus: The Caste System and its Implications*, complete revised English edition (Chicago: University of Chicago Press).

– (1986), *Essays on Individualism: Modern Ideology in Anthropological Perspective* (Chicago: University of Chicago Press).

Dumont, L. and Pocock, D.F. (1957), 'For a Sociology of India', *Contributions to Indian Sociology,* 1, 8–22.

Durkheim, E. (1961) {1915}, *'Elementary Forms of Religious Life'*, trans. J.B. Swan (New York: Collier).

Eriksen, A. (2005a), *Silent Movement: Transformations of Gendered Social Structures on Ambrym, Vanuatu.* (University of Bergen: Thesis for the degree of Dr. Polit.).

– (2005b), 'The Gender of the Church: Conflicts and Social Wholes on Ambrym, Vanuatu', *Oceania,* 75:3, 284–300.

– (2006), 'On the Value of the Church: The Gendered Dynamics of an Inverted Hierarchy on North Ambrym, Vanuatu', *Paideuma*, 52, 91–106.

– (2006), 'Expected and Unexpected Cultural Heroes: Reflections on Gender and Agency of Conjuncture on Ambrym, Vanuatu', *Anthropological Theory*, 6:2, 227–49.

Fortes, M. (1953), 'The Structure of Unilineal Descent Groups', American *Anthropologist* 55:17–41.

Foster, R.J. (1995), Social Reproduction and History in Melanesia. (Cambridge: Cambridge University Press).

Fox, J.J. (1989), 'Category and Complement: Binary Ideologies and the Organization of Dualism in Eastern Indonesia', in D. Maybury-Lewis and U. Almagor (eds), *The Attraction of Opposites: Thought and Society in a Dualistic Mode*, pp 33–56. (Ann Arbor: University of Michigan Press).

– (1994), 'Reflections on 'Hierarchy' and 'Precedence', *History and Anthropology,* 7:1–4, 87–109.

– (1997), 'Place and Landscape in Comparative Austronesian Perspective', in *The Poetic Power of Place*, James J. Fox, (ed.) (A publication of the Department of Anthropology published in association with The Comparative Austronesian Project, Research School of Pacific and Asian Studies, The Australian National University, Canberra).

Frater, M. (1922), *Midst Volcanic Fires* (London: James Clark and Co).

Geismar, H. (2005), 'Copyright in Context: Carvings, Carvers and Commodities in Vanuatu', *American Ethnologist* 33:3, 437–59.

Gell, A. (1992), 'Inter Tribal Commodity Barter and Reproductive Gift Exchange in Old Melanesia', in C. Humphrey and S. Hugh Jones (eds), *Barter, Exchange and Value. An Anthropological Approach*, pp. 142–69, (Cambridge: Cambridge University Press).

– (1998), *Art and Agency: An Anthropological Theory* (Oxford: Clarendon Press).

– (1999), *The Art of Anthropology: Essays and Diagrams*, E. Hirsch (ed.), London School of Economics Monographs on Social Anthropology, vol. 67 (London: Athlone Press).

Gewertz, D. and Errington, F. (1987), *Cultural Anthropology and a Feminist Alternative: An Analysis of Culturally Constructed Gender Interests in Papua New Guinea* (Cambridge: Cambridge University Press).

– (1991), *Twisted Histories and Altered Contexts: Representing the Chambri in a World System* (Cambridge: Cambridge University Press).

– (1999), *Emerging Class in Papua New Guinea* (Cambridge: Cambridge University Press).

Giddens, A. (1990), *The Consequences of Modernity* (Cambridge: Polity Press).

Godelier, M. (1986), *The Making of Great Men* (Cambridge: Cambridge University Press).

Goody, J. (1973), 'Bridewealth and Dowry in Africa and Eurasia', in J. Goody and S.J. Tambiah (eds), *Bridewealth and Dowry*, pp. 1–59. (Cambridge: Cambridge University Press).

Gregory, C. (1982), Gifts and Commodities (London: Academic Press).

Grosz, E. (1989), *Sexual Subversions* (London: Allen and Unwin).

Gupta, A. and Fergusen, J. (1997), 'Beyond Culture: Space, Identity, and the Politics of Difference', in A. Gupta and J. Ferguson (eds), Culture, Power, Place: Explorations in Critical Anthropology, pp 33–51. (Durham, NC: Duke University Press).

Harrison, S. (1985), 'Ritual Hierarchy and Secular Equality in a Sepik River Village', American Ethnologist, 12:3, 413–26.

– (1993), 'Transformations of Identity in Sepik Warfare', in M. Strathern (ed.) Shifting Contexts, pp. 81–99 (London and New York: Routledge).

Hermann, E. (1992), 'The Yali Movement in Retrospect: Rewriting History, Redefining 'Cargo Cult'', Oceania 63:1, 55–71.

Hirsch, E. (1995), 'Introduction: Landscape: Between Place and Space', in E. Hirsch and M. O'Hanlon (eds), The Anthropology of Landscape. Perspectives on Place and Space, pp. 1–30. (Oxford Studies in Social and Cultural Anthropology: Oxford University Press).

Hobsbawm, E. and Ranger, T. (eds) (1983), The Invention of Tradition (Cambridge: Cambridge University Press).

Howell, S. (1985),'Equality and Hierarchy in Chewong Classification', in R.H. Barnes, D. de Coppet and R. J. Parkin (eds), *Contexts and Levels*, pp. 167–80 (Oxford: JASO Occasional Papers no. 4).

Hviding, E. (1996), *Guardians of the Marovo Lagoon; Practice, Place and Politics in Maritime Melanesia* (Honolulu: University of Hawaii Press).

– (2003), 'Disentangling the *Butubutu* of New Georgia: Cognatic Kinship in Thought and Action', in I. Hoëm and S. Roalkvam (eds), *Oceanic Socialities and Cultural Forms: Ethnographies of Experience*, 71–113 (Oxford: Berghahn Books).

Hyslop, C. (1999), 'The Linguistics of Inhabiting Space: Spatial Reference in the North East Ambae Language', *Oceania,* 70:1, 25–42.

Iteanu, A. (1989), 'Sacred and Profane Revisited: Durkheim and Dumont Considered in the Orokaiva Context', *Ethnos* 55:3–4,169–83.

Jebens, H. (2005), *Pathways to Heaven: Contesting Mainline and Fundamentalist Christianity in Papua New Guinea.* (Oxford: Berghahn Books).

– (ed.) (2004), *Cargo, Cult and Culture Critique* (Honolulu: Hawaii University Press).

Jolly, M. (1987), 'The Forgotten Women: A History of Migrant Labour and Gender Relations in Vanuatu', *Oceania* 58:2, 119–39.

– (1989), Sacred Spaces: Churches, Men's Houses and Households in South Pentecost, Vanuatu. In M. Jolly and M. Macintyre (eds), *Family and Gender in the Pacific: Domestic Contradictions and the Colonial Impact*, Cambridge University Press, Cambridge, 213–35.

– (1991a), 'To Save the Girls for Brighter and Better Lives': Presbyterian Mission and Women in the South of Vanuatu: 1848–1870', *Journal of Pacific History* 26:1, 27–48.

– (1991b), 'Gifts, Commodities and Corporeality: Food and Gender in South Pentecost, Vanuatu', *Canberra Anthropology* 14:1, 45–66.

– (1992), 'Spectres of Inauthenticity', *The Contemporary Pacific*, 4:1, 3–27.

– (1994), 'Hierarchy and Encompassment. Rank, Gender and Place in Vanuatu and Fiji', *History and Anthropology,* 7:1–4,133–67.

– (1995), *Women of the Place: Kastom, Colonialism and Gender in Vanuatu.* (Philadelphia: Harwood Academic Publishers).

– (2003), 'Epilogue', *Oceania,* 74:1–2, 134–147.

Jolly, M. and MacIntyre, M. (eds) (1989), *Family and Gender in the Pacific. Domestic Contradictions and the Colonial Impact.* (Cambridge: Cambridge University Press).

Josephides, L. (1985), *The Production of Inequality: Gender and Exchange Among the Kewa* (London: Tavistock).

Kapferer, B. (2005), *The Retreat of the Social: The Rise and Rise of Reductionism. Critical Interventions: A Forum for Social Analysis.* (Oxford: Berghahn Books).

Keesing, R. (1981), [1976], *Cultural Anthropology: A Contemporary Perspective* (New York: Holt, Rhinehart and Winston).

– (1982), *Kwaio Religion: The Living and the Dead in a Solomon Island Society* (New York: Columbia University Press).

– (1988), Melanesian Pidgin and the Oceanic Subtrate (Stanford: Stanford University Press).

– (1989), 'Creating the Past: Custom and Identity in Contemporary Pacific', The Contemporary Pacific 1, 19–42.

– (1992), Custom and Confrontation: The Kwaio Struggle for Cultural Autonomy (Chicago: University of Chicago Press).

– (1993), 'Kastom Re-examined', Anthropological Forum 6:4, 587–97.

Keesing, R. and Tonkinson, R. (1982), 'Reinventing Traditional Culture: The Politics of Kastom in Island Melanesia', Mankind 13:4, 297–399.

Kelly, R. (1993), Constructing Inequality: The Fabrication of a Hierarchy of Virtue Among the Etoro (Ann Arbor: University of Michigan Press).

Lamb, R. (1905), *Saints and Savages: The Story of Five Years in the New Hebrides* (Sydney: William Blackwood and Sons).

Lane, B. and Lane, R. (1956), 'A Re-interpretation of the Anomalous Six Section Marriage System of Ambrym, New Hebrides', in *Southwestern Journal of Anthropology* 12:406–14.

–(1958), 'The Evolution of Ambrym Kinship' *Southwestern Journal of* Anthropology 14:107–35.

Larcom, J. (1982), 'The Invention of Convention', Mankind, 13:4, 330–37.

Lattas, A. (1991), 'Sexuality and Cargo Cults: The Politics of Gender and Procreation in West New Britain', Cultural Anthropology, 6:2, 230–56.

– (2004), 'Towards a History of Travel in Melanesia: Shamanism, Dreams and Modernity', unpublished manuscript.

Layard, J. (1942), Stone Men of Malekula (London: Chatto and Windus).

Lindstrom, L. (1982), 'Leftemap Kastom: The Political Tradition on Tanna', Mankind, 13:4, 316–29.

– (1993a), *Cargo Cults: Strange Stories of Desire from Melanesia and Beyond* (Honolulu: University of Hawaii Press).

– (1993b), 'Cargo Cult Culture: Toward a Genealogy of Melanesian Kastom', *Anthropological Forum* 6:4, 316–29.

– (1997a), 'Chiefs in Vanuatu Today', *Chiefs Today: Traditional Pacific Leadership and the Postcolonial State*, L. Lindstrom and G. White (eds) (Stanford: Stanford University Press).

– (1997b), 'Introduction: Chiefs Today', in *Chiefs Today: Traditional Pacific Leadership and the Postcolonial State*, L. Lindstrom and G. White (eds) (Stanford: Stanford University Press).

Lindstrom, L. and White, G. (eds) (1993), Special Issue *Anthropological Forum* 6:4, 316–29.

Löffler L.G. (1960), 'The Development of the Ambrym and Pentecost Kinship Systems', *Southwestern Journal of Anthropology* 16:442–61.

Markham, A.H (1873), *The Cruise of the Rosario* ... (London: Sampson Low, Morston, Low and Seale).

Mauss, M. (1990) [1925], *The Gift: Form and Function of Exchange in Archaic Societies* (London: Routledge).

McDougall, D. (2003), 'Fellowship and Citizenship as Models of National Community: United Church Women's Fellowship in Ranongga, Solomon Islands', *Oceania*, 74:1–2, 61–81.

Meggitt, M. J. (1977), *Blood is Their Argument: Warfare Among the Mae Enga Tribesmen of the New Guinea Highlands* (Palo Alto: Mayfield Publishing Company).

Meillasoux, C. (1964), *L'Antropologie Economique des Gouro de Cote d'Ivoire* (Paris: Mouton).

Miles, W.F.S. (1998), *Bridging Mental Boundaries in a Postcolonial Microcosm: Identity and Development in Vanuatu* (Honolulu: University of Hawaii Press).

Miller, G. (1981), *Live: A History of Church Planting in the New Hebrides, New Republic of Vanuatu to 1880, Book 2* (Presbyterian Church of Australia, Sidney: Bridge Printery).

– (1989), *Live: A History of Church Planting in the Republic of Vanuatu, the Northern Islands 1881–1948*, (Australia: Mission Publications).

Moore, H. (1988), *Feminism and Anthropology* (Cambridge: Polity Press).

Mosko, M. (1994), 'Transformations of Dumont: The Hierarchical, the Sacred and the Profane in India and Ancient Hawaii', *History and Anthropology*, 7:1–4, 19–87.

Murray, C. (1887), 'The Diary of Rev. Charles Murray', unpublished manuscript, Presbyterian Church Archives, Knox College, Dunedin, New Zealand.

Ortner, S. B. (1974), 'Is Female to Male as Nature is to Culture?', *Women, Culture and Society*, M.Z. Rosaldo and L. Lamphere (eds), pp. 67–89, (Palo Alto: Stanford University Press).

– (1984), 'Theory in Anthropology Since the Sixties', *Comparative Studies in Society and History* 26:1, 126–166.

Paini, A. (2002), 'The Kite is Tied to You: Custom, Christianity and Organization among Kanak Women of Drueulu, Lifou, New Caledonia', *Oceania*, 74:1–2, 81–98.

Paton, W.F. (1971a), *Ambrym (Lonwolwol) Dictionary*. Pacific Linguistics series, C- No.21 (Canberra: The Australian National University).

– (1971b), *Tales of Ambrym*. Pacific Linguistics Series, D-10 (Canberra: The Australian National University).

– (1979), *Customs of Ambrym*. Pacific Linguistics Series, D-22 (Canberra: The Australian National University).

Patterson, M. (1976), *Kinship, Marriage and Ritual in North Ambrym*. PhD dissertation. (University of Sidney).

– (1981), 'Slings and Arrows: Rituals of Status Acquisition in North Ambrym', in Allen (ed.).

– (2002), 'Moving Histories: An Analysis of Place and Mobility in North Ambrym, Vanuatu', *The Australian Journal of Anthropology*, 13:2, 200–18.

Philibert, J. M. (1992), 'Social Change in Vanuatu', *Social Change in the Pacific Islands*, A.B. Robillard (ed.), pp. 98–133, (London and New York: Keagan Paul International).

Price, C.A. and Baker, E. (1976), 'Origin of Pacific Labourers in Queensland, 1863–1904: A Research Note', *The Journal of Pacific History* 11, 106–121.

Radcliffe-Brown, A. (1927), 'The regulation of marriage in Ambrym', *Journal of the Royal Anthropological Society* 57:343–8.

Rio, K. M. (1997), *Standing Drums in Vanuatu: The Cultural Biography of a National Symbol*, unpublished thesis (Hovedfagsoppgave at the University of Bergen).

– (2002a), *The Third Man: Manifestations of Agency on Ambrym Island, Vanuatu*, (PhD dissertation, University of Bergen).

– (2002b), 'The Sorcerer as an Absented Third Person: Formations of Fear and Anger in Vanuatu', *Social Analysis*, 46:2, 129–154. Also in B. Kapferer (ed.), *Beyond Rationalism: Sorcery, Magic and Ritual in Contemporary Realities* (Oxford: Berghahn Books).

Robbins, J. (2002), 'My Wife Can't Break Off Part of her Belief and Give it to Me: Apocalyptic Interrogations of Christian Individualism Among the Urapmin of Papua New Guinea', *Paideuma* 48:189–206.

– (2004), *Becoming Sinners: Christianity and Moral Torment in a Papua New Guinea Society* (Berkley: University of California Press).

– (2007) Continuity Thinking and the Problem of Christian Culture: Belief, Time, and the Anthropology of Christianity, *Current Anthropology* 48:1, 5–39.

Robbins, J and Wardlow, H. (eds) (2005), *The Making of Global and Local Modernities in Melanesia* (Aldershot: Ashgate).

Rodman, M. (1987), *Masters of Tradition* (Vancouver: University of British Columbia Press).

Rivers, W.H.R. (1915), 'Descent and Ceremonial in Ambrim', *Journal of the Royal Anthropological Society* 45:229:32.

Rubinstein, R.L. (1981), 'Knowledge and Political Process on Malo', Allen, M. (ed.), *Vanuatu: Politics, Economics and Ritual in Island Melanesia* (Sydney: Academic Press Australia).

Sahlins, M. (1962), *Moala: Culture and Nature on a Fijian Island* (Ann Arbor: University of Michigan Press).

– (1963), 'Poor Man, Rich Man, Big Man, Chief: Political Types in Melanesia and Polynesia', *Comparative Studies in Society and History* 5: 285–303.

– (1972), *Stone Age Economics* (New York: Aldine De Gryter).

– (1981), *Historical Metaphors and Mythical Realities: Structure of the Early History of the Sandwich Islands Kingdom*. ASAO Special Publications No. 1. (Ann Arbor: The University of Michigan Press).

– (2000) [1982], 'Individual Experience and Cultural Order', reprinted in *Culture in Practice*, pp. 277–293 (New York: Zone Books).

– (1985), *Islands of History* (Chicago: University of Chicago Press).

– (2000) [1993], 'Goodbye to Tristes Tropes: Ethnography in the Context of Modern World History', reprinted in *Culture in Practice*, pp. 471–501 (New York: Zone Books).

– (1999), 'Two or Three Things I know About Culture', *Journal of the Anthropological Institute*, 5:4, 399–421.

– (2004), *Apologies to Thucidides: Understanding History as Culture and Vice Versa* (Chicago: University of Chicago Press).

Scarr, D. (1967a), *Fragments of Empire: A History of the Western Pacific High Commission 1877–1914* (Canberra: Australian National University Press, London: C. Hurst and Co.).

– (1967b), 'Recruits and Recruiters: A Portrait of the Pacific Island Labour Trade', *The Journal of Pacific History*, 2: 5–25.

Scheffler, H. (1970), 'Ambrym Revisited: A Preliminary Report', *Southwestern Journal of Anthropology*, 26:52–66.

Seligman, B.Z. (1927), 'Bilateral Descent and the Formation of Marriage Classes', *Journal of the Royal Anthropological Institute,* Vol. 57: 349–75.

– Sexton, L. (1982), A Women's Savings and Exchange System in Highland Papua New Guinea. *Oceania* 52, 167–198.

Shineberg, Dorothy (undated) database, unpublished, in A. Eriksen's files.

Siegel, J. (1985), 'Notes and Documents: Origins of Pacific Island Labourers in Fiji', *The Journal of Pacific History*, 20, 42–54.

Sommerville, B.T. (1894), 'Notes of Some Islands in the New Hebrides', *Journal of the Royal Anthropological Institute* 23:2–21, 363–93.

Speiser, F. (1996) [1923], Ethnology of Vanuatu: An Early Twentieth Century Study (Honolulu: University of Hawaii Press).

Steel, R.D.D. (1880), 'The New Hebrides and Christian Missions ...' (London: James Nisbet and Co.).

Stewart, P.J. and Strathern, A. (eds) (1997), Millennium Markers (Center for Pacific Studies: James Cook University).

– (eds) (2000a), Millennial Countdown in New Guinea. Special issue of *Ethnohistory*, 47:1.

– (eds) (2000b), *Identity Work: Constructing Pacific Lives*. ASAO (Association for Social Anthropology in Oceania) Monograph Series No. 18 (Pittsburgh: University of Pittsburgh Press).

Stewart, P.J., Strathern, A. and Robbins, J. (eds) (2001), Pentecostal and Charismatic Christianity in Oceania. Special Issue of the *Journal of Ritual Studies* 15:2.

Strathern, A. (1971), *The Rope of Moka: Big-men and Ceremonial Exchange in Mount Hagen, New Guinea* (Cambridge: Cambridge University Press).

Strathern, A. (1980), 'The Central and the Contingent: Bridewealth Among the Melpa and the Wiru', in *The Meaning of Marriage Payments*, J. Comaroff (ed.) (London: Academic Press).

Strathern, A. and P.J. Stewart (2000), *Arrow Talk: Transaction, Transition, and Contradiction in New Guinea Highlands History* (Kent, OH: Kent State University Press).

Strathern, M. (1984), 'Subject or Object? Women and the Circulation of Valuables in Highland New Guinea', in R. Hirschon (ed.), *Women and Property, Women as Property* (London: Croom Helm).

– (1988), *The Gender of the Gift* (Berkeley, CA: California University Press).

– (1993), 'Making Incomplete: A Comment on Female Initiation in Melanesia, in *Carved Flesh/Cast Selves: Gendered Symbols and Social Practices*, in Broch-Due, I. Rudie, T. Bleie (eds) (Oxford: Berg).

– (1993), 'The Nice Thing About Culture is That Everyone Has It', in Shifting Contexts: Transformations in Anthropological Knowledge, M. Strathern (ed.) (London and New York: Routledge).

– 1995 [1972], *Women in Between, Female Roles in a Male World: Mount Hagen, New Guinea* (London: Rowman and Littlefield Publishers, Inc).

– (1996), 'Cutting the Network', *Journal of the Royal Anthropological Institute*, 2:3, 517–535.

Thomas, N. (1989), *Out of Time: History and Evolution in Anthropological Discourse* (Cambridge: Cambridge University Press).

– (1992), 'The Inversion of Tradition', *American Ethnologist*, 19:2, 213–32.

Tonkinson, R. (1981), 'Church and Kastom in Southeast Ambrym', in Allen (ed.).

Toren, C. (1989), 'Drinking Cash: The Purification of Money Through Ceremonial', in Bloch and Parry (eds), *Money and the Morality of Exchange*, pp. 142–164 (Cambridge: Cambridge University Press).

– (1990), *Making Sense of Hierarchy: Cognition as Social Process in Fiji* (London School of Economics, Monographs on Social Anthropology, no. 61).

Van Trease, H. (1987), *Politics of Land in Vanuatu* (Suva, Fiji: IPS, USP).

Wagner, R. (2001), *An Anthropology of the Subject* (Berkeley, CA: University of California Press).

Wardlow, H. (2006), *Wayward Women: Sexuality and Agency in a New Guinea Society* (Berkeley, CA: University of California Press).

Weiner, J.F. (1991), *The Empty Place: Poetry, Space and Being Among the Foi of Papua New Guinea* (Bloomington: Indiana University Press).

White, G.M. (1991), *Identity through History, Living Stories in a Solomon Island Society* (Cambridge Studies in Social Anthropology: Cambridge University Press).

– (1993), 'Three Discourses on Custom', in *Anthropological Forum* (eds), Lindstrom and White, Special Issue, vol. 6:4, 475–494.

Index